GW00693871

Prudent for a Purpose:
Working for a Stronger and Fairer Britain

Economic and Fiscal Strategy Report and
Financial Statement and Budget Report
March 2000

Return to an Order of the House of Commons dated 21 March 2000.

Copy of Economic and Fiscal Strategy Report and Financial Statement and Budget Report – March 2000 as laid before the House of Commons by the Chancellor of the Exchequer when opening the Budget.

Stephen Timms
Her Majesty's Treasury
21 March 2000

Ordered by the House of Commons to be printed 21 March 2000

LONDON: THE STATIONERY OFFICE

£35

House of Commons No. 346

The Economic and Fiscal Strategy Report and Financial Statement and Budget Report contain the Government's assessment of the medium-term economic and budgetary position. They set out the Government's tax and spending plans, including those for public investment, in the context of its overall approach to social, economic and environmental objectives. After approval by Parliament for the purposes of Section 5 of the European Communities (Amendment) Act 1993, these reports will form the basis of submissions to the European Commission under Article 99 (ex Article 103) and Article 104 (ex Article 104c) of the Treaty establishing the European Union.

CONTENTS

OVERVIEW

1.1 The Government is pursuing a comprehensive and coordinated strategy to fulfil Britain's national economic potential and deliver the objective of high and stable levels of growth and employment – with rising living standards for all.

1.2 Over the past three years, the Government has been building a platform of economic stability, locking in low inflation and bringing the public finances under control. Through measures to promote enterprise and fairness and build a stronger and fairer Britain, Budget 2000 takes further steps towards meeting the Government's long-term goals – with new measures to boost productivity, encourage work, support families and communities, and protect the environment.

1.3 As a result of a commitment to stability and prudence, the Budget ensures that the Government remains on track to meet its fiscal rules and locks in the fiscal tightening over the next two years to an even greater extent than projected in Budget 99, while releasing substantial new resources for education, health, transport, law and order, tackling child poverty and supporting pensioners.

Budget 2000, *Prudent for a Purpose: Working for a Stronger and Fairer Britain*, **comprises the Economic and Fiscal Strategy Report (EFSR) and the Financial Statement and Budget Report (FSBR). The EFSR sets out:**

- **a coherent and coordinated framework and strategy to meet the Government's objectives;**

- **a progress report on what the Government has achieved so far; and**

- **how Budget 2000 measures contribute to each element of the strategy.**

The FSBR provides:

- **a summary of each of the main Budget measures; and**

- **updated forecasts for the economy and the public finances.**

1.4 Full details of the Government's economic strategy are described in the November 1999 Pre-Budget Report. The EFSR follows the same structure as the Pre-Budget Report, focusing on the following key elements:

- delivering macroeconomic stability;

- meeting the productivity challenge;

- increasing employment opportunity for all;

- ensuring fairness for families and communities; and

- protecting the environment.

DELIVERING MACROECONOMIC STABILITY

1.5   Chapter 2 describes the Government's framework for macroeconomic policy and prospects for the UK economy and the public finances (full details of which are set out in Chapters B and C of the FSBR).

The new framework 1.6   Since coming into office, the Government has introduced new frameworks for both monetary and fiscal policy, both of which are highly transparent, forward-looking and underpinned by legislation:

- a new monetary framework to deliver low inflation, giving the Bank of England responsibility for setting interest rates to meet the Government's symmetrical inflation target;

- a new fiscal framework based on a prudent approach to the public finances and underpinned by two strict fiscal rules – the golden rule and the sustainable investment rule; and

- a new public spending framework, integrated into the fiscal framework, to deliver greater certainty for long-term planning and remove the previous bias against investment.

1.7   Early indications are that the new frameworks are delivering significant benefits. In contrast to the boom and bust of the past, the UK economy has enjoyed a period of stability and steady growth since the introduction of the frameworks – with employment rising to record levels. Inflation has remained close to target and interest rates have been lower and more stable than in the past. At the same time, the new fiscal framework has restored the public finances to a healthy and sustainable position, while allowing fiscal policy to support monetary policy through the economic cycle.

The economic forecast 1.8   Economic developments over the past year have broadly confirmed the judgements taken in the Budget 99 forecast, with the pause in UK growth at the end of 1998 being short lived and stronger activity spreading to most sectors and regions of the UK economy through last year. Unemployment has fallen to 20-year lows. The Budget 2000 forecast shows that:

- RPIX inflation is expected to remain below the $2^1/_2$ per cent target throughout this year, rising back to target by early 2001;

- GDP is expected to grow by $2^3/_4$ to $3^1/_4$ per cent in 2000, up from 2 per cent in 1999 and a little stronger than expected at the time of the Pre-Budget Report. Growth of $2^1/_4$ to $2^3/_4$ per cent is forecast for both 2001 and 2002; and

- there are clear upside risks to the outlook for activity and inflation, highlighting the importance of the Government's forward-looking policy framework and the need for responsible wage bargaining and price setting across the economy. But there are also downside risks associated with imbalances in the world economy, particularly in Japan and the US.

Fiscal developments and prospects 1.9   Latest fiscal outturns have been stronger than expected at the time of Budget 99. While some of this improvement in the public finances in 1999–2000 reflects stronger than expected growth, much of it appears to have been structural. The surplus on current budget in 1999–2000 is now estimated to be £17.1 billion, compared with a Budget 99 forecast of £2 billion.

I.10 Against this background of a significant improvement in the public finances in 1999–2000, which is projected to persist, large surpluses expected on the current budget would imply a fiscal tightening well in excess of that anticipated at the time of Budget 99. It is against this outlook that the Budget 2000 decisions have been taken.

I.11 The Government's Budget judgement ensures that the fiscal rules will continue to be met over the coming years, including under a more cautious case, and that the outcome of the Budget is consistent with the Government's continuing commitment to prudence and responsibility. The Budget locks in the fiscal tightening over the next two years to an even greater extent than projected in Budget 99, while releasing substantial new resources for the Government's key public service priorities.

I.12 In the Budget the Government is:

- implementing a Budget package to promote enterprise and work and release extra resources to tackle child and pensioner poverty, as set out in Table 1.2;

- setting firm overall spending limits for the period of the 2000 Spending Review allowing:

  - current spending to increase by $2\frac{1}{2}$ per cent a year in real terms in the three years to 2003–04, in line with the Government's neutral view of the economy's trend rate of growth;

  - a more than doubling of net investment, rising to 1.8 per cent of GDP by 2003–04. This makes a significant further contribution to tackling the legacy of underfunding of Britain's public infrastructure, while remaining consistent with the sustainable investment rule; and

- allocating an additional £3 billion of current spending in 2001–01 and an additional £1 billion of capital spending within DEL in 2000–01.

Table 1.1: Fiscal balances comparison with Budget 99[1]

	Outturn[2]	Estimate	Projections	
	1998-99	1999-00	2000-01	2001-02
Fiscal balances (£ billion)				
Surplus on current budget – Budget 99	4.1	2	4	8
Surplus on current budget – Budget 2000	7.5	17.1	14	16
Net borrowing – Budget 99	–1.0	3	3	1
Net borrowing – Budget 2000	–2.8	–11.9	–6	–5
Cyclically-adjusted budget balances (per cent of GDP)				
Surplus on current budget – Budget 99	0.2	0.6	1.0	1.1
Surplus on current budget – Budget 2000	0.6	1.8	1.3	1.3
Net borrowing – Budget 99	0.1	0.0	–0.2	–0.1
Net borrowing – Budget 2000	–0.1	–1.2	–0.5	–0.3
Debt ratio (per cent of GDP)				
Public sector net debt – Budget 99	40.6	39.4	38.2	36.8
Public sector net debt – Budget 2000	39.7	37.1	35.1	33.6

[1] Excluding windfall tax receipts and associated spending.

[2] The 1998–99 figures were estimates in Budget 99.

Meeting the fiscal rules 1.13   Over the projection period, the surplus on the current budget is projected to fall gradually to 0.7 per cent of GDP by 2004–05. Consistent with the need to maintain a cautious approach, this profile shows that the Government is well on track to meet its golden rule over the projection period, with the average surplus on the current budget from 1999–2000 falling from 1.7 per cent of GDP in 2000–01 to 1.4 per cent of GDP in 2004–05. The cyclically-adjusted current budget also remains comfortably in surplus throughout the projection period.

1.14   Net debt has declined continuously as a proportion of GDP since 1996–97, when it stood at 44 per cent of GDP. By the end of March 2000, it is projected to be 37 per cent of GDP. This is consistent with meeting the sustainable investment rule. The Budget 2000 projections show a decline in net debt over the projection period, stabilising at 32$\frac{1}{2}$ per cent of GDP by 2004–05 reflecting the sustained improvement in the position of the public finances. This is consistent with the projected more than doubling in net investment over the same period.

1.15   As required by the *Code for Fiscal Stability*, Annex A of the EFSR presents illustrative long-term fiscal projections and examines the long-term sustainability of the public finances. This indicates that the UK has a broadly sustainable fiscal position in the long term.

MEETING THE PRODUCTIVITY CHALLENGE

1.16   Britain's productivity performance lags behind that of other major countries. Chapter 3 describes the action which the Government has taken since coming into office to tackle this productivity gap and the further steps which are being taken in Budget 2000 to help make Britain the most competitive environment for business in the world and promote balanced growth across all the regions of Britain. The Government's long-term ambition for the next decade is that Britain will have a faster rise in productivity than its main competitors, as it closes the productivity gap.

Measures already announced 1.17   The Government has already taken significant steps to increase competition, enterprise and innovation, skills, investment and public sector productivity – the five key drivers of productivity performance:

- **competition:** the new Competition Act came into force in March 2000, giving tough new powers to the Office of Fair Trading to curb anti-competitive behaviour;

- **enterprise and innovation:** measures to improve the science base and the commercialisation of research from universities and Public Sector Research Establishments, the introduction of the new R&D tax credit and the launch of the Small Business Service in April 2000, together with a range of measures to promote enterprise opportunities in deprived areas;

- **skills:** in addition to substantial additional resources for education, individual learning accounts and UfI Limited (the company taking forward the University for Industry concept) will from this year increase opportunities for life-long learning. The Government's long-term ambition, as discussed in Chapter 5, is that by the end of the decade 50 per cent of Britain's young people will be going on to higher education;

- **investment:** corporation tax rates have been cut to their lowest ever level and the new 10p rate for the smallest companies from April 2000 will benefit 270,000 businesses; and

- **public sector productivity:** the Government has set output and efficiency targets for public service delivery through Public Service Agreements. The Public Sector Productivity Panel is working with government departments to identify and tackle key areas for improvement, and the new Office of Government Commerce will streamline government procurement processes and should deliver £1 billion of efficiency savings over the next three years.

Budget **1.18** Budget 2000 includes a further package of measures to increase productivity, boost **measures** enterprise and support small businesses across all regions of Britain:

- **major reforms to capital gains tax** from April 2000 to strengthen the incentives for entrepreneurial investment, including a shortening of the business assets taper from 10 to 4 years and a much wider definition of business assets. All shareholdings in unquoted trading companies will qualify, and in quoted trading companies all employee shareholdings will qualify, as will other shareholdings over 5 per cent;

- permanent **40 per cent capital allowances** for small and medium-sized enterprises (SMEs);

- further steps to support e-commerce, with new discounts for electronic filing of tax returns, the introduction of **100 per cent first year capital allowances for small firms buying ICT equipment, and a £60 million package to help get more small firms on-line and deliver services to them electronically;**

- an increase from 10 to 15 in the number of employees in small companies eligible for the new **Enterprise Management Incentives** scheme to be introduced in April 2000, and final details – following consultation – of the new **all-employee share ownership plan** and **corporate venturing tax relief** from April 2000;

- a **£1 billion target umbrella fund to finance enterprise growth** to be taken forward by the Small Business Service and Regional Development Agencies to provide better access to venture capital for small, growth firms in the regions;

- following the **Banking Review** by Don Cruickshank, the Government is bringing forward a package of measures designed to reduce prices and improve services for consumers and SMEs and promote innovation in banking;

- Paul Myners, Chairman of Gartmore Investment Management, will look at whether there are factors discouraging **institutional investors** from investing in smaller companies. He will shortly be launching a consultation exercise and will report back with recommendations by the next Budget; and

- changes to the **work permits system** to enable UK employers to recruit skilled people from overseas where there are skills shortages and to enhance the UK's image as an attractive location for talented overseas students and entrepreneurs.

1.19 The Secretary of State for Trade and Industry will be making further announcements shortly.

INCREASING EMPLOYMENT OPPORTUNITY FOR ALL

1.20   Chapter 4 describes the Government's aim to deliver employment opportunity for all – the modern definition of full employment. Its long-term economic ambition is that by the end of the decade there will be a higher percentage of people in employment than ever before. The Government is taking steps to help match the large number of vacancies in regions across the country to people in neighbouring unemployment blackspots. It is determined to help into work those who are unemployed and those who are outside the labour market but would like to find work.

Measures   **1.21**   To deliver employment opportunity for all, the Government has already introduced an
already   ambitious set of reforms built on the evidence of what works: helping people to move from
announced   welfare to work, helping to make work pay, and helping people to secure progression once in work:

- **welfare to work:** over 750,000 people have already participated in the range of New Deal programmes with almost 260,000 moving into jobs. April 2000 will see the introduction of 15 Employment Zones in areas of particularly high unemployment and enhanced provision to intensify contact between the Employment Service and the long-term unemployed; and

- **making work pay:** through tax and benefit reforms including the Working Families' Tax Credit, reform of NICs, the new 10p rate of income tax from April 1999 and the cut in the basic rate to 22p from April 2000 – the lowest rate for 70 years. This is underpinned by the National Minimum Wage, the adult rate of which will be increased to £3.70 an hour from October 2000.

Budget   **1.22**   Budget 2000 builds on these measures, taking further steps to secure employment
measures   opportunity for all:

- from autumn 2000, special Action Teams will help to match unemployed people to suitable vacancies in neighbouring areas in 20 of Britain's communities suffering from the highest unemployment and lowest employment, along with additional support in the 15 Employment Zone areas;

- as outlined in the Pre-Budget Report, there will be a national rollout of an Intensive Gateway within the New Deal for 18 – 24 year olds from June 2000, and a national extension and intensification of the New Deal for 25 plus from April 2001;

- extended choices will be available to lone parents so that, from April 2001, all lone parents on Income Support with children over the age of five will be required to meet with a specialist personal adviser who will guide them through their choices – including help to try work, help to move into part-time or full-time work and the opportunity to undertake education and training;

- the first stage of work to develop a nationwide service to help disabled people find work and testing the effectiveness of help for people when they become ill in work with job retention and rehabilitation pilots;

- a new Job Grant of £100 from spring 2001 to ease the transition from welfare to work, together with a 4-week Income Support for Mortgage Interest (ISMI) run-on and simplified rules for the Housing Benefit Extended Payments Scheme;

- additional support for working families with an increase in the under-16 child credit in the Working Families' Tax Credit from June 2000 (matched by increases in the Disabled Person's Tax Credit and income-related benefits); and

- a new employment tax credit from 2003, to be brought in alongside the integrated child credit, to extend the principle of the Working Families' Tax Credit to people without children.

FAIRNESS FOR FAMILIES AND COMMUNITIES

I.23   As discussed in Chapter 5, the Government is committed to building a fairer and more inclusive society in which everyone has the opportunity to benefit from higher living standards. In particular, it is pursuing an extensive programme to tackle the causes of poverty. The Government's long-term economic ambition is to halve child poverty by the end of the next decade, as it moves towards its aim to abolish child poverty within 20 years. The Government is also working hard to ensure that individuals and communities have access to high quality public services, including good schools and a modern health service.

Measures already announced

I.24   The key elements of the Government's strategy to meet these aims, and the measures which it has already introduced to help do so, include:

- support for families and children: through further increases in universal Child Benefit from April 2000, targeted support through the Working Families' Tax Credit and Income Support and, from April 2001, the new Children's Tax Credit which replaces the married couple's allowance following its withdrawal in April 2000;

- fairness for pensioners: with a minimum income guarantee uprated by earnings for the poorest pensioners, a £100 winter fuel payment for every pensioner household, and the concessionary TV licences for those aged 75 and over; and

- delivering high quality public services: significant additional resources for health and education over the three years from April 1999 as part of the 1998 Comprehensive Spending Review.

Budget measures

I.25   Budget 2000 takes further steps to support families and tackle child poverty, help pensioners, promote saving, improve public services and ensure a fair and efficient tax system.

Families and children

To provide further support for families and children:

- the under-16 child credit in the Working Families' Tax Credit will be increased by a further £4.35 a week from June 2000. This will be matched in the Disabled Person's Tax Credit, the under-16 child allowance in Income Support and income-related benefits;

- an additional 50 pence a week will be added to the Children's Tax Credit when it is introduced in April 2001, making it worth up to £442 a year – more than twice the value of the married couple's allowance which it replaces;

- a package of measures will help low-income mothers support their children in the early months, including an increase of £100 to £300 in the Sure Start Maternity Grant from summer 2000;

- continued consultation on the new Children's Fund which will be set up as part of the 2000 Spending Review, including a network of Children's Funds; and

- a new integrated child credit from 2003, which will bring together the different stands of support for children in the Working Families' Tax Credit, Income Support and the Children's Tax Credit into a seamless system of support for children built on the foundation of universal Child Benefit.

The measures introduced so far in this Parliament will lift 1.2 million children out of poverty and mean that by 2001 the tax burden on a typical family on average earnings with two children will be at its lowest since 1972.

Pensioners

To provide further support and security for pensioners, Budget 2000:

- builds on the five-fold increase in the winter fuel payment announced in Budget 99, with a further increase from £100 to £150 for every 60+household;

- doubles the lower capital limit attached to the minimum income guarantee to £6,000 and increases the upper limit to £12,000 to reward pensioners who have managed to save something for their retirement; and

- announces the Government's intention to look at opportunities to develop the minimum income guarantee, whether through an income taper or other measures, to reward pensioners who have made some provision for their retirement.

As a result of measures announced in this and previous Budgets, over the course of the current Parliament the Government will be spending an additional £6.5 billion on pensioners.

Savings

To help promote savings opportunity for all, the Budget announces that:

- the Government has decided to retain the current £7,000 Individual Savings Account (ISA) contribution limit for 2000–01, rather than reduce it to £5,000 as previously planned.

Modernising public services

As a result of prudent management of the public finances, Budget 2000 sustains and increases for the next four years the investment the Government has already made in Britain's key public services. Within the firm overall spending limits set by this Budget, spending will be focused on the public's priorities. The Budget announces:

Health:

- an immediate additional £2 billion for the NHS in 2000–01 including extra resources from a rise in tobacco duties;

- 6.1 per cent average annual real terms growth over the next four years – the longest period of sustained high growth in the history of the NHS; and

- NHS reforms to tackle variations in efficiency, performance and health outcomes to ensure that a step change in resources can achieve a step change in results.

Education:

- an immediate boost for education of £1 billion across the UK providing more money for schools and for helping young people to stay on at school.

Transport:

- an additional £280 million, available across the UK for transport, including new money for both road and public transport schemes.

Tackling crime:

- an extra £285 million available for the fight against crime. Capital modernisation projects totalling £185 million have been approved for criminal justice agencies. Another £100 million will be available for modernising policing across the UK.

In addition, Budget 2000 is putting an immediate extra £200 million into the Government's Captial Modernisation Fund to support innovative capital projects which will improve service delivery. Further allocations from the £2.7 billion Capital Modernisation Fund will be announced in the coming weeks.

A fair and efficient tax system

The Government is committed to addressing unfairness in the taxation system. Measures in Budget 2000 to help promote a fair and efficient tax system include:

- Budget 2000 increases the rate of tobacco duties by 5 per cent in real terms with immediate effect. This will release extra resources which will be included in the additional £2 billion for the NHS in 2000–01. Further details of the Government's strategy to tackle tobacco smuggling will be announced on 22 March;

- from April 2001, air passenger duty on economy flights within the European Economic Area (EEA) will be reduced from £10 to £5 and flights from the Scottish Highlands and Islands will be removed from duty. The rate for club and first class fares for destinations outside the EEA will rise from £20 to £40, with other rates unchanged. Part of the cost of these changes will be met by removing the exemption from duty of return flights within the UK, a modification necessary to comply with European law;

- an increase in the rates of stamp duty for property transactions above £250,000. 95 per cent of residential property transactions will be unaffected; and;

- the Budget also demonstrates the Government's continuing commitment to protect the revenue base by tackling tax abuse across the entire system, with a range of measures designed to ensure that both individuals and businesses pay their fair share of taxes.

PROTECTING THE ENVIRONMENT

I.26   Economic growth needs to take place in a way which ensures the effective protection of the environment and the prudent use of natural resources. Chapter 6 describes the Government's strategy for protecting the environment, for both current and future generations. Budget 99 included the largest package of environmental tax reforms ever announced in the UK. Budget 2000 implements and delivers the key reforms, putting in place policies to tackle climate change, improve air quality, regenerate Britain's cities and protect the countryside.

Measures already announced

I.27   The Government has already announced a range of measures designed to meet its environmental objectives, including:

- a climate change levy, to be introduced in April 2001, to encourage energy efficiency in business and help reduce greenhouse gas emissions. All the revenue raised will be fully recycled back to business through a 0.3 percentage point cut in employers' NICs and additional support for energy efficiency measures;

- supporting integrated transport with reduced Vehicle Excise Duty (VED) for cars with the smallest engines, improvements to the transport system and tax measures to promote environmentally-friendly commuting; and

- a five-year programme of annual increases in the standard rate of landfill tax from April 2000, as part of the Government's strategy to promote more sustainable waste management.

Budget measures

I.28   Budget 2000 includes further measures to tackle climate change, improve air quality, regenerate Britain's cities and protect the countryside:

- reforms to VED to encourage the use of more environmentally-friendly vehicles, including an extension of the reduced rate of VED for existing cars to cars with engines up to 1,200cc and a new graduated VED system for new cars based on their carbon dioxide (CO_2) emissions – both from March 2001;

- a revenue-neutral reform of company car taxation from April 2002 to encourage the take-up of vehicles which have lower CO_2 emissions and use environmentally-friendly fuels;

- reforms to lorry VED, including allowing 44-tonne lorries meeting Euro II emissions standards onto UK roads from early 2001, at favourable VED rates;

- a new fiscal incentive to use ultra-low sulphur petrol and the freezing of the duty rate on road fuel gases;

- further refinements to the detailed design of the climate change levy to increase its environmental effectiveness while protecting competitiveness;

- further encouragement for emissions trading;

- an extension of the reduced rate of VAT for the installation of energy saving materials to all homes, and the introduction of capital allowances to underpin the Government's Affordable Warmth Programme;

- new relief from stamp duty for some Registered Social Landlords to encourage social housing provision and make better use of the existing housing stock;

- a possible relief from stamp duty for new developments on brownfield sites, with consultation on how this measure might be best targeted to help meet the Government's objective to encourage better use of brownfield land;

- a new aggregates levy from April 2002 to tackle the environmental costs associated with quarrying and encourage the use of recycled materials. All of the revenues will be returned to business through a cut in employers' national insurance contributions and a new Sustainability Fund to deliver environmental benefits to the local communities affected by quarrying; and

- further discussions on a possible voluntary package of measures to reduce the environmental impacts of the use of pesticides.

I.29   Table 6.1 of the EFSR shows how the Government's environmental tax measures fit in to the overall framework of the Governments environmental policy. An environmental assessment of these measures is detailed in Table 6.2 of the EFSR.

IMPACT OF BUDGET MEASURES ON HOUSEHOLDS

I.30   The measures in this and previous Budgets support the Government's objectives of promoting and rewarding work, while giving extra support to pensioners and families with children.

I.31   By April 2001, when personal tax and benefit measures from this and previous Budgets have come into effect:

- on average, households will be £460 a year better off;

- on average, families with children will be £850 a year better off; and

- the tax burden on a single-earner family on average earnings with two children will be the lowest since 1972.

Living standards

- for a single-earner family with two children on £25,000 a year, real living standards will have risen by 10 per cent over the Parliament; and

- as a result of the Working Families' Tax Credit, for a single-earner family with two children on £12,500 a year, real living standards will rise by 20 per cent this year, the largest annual rise for 25 years.

Supporting working families

- a single-earner family with two children on £25,000 a year will be £370 a year better off;

- a single-earner family with two children on £12,500 will be £2,600 a year better off; and

- no family with someone in full-time work will get less than £214 a week, over £11,000 a year.

Tackling poverty

- the poorest two-child family on income support will be £1,500 a year better off;

- 1.2 million children will be lifted out of poverty; and

- for a 75-year old pensioner on the minimum income guarantee, annual income in April 2001 will be over £950 higher than in 1997. For a 75-year old couple it will be £1,350 higher.

I.32   Charts 1.2 and 1.3 on page 14 provide an indication of where taxpayers' money will be spent in the year ahead and where taxes come from. These figures take account of the additional increases in spending in 2000–01 announced in Budget 2000.

Table 1.2: Budget 2000 Measures

	(+ve is an Exchequer yield)			£ million
	2000–01 indexed	**2001–02 indexed**	**2002–03 indexed**	**2000–01 non-indexed**
MEETING THE PRODUCTIVITY CHALLENGE				
1 New all-employee share plan	-120	-280	-370	-120
2 Abolition of stamp duty on intellectual property	-5	-5	-5	-5
3 Corporate venturing scheme	-5	-25	-50	-5
4 Capital gains tax reform	0	-225	-275	0
5 Abolition of withholding tax on international bonds and foreign dividends	0	-300	*	0
Small business				
6 Enterprise Management Incentives	-30	-50	-60	-30
7 EIS/VCTs: reduction in minimum holding period and technical changes	-5	-15	-25	-5
8 Permanent first year capital allowances for small and medium sized enterprises at 40%	*	-190	-330	*
9 First year capital allowances for small enterprises for information and communication technology at 100% for three years	0	-90	-90	0
10 Discount for filing of tax returns over the internet and electronic payment	-5	-30	0	-5
Large business				
11 Extending group rules for corporation tax losses and company gains	-60	-100	-65	-60
12 Changes to double taxation relief	+40	+140	+120	+40
13 Reduction in interest rates on overdue quarterly instalments and de-minimis limit for CT instalments raised to £10,000	-5	*	*	-5
INCREASING EMPLOYMENT OPPORTUNITY FOR ALL				
14 Income tax: indexation of allowances and limits	0	0	0	-470
15 Reduction in employer national insurance contribution rate by 0.1 percentage points from April 2002	0	0	-350	0
Transition to work package				
16 £100 Job Grant	0	-20	-20	0
17 Income Support Mortgage Interest run-on for 4 weeks on taking work	0	-10	-10	0
18 Income Support Mortgage Interest 52 week linking rule	0	-5	-5	0
19 Simplification of Housing Benefit Extended Payments Scheme	0	-15	-15	0
20 Increasing £15 earnings disregard in income-related benefits to £20	0	-20	-20	0
FAIRNESS FOR FAMILIES AND COMMUNITIES				
Measures for families with children				
Tackling child poverty				
21 Increase Children's Tax Credit by £0.50 from April 2001	0	-100	-130	0
22 Increase Working Families' Tax Credit under 16 child credit and income related benefits by £4.35 from June 2000 and October 2000 respectively	-665	-1,260	-1,295	-665
Maternity package				
23 Extension of Working Families' Tax Credit to those receiving maternity pay	0	-40	-80	0
24 Increase Sure Start Maternity Grant by £100	-5	-20	-20	-5
Fairness to pensioners				
25 Increase minimum income guarantee capital limits for pensioners from April 2001	0	-145	-145	0
26 £150 Winter Allowance from December 2000	-430	-430	-430	-430
Securing the tax base				
27 Capital gains tax: use of trusts and offshore companies	0	+120	+125	0
28 Stamp duty: transfer of property and company reorganisations	+50	+100	+100	+50
29 Life assurance company taxation: modification of apportionment rules	+50	+115	+120	+50

Table 1.2: Budget 2000 Measures

		(+ve is an Exchequer yield)		£ million
	2000–01 indexed	**2001–02 indexed**	**2002–03 indexed**	**2000–01 non-indexed**
30 Insurance companies and Lloyds: reserves	0	+30	+120	0
31 Rent factoring	+20	+50	+80	+20
32 Controlled Foreign Companies	+40	+120	+150	+40
33 Petroleum Revenue Tax: preventing misuse of safeguard relief	0	+10	+30	0
34 VAT: capital asset disposals	+5	+5	+5	+5
Duties and other tax changes				
35 Relaxation for flights from Scottish Highlands and Islands from April 2001	0	-5	-5	0
36 Other reforms to Air Passenger Duty	-5	-75	-85	0
37 Stamp duty: 3 per cent rate for transfer of land and property above £250,000 and 4 per cent above £500,000	+290	+295	+365	+290
38 Stamp duty: Registered Social Landlords	-10	-20	-20	-10
39 Enhancement to charities tax package	0	-5	-15	0
40 Alcohol: freeze duty on spirits and revalorise all other alcohol duties	-25	-25	-20	+140
41 VAT: reduced rates on sanitary protection	-10	-35	-35	-10
42 Inheritance tax: index threshold	0	0	0	-15
43 Extending current Individual Savings Account subscription limits for 1 year to April 2001	-40	-70	-75	-40
44 5% real increase to tobacco duty	+235	+405	+415	+375
45 Reform of amusement machine licence duty	-5	*	*	-5
46 VAT: indexation of registration and deregistration thresholds	0	0	0	-5
47 Construction industry scheme: reducing the deduction rate	-150	-50	-50	-150
48 VAT: exemption	+15	+15	+15	+15
49 VAT: credit supplies	-20	-20	-20	-20
PROTECTING THE ENVIRONMENT				
50 Revalorisation of hydrocarbon oil duties	0	0	0	+715
51 Ultra low sulphur petrol – introducing a 1p differential with unleaded petrol	*	-15	-35	*
52 VAT: revalorisation of fuel scale charges for business cars	0	0	0	+60
53 Extending reduced VAT rate for energy saving materials	-35	-35	-35	-35
54 Affordable warmth scheme: capital allowances	*	-10	-20	*
55 Aggregates levy	0	0	+385	0
Vehicle Excise Duty:				
56 Reduce VED rates for goods vehicles	-45	-45	-45	-45
57 Introduction of graduated VED system for new cars from March 2001	0	-80	-140	0
58 Increase threshold for reduced VED rates for private and light goods vehicles tax class to 1,200cc (from 1,100cc) from March 2001	-120	-120	-120	-120
59 Revalorisation of VED rates for existing Private and Light Goods Vehicles deferred until March 2001	-110	0	0	-110
TOTAL	**-1,165**	**-2,580**	**-2,480**	**-570**

*negligible.

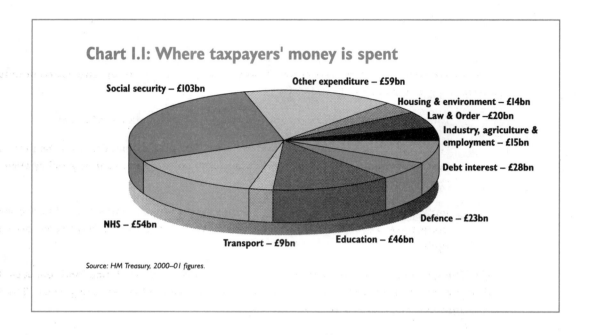

Chart 1.1: Where taxpayers' money is spent

- Social security – £103bn
- Other expenditure – £59bn
- Housing & environment – £14bn
- Law & Order – £20bn
- Industry, agriculture & employment – £15bn
- Debt interest – £28bn
- Defence – £23bn
- Education – £46bn
- Transport – £9bn
- NHS – £54bn

Source: HM Treasury, 2000–01 figures.

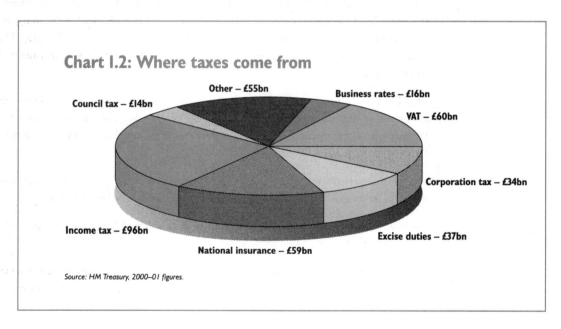

Chart 1.2: Where taxes come from

- Other – £55bn
- Council tax – £14bn
- Business rates – £16bn
- VAT – £60bn
- Corporation tax – £34bn
- Excise duties – £37bn
- National insurance – £59bn
- Income tax – £96bn

Source: HM Treasury, 2000–01 figures.

2 DELIVERING MACROECONOMIC STABILITY

The forward-looking macroeconomic framework put in place by the Government is delivering greater economic stability:

- the monetary policy framework is delivering low and stable inflation;

- the fiscal policy framework has restored the public finances to a healthy and sustainable position and allowed fiscal policy to support monetary policy through the cycle; and

- early indications suggest that the economy may have completed a full economic cycle since 1997–98. If so, the Government met both of its fiscal rules over the cycle.

The Budget maintains the commitment to stability and prudence and ensures the Government remains on track to meet the fiscal rules and deliver steady growth. The key messages in this chapter are:

- latest fiscal outturns and projections are better than expected, with much of the improvement being structural. This Budget locks in the fiscal tightening over the next two years to an even greater extent than projected in Budget 99, while releasing substantial new resources for the Government's key public service priorities;

- The Government's Budget judgement ensures that the fiscal rules will be met over the coming years and that the outcome of the Budget is consistent with the continuing commitment to prudence and responsibility. In the Budget the Government is:

  - implementing a Budget package to promote enterprise and work and release extra resources to tackle child and pensioner poverty;

  - setting firm overall limits for public spending for the period of the 2000 Spending Review, allowing;

    - current spending to increase by $2\frac{1}{2}$ per cent a year in real terms in the three years to 2003-04, in line with the Government's neutral view of the economy's trend rate of growth; and

    - a more than doubling in net investment, rising to 1.8 per cent of GDP by 2003-04. This makes a significant further contribution to tackling the legacy of underfunding of Britain's public infrastructure while remaining consistent with the sustainable investment rule.

    - allocating an additional £3 billion of current spending in 2000-01 and an additional £1 billion of capital spending within DEL in 2000-01.

The Government will continue to entrench the monetary and fiscal frameworks, delivering stability and steady growth and avoiding a return to the boom and bust of the past.

THE MACROECONOMIC FRAMEWORK

Delivering   **2.1**   The UK has a history of poor economic performance in comparison with other G7
stability   economies. Much of the blame for this poor performance can be attributed to policy errors
made in the past. The Government's macroeconomic framework has been designed to avoid
a repeat of mistakes which led to boom and bust cycles and relative underperformance. In the
face of the uncertainty and unpredictability of ever more rapid financial flows, the
Government believes it is vital to:

- set clear, long-term policy objectives;

- adopt predictable, well-understood procedural rules for monetary and fiscal
  policymaking; and

- keep markets properly informed, and ensure that objectives and the relevant
  institutions which implement them are seen to be credible, through increased
  openness, accountability and transparency.

2.2   In keeping with this approach, the Government introduced new frameworks for the
operation of both monetary and fiscal policy. These frameworks are highly transparent,
forward-looking and are underpinned by legislation. Their design helps prevent
macroeconomic policy being set on the basis of short-term political interests, rather than in
the interests of the economy and country as a whole. This macroeconomic framework is
delivering much more stable growth and employment than in the past, based on low inflation
and sound public finances.

The monetary   **2.3**   Price stability is a key requirement for achieving the Government's central economic
framework   objective of high and stable levels of growth and employment. Low and stable inflation helps
individuals and businesses to plan for the long term. This in turn improves the quality and
quantity of long-term investment, both in physical and human capital, and helps raise
productivity.

2.4   The UK's poor inflation record over most of the past 30 years reflected shortcomings in
the previous design and conduct of monetary policy. In the past, objectives were often
inappropriate or unclear, roles and responsibilities were ill-defined, and a lack of
transparency hindered the accountability and credibility of policymakers.

2.5   On entering office, the Government undertook fundamental reforms of the monetary
policy framework. Recognising the importance of price stability, the Government made this
the key objective of monetary policy. The objective was defined as a single and unambiguous
inflation target to avoid any risk of a return to policies (such as attempting to target both
inflation and the exchange rate) that caused instability in the past. Thus a clear inflation
target of $2^1/_2$ per cent for the annual increase in the Retail Prices Index excluding mortgage
interest payments (RPIX) was set and is reaffirmed in this Budget. To ensure that monetary
policy is forward-looking and supports the Government's growth and employment objectives
the Government also made the inflation target symmetrical, so that deviations below target
are treated equally seriously as those above.

2.6   The Government's monetary policy framework also sets out clear roles and
responsibilities: the Government sets the inflation target, while the task of the Bank of
England's Monetary Policy Committee (MPC) is to set interest rates to meet that target.
Interest rate decisions are thus now made by independent experts, unencumbered by short
term political pressures. The MPC's decisions are based on rigorous analysis and take into
account all available information, including regional and sectoral information provided by
the Bank's network of 13 regional agents, which covers the whole of the UK.

2.7   The inflation target applies at all times, and the MPC is accountable for any deviations from it. The framework recognises, however, that any economy can at some point be subject to unexpected events which can cause inflation to depart from its desired level. In such cases, the onus is on the MPC to explain how it proposes to return inflation back to target. If inflation is more than one percentage point below or above the target, the Governor of the Bank of England is required to write an open letter to the Chancellor, explaining why this divergence has occurred, the policy action being taken to deal with it, the period within which inflation is expected to return to target, and how this approach is consistent with the Government's objectives for growth and employment.

2.8   The granting of operational independence to the Bank was also accompanied by a range of measures aimed at improving the transparency and accountability of monetary policy. Minutes of the MPC's meetings are published within two weeks of its decisions, while the quarterly *Inflation Report* reviews recent monetary policy decisions, assesses developments in inflation and indicates the expected approach to meeting the Bank's objectives. In addition, members of the MPC are subject to full scrutiny by Parliament, through the Treasury Committee and a specially established House of Lords Committee.

2.9   A key feature of the monetary policy framework is the forward-looking and pro-active approach taken by the MPC. Inflation outturns have been a poor guide to prospects in previous cycles (see Box B4). This highlights the fact that policymakers need to look ahead when making decisions, given that the effects of monetary policy flow through to inflation with a lag, and because upward or downward pressures on inflation take time to build following either an upturn or a slowing in growth. The new monetary arrangements provide a more credible framework in which unexpected developments can be addressed as they arise. By acting promptly, policymakers can help to contain inflationary pressures, thereby reducing volatility in both inflation and output.

The fiscal framework   **2.10**   The Government has also introduced a new framework for fiscal policy to ensure that the same high standards of transparency, responsibility and accountability which now underpin monetary policy also apply to fiscal policy decisions.

2.11   The previous fiscal framework left the Government, on taking office, faced with a large structural deficit, low net investment, rising public debt and falling public sector net worth. This situation had come about, in part, as a result of a lack of clear and transparent fiscal objectives, together with fiscal reporting that did not permit full and effective public and parliamentary scrutiny.

2.12   The Government therefore implemented a new framework for fiscal policy based on a set of five central principles – transparency, stability, responsibility, fairness (including between generations) and efficiency. These principles were enshrined in the Finance Act 1998 and repeated in the *Code for Fiscal Stability*, approved by the House of Commons in December 1998. The Code explains how these principles are to be reflected in the formulation and implementation of fiscal policy in practice.

2.13   As outlined in the March 1999 EFSR, the Government is committed to ensuring that households are fully informed about tax and spending decisions and in due course intends to amend the *Code for Fiscal Stability* to guarantee this. It is considering the most effective way to take this forward, including the distribution to households of a leaflet, as set out last year.

2.14   The Government's key objectives for fiscal policy are:

- over the medium term, ensuring sound public finances and that spending and taxation impact fairly both within and across generations. In practice, this requires that:

  - the Government meets its key tax and spending priorities while avoiding an unsustainable and damaging rise in the burden of public debt; and

  - as far as possible, those generations who benefit from public spending also meet the costs of the services they consume.

- over the short term, supporting monetary policy where possible, by:

  - allowing the automatic stabilisers to play their role in smoothing the path of the economy in the face of variations in demand; and

  - where prudent and sensible, providing further support to monetary policy through changes in the structural (cyclically-adjusted) fiscal position.

2.15   These objectives are reflected in the Government's two strict fiscal rules, against which the performance of fiscal policy may be judged:

- the golden rule: over the economic cycle, the Government will borrow only to invest and not to fund current spending; and

- the sustainable investment rule: public sector net debt as a proportion of GDP will be held over the economic cycle at a stable and prudent level.

2.16   The golden rule is met if, on average over a complete economic cycle, the current budget is in balance or surplus. The Government has also said that, other things equal, a reduction in net public sector debt to below 40 per cent of GDP over the economic cycle is desirable.

The public spending framework

2.17   The Government has also implemented a new regime for planning and controlling public spending with the following main features:

- three-year plans have been set for all the main government departments through Departmental Expenditure Limits (DEL). These limits provide departments with a solid basis for planning and an incentive to manage their own costs effectively. A spending review is taking place currently, and will be completed by July 2000 (see Box 2.2);

- Annually Managed Expenditure (AME), which cannot reasonably be subject to firm multi-year limits, is subject to tough annual scrutiny as part of the Budget process; and

- within DEL and AME – which together equate to Total Managed Expenditure (TME) – a distinction is made between current and capital spending for each department, consistent with the distinction in the fiscal rules. This removes the bias against investment inherent under the previous planning regime.

2.18   Each department is also committed, through Public Service Agreements (PSAs), to testing performance and efficiency targets for the modernisation of public services. Departments have also drawn up Departmental Investment Strategies (DIS), first published in March 1999, to show how they manage capital effectively and how investment decisions are taken on a robust basis so as to maximise the benefits of the extra investment.

Performance of the frameworks

2.19   The new monetary policy framework has been in operation now for almost three years. As Chart 2.1 demonstrates, the MPC's record so far in meeting the Government's inflation target is a good one. Since May 1997, RPIX inflation has averaged 2.5 per cent, moving in a narrow band between a low of 2.1 per cent and a high of 3.2 per cent.

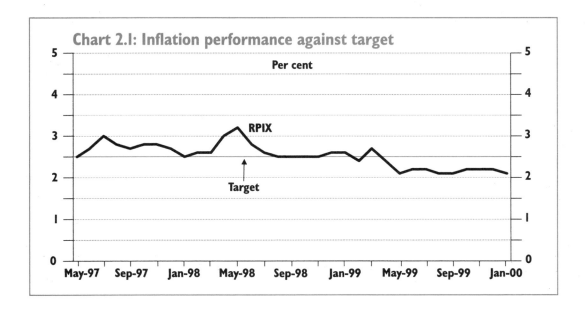

Chart 2.1: Inflation performance against target

2.20   Survey and financial market data also suggest that the MPC has established a high degree of credibility, with inflation expected to remain close to target in the future. Since the Government's monetary policy framework was introduced, expectations of inflation ten years ahead have fallen from over 4 per cent to around $2\frac{1}{2}$ per cent, consistent with the inflation target.

Chart 2.2: Inflation expectations 10 years ahead

2.21 The MPC has acted quickly and pre-emptively to maintain price stability[1]:

- from mid to late 1997, the MPC raised interest rates four times and successfully headed off mounting inflationary pressures;

- between late 1998 and the first half of 1999, the MPC cut rates aggressively in response to the global downturn, action that not only lessened the risk of a significant undershoot of the inflation target but which was also widely credited with helping to avoid a sharp slowdown in domestic activity; and

- since autumn 1999, the MPC has again moved pre-emptively, in four measured steps, to avoid a build up of inflationary pressures. Base rates have been raised to 6 per cent in response to the improved global economic outlook, strong growth in consumer spending and tighter labour market countries.

2.22 By focusing on price stability, the Government's monetary policy framework has allowed interest rates to be lower and more stable than in the past. Despite recent increases, official rates remain well below their latest peak and are less than half the level seen in the late 1980s and early 1990s. In addition, long-term interest rates are at historically low levels and are currently below equivalent rates in other major European countries.

2.23 The new fiscal framework has restored the public finances to a healthy and sustainable position, while allowing fiscal policy to support monetary policy through the economic cycle. The necessary fiscal tightening during 1997–98 supported monetary policy when the economy was above trend, and Budget 99 locked in that tightening. The Budget 2000 projections show this tightening is more than locked in, with the Government continuing to meet the fiscal rules, including on more cautious assumptions.

2.24 Early indications suggest that the new macroeconomic framework is delivering valuable results. In contrast to the boom and bust of the past, the UK economy has enjoyed a period of stability and steady growth since the introduction of the new monetary and fiscal policy frameworks, (see Chart B3), with output and employment at high and stable levels. With its focus on economic stability, increased employment opportunity, higher productivity, and responsibility in wage setting, the Government is aiming for stronger sustained growth.

2.25 A high degree of economic stability will also help to provide the foundations for the necessary convergence should the UK decide to join EMU in the next Parliament (see Box 2.1).

---

[1] See *The New Monetary Policy Framework*, HM Treasury, October 1999, for a more detailed assessment.

Box 2.1: EMU AND EMU PREPARATIONS

The UK economy is closely linked to the economies of the eleven member countries of EMU. Almost 50 per cent of the UK's trade is with the euro zone and the UK and the euro area are each other's largest trade and investment partners. The Government is therefore committed to playing its part in ensuring a successful single currency.

Government policy on UK membership of the single currency remains as set out by the Chancellor of the Exchequer in a statement to Parliament in October 1997, and as restated by the Prime Minister when he launched the first Outline National Changeover Plan in February 1999.

The determining factor underpinning any Government decision on membership of the single currency is whether the economic case for the UK joining is clear and unambiguous. Because of the magnitude of the decision, the Government believes – as a matter of principle – that if the decision to enter is taken by Government, it should be put to a referendum of the British people. Government, Parliament and the people must all agree.

The Government has set out five economic tests which will have to be met before any decision to join can be taken. These are: whether the UK has achieved sustainable convergence with the economies of the single currency; whether there is sufficient flexibility in the UK economy to adapt to change and unexpected economic events; whether joining the single currency would create better conditions for business to make long term decisions to invest in the UK; the impact membership would have on our financial services industry; and, ultimately, whether the single currency would be good for employment. The Government has said that it will produce another assessment of the five tests early in the next Parliament.

The Government is committed to ensuring that preparations are made so that, should the economic tests be met, the British people would be in a position to exercise genuine choice in a referendum. The Government has recently published its second Outline National Changeover Plan, which shows that, through making targeted preparations during 1999, the UK has maintained the option to make a decision early in the next Parliament, for a smooth and cost-effective changeover should Government, Parliament and the people - in a referendum – decide to join. This has been achieved both by preparations in the public sector, and through a co-ordination of planning effort across the whole economy.

The Government has also been helping small and medium sized enterprises (SMEs) to consider what impact the euro has on the way they do business. Some three quarters of a million SMEs have trading links with the European Union. The Government will continue to work with business to provide them with the information that they need. Further details are set out in the Treasury's Third Report on Euro Preparations.

RECENT ECONOMIC AND FISCAL DEVELOPMENTS

Recent economic developments

2.26   The past 18 months have provided an important test for the Government's monetary and fiscal frameworks. This time last year, many commentators foresaw weak short-term prospects for the UK economy. Global financial turbulence from summer 1998 prompted a period of slow growth in UK export markets and delivered a severe shock to global and domestic confidence. UK economic growth came to a temporary standstill in late 1998, mainly due to falling export volumes. Business surveys also deteriorated sharply, though these were clearly heavily influenced by global conditions, as domestic demand, particularly investment spending, remained quite firm.

2.27 The Budget 99 forecast, by contrast, projected much greater buoyancy in UK activity. With inflation under control, helped by a significant fiscal tightening during 1997 and 1998, monetary policy was able to respond pro-actively to events. By the time of Budget 99, base rates had already been reduced by 2 percentage points from a relatively low peak of $7\frac{1}{2}$ per cent in mid-1998, and subsequently fell to a trough of 5 per cent in summer 1999. With private sector balance sheets in good health, the prospect of continued growth in domestic demand underpinned the more buoyant Budget 99 forecast of 1 to $1\frac{1}{2}$ per cent growth in 1999, strengthening in 2000 as trade pressures eased.

2.28 Developments over the past year broadly confirm those Budget forecasts. Activity strengthened rapidly through 1999, with quarterly GDP growth rising from 0.4 per cent in the first quarter of 1999 to an average rate of 0.9 per cent during the second half. The balance of growth also improved in 1999, with manufacturing output and export volumes recovering rapidly from mid-year, and all regions of the UK sharing in the strengthening in activity (see Box B1). GDP rose by 2 per cent overall in 1999, exceeding the upper end of the Budget 99 forecast range. Underlying strength in private sector demand has in fact been much greater than anticipated. Household consumption growth, in particular, significantly exceeded all earlier forecasts.

2.29 The labour market also performed strongly in 1999, with LFS employment rising by 290,000 during the course of the year. The strengthening of output growth did, however, outstrip employment gains, yielding a marked recovery in non-oil productivity growth to over $1\frac{1}{2}$ per cent by the fourth quarter of 1999. Broadly as anticipated in the Pre-Budget Report forecast, this is now much closer to the rate underpinning the Government's neutral $2\frac{1}{2}$ per cent estimate for trend output growth. Growth in unit wage costs eased somewhat through 1999 as a consequence.

2.30 Unemployment has declined further with both the claimant count and ILO measures now standing at 20-year lows, and the employment rate approaching its previous peak. It seems quite likely that the sustainable level of unemployment has fallen over recent years, though the recent upturn in earnings growth sounds a cautionary note. The key to further sustained increases in the employment rate therefore lies increasingly in expanding the effective supply of labour by re-attaching the inactive to the labour market and further tackling persistent long-term unemployment. This will be helped by continued improvements in regional labour market balance reflected, for example, in lower dispersion in ratios of unemployment to vacancies across the UK (see Box B2). The Government's strategy to increase employment opportunity for all is described in Chapter 4.

2.31 RPIX inflation has remained just below target since April 1999. Underlying price deflation in the retail goods sector more than accounts for these subdued outturns. Sterling's strength and falling import prices have sharpened competitive pressures on domestic producers and retailers, with retail goods inflation rates recently at 40-year lows in many sectors. Core service sector inflation, by contrast, rose to $5\frac{1}{2}$ per cent during the course of 1999. With services less directly exposed to sterling, this provides a much clearer reflection of the rapid growth in demand and a tight labour market. Nominal earnings have accelerated sharply recently and are now growing in excess of the $4\frac{1}{2}$ per cent rate that the Bank of England has said is consistent with the inflation target in the medium term.

Recent fiscal developments

2.32 The decisions taken in Budget 99 were designed to lock in the substantial fiscal tightening that had been achieved since 1997–98, and allowed fiscal policy to support monetary policy over the cycle. In the event, stronger than anticipated growth, coupled with other structural factors, improved the position of the public finances beyond that projected in Budget 99.

2.33   The surplus on the current budget in 1999–2000 is now estimated to be £17.1 billion, compared with a forecast of £2 billion at the time of Budget 99. A similar improvement is observed for public sector net borrowing (PSNB). A repayment of £11.9 billion is now expected in 1999–2000, compared with a projected deficit of £3 billion in Budget 99. These surpluses are also higher than expected at the time of the Pre-Budget Report.

Table 2.1: Changes in the surplus on current budget and net borrowing

	£ billion	
	Outturn	**Estimate**
	1998–99[3]	**1999–00**
Surplus on current budget[1,2]		
Budget 99	4.1	2
Contribution due to higher receipts	1.6	11.4
Contribution due to lower spending	1.8	3.3
Budget 2000	**7.5**	**17.1**
Net borrowing[1,2]		
Budget 99	**–1.0**	**3**
Contribution due to higher receipts	–1.6	–11.4
Contribution due to lower spending	–0.2	–3.3
Budget 2000	**–2.8**	**–11.9**

[1] Excluding windfall tax receipts and associated spending.

[2] Figures may not sum due to rounding.

[3] 1998-99 figures were estimates in Budget 99.

2.34   Higher than expected surpluses in 1999–2000 primarily reflect:

- higher than projected receipts of £11.4 billion, due to:
  - a more favourable composition of GDP; and
  - higher than expected GDP growth;
- lower than projected current expenditure of £3.3 billion.

2.35   It is important to distinguish between the cyclical and structural components of the fiscal improvement. Cyclical adjustment is not an exact science, as neither the level nor the growth of potential output is directly observable. However, based on the Treasury's methodology for cyclical adjustment[2], while some of the improvement in the public finances in 1999–2000 reflects stronger than anticipated growth, much of the improvement appears to have been structural.

2.36   Table 2.2 shows the cumulative fiscal tightening that has taken place since 1996-97. The 4.2 per cent of GDP cumulative tightening to 1999-2000 is equivalent to nearly £40 billion.

Table 2.2: The fiscal tightening – cumulative change since 1996–97

	Percentage points of GDP		
	Outturns		**Estimate**
	1997–98	**1998–99**	**1999–2000**
Public sector net borrowing (cyclically-adjusted)[1]			
Budget 99	–2.0	–3.0	–3.2
PBR 99	–1.8	–3.0	–3.2
Budget 2000	–1.8	–3.1	–4.2

[1] Excluding windfall tax receipts and associated spending.

[2] The Treasury's methodology for cyclical adjustment is set out in *Fiscal Policy: Public Finances and the Cycle*, HM Treasury, March 1999.

Performance over the cycle   **2.37**   The two fiscal rules are set over the economic cycle. This provides an inbuilt capacity for fiscal policy to respond to changing economic circumstances. The economy was judged to have been on trend in the first half of 1997. Output fell below trend towards the end of 1998, but only for a very short time, before returning to trend again in the middle of 1999. Thus, early indications suggest the economy may have completed a full economic cycle – albeit a short and shallow one by historical standards – since 1997–98. Given the closeness to trend and possible measurement errors, this conclusion can only be provisional at this stage. If the monetary and fiscal frameworks are successful, a reduction of cyclical movements in the economy over time is to be expected.

2.38   Based on this assessment, the Government met both its fiscal rules over this short cycle. For the period 1997–98 to 1999–2000, the average annual surplus on the current budget was 0.7 per cent of GDP. This contrasts with the cycle from 1986–87 to 1997–98 during which there was an average annual current budget deficit of 2 per cent of GDP. The sustainable investment rule has also been met, with net debt standing at 37.1 per cent of GDP in 1999–2000.

THE ECONOMIC AND FISCAL OUTLOOK

2.39   The health of the public finances and the state of the economy are interdependent. This section looks first at the economic outlook before examining what this means for the public finances, and the implications for this year's Budget decisions.

Economic outlook   **2.40**   Latest economic indicators have yet to provide clear evidence of any slowing in domestic demand growth in early 2000. Household spending in particular looks set for continued robust growth in the short term.

Table 2.3: Summary of forecast

	1999	2000	Forecast 2001	2002
GDP growth (per cent)	2	$2^{3}/_{4}$ to $3^{1}/_{4}$	$2^{1}/_{4}$ to $2^{3}/_{4}$	$2^{1}/_{4}$ to $2^{3}/_{4}$
RPIX inflation (per cent, Q4)	$2^{1}/_{4}$	$2^{1}/_{4}$	$2^{1}/_{2}$	$2^{1}/_{2}$

2.41   Domestic demand is expected to grow by $3^{1}/_{2}$ to 4 per cent in 2000, a full percentage point higher than forecast in the Pre-Budget Report. Consumer confidence remains at very high levels, boosted by the recent sharp acceleration in house prices. The saving ratio is now expected to fall to $5^{1}/_{2}$ per cent this year, with the result that much stronger growth in household consumption of $3^{1}/_{2}$ to $3^{3}/_{4}$ per cent is now forecast in 2000. Stronger domestic demand growth overall is likely to be offset by a weaker net trade performance. This partly reflects correspondingly faster growth in import volumes, but also slower growth in export volumes reflecting sterling's recent strengthening. GDP is expected to grow by $2^{3}/_{4}$ to $3^{1}/_{4}$ per cent in 2000, an upward revision of $^{1}/_{4}$ percentage point since the Pre-Budget Report forecast.

2.42   RPIX inflation is currently a little below the Government's $2^{1}/_{2}$ per cent target and some downward price pressures can be expected to persist for a while. This creates headroom for above trend growth this year, with the output gap projected to rise to around $^{1}/_{2}$ per cent of GDP by the end of the year. Hence, it is vital that the economy does not exceed its trend growth rate in later years, so more sustainable rates of expansion in domestic demand must be achieved[3]. The MPC has pre-emptively increased interest rates by a full percentage point since September 1999. Much in line with the independent consensus, GDP growth is expected to ease back to its trend rate of $2^{1}/_{4}$ to $2^{3}/_{4}$ per cent in both 2001 and 2002.

---

[3] See *Trend Growth - Prospects and Implications for Policy*, HM Treasury, November 1999.

2.43   RPIX inflation is forecast to remain below target throughout 2000, with sterling's recent appreciation sustaining competitive pressures and accounting for the more persistent inflation undershoot compared to the Pre-Budget Report forecast. However, firms' margins are unlikely to continue to be squeezed at their current rate and rising import prices are expected to make a much stronger contribution to inflation from now on. These factors are likely to offset a gradual easing in domestic costs growth, returning RPIX inflation to $2\frac{1}{2}$ per cent by early 2001.

2.44   There are clear upside risks to the outlook. Stronger than expected growth in domestic demand would lead to greater labour market cost pressures and a sharper rise in RPIX inflation during the course of 2001. In particular, recent rapid growth in house prices, transactions and borrowing could lead to much stronger growth in household consumption than forecast. Accelerating house prices would pose some risk to economic stability.

2.45   These risks highlight the importance of the Government's forward-looking policy framework. While house price inflation and activity is likely to remain robust in the near-term, pressures should ease later in 2000 and into 2001 as higher purchase prices, mortgage rates and some easing in real income growth act to curtail housing demand. The removal of MIRAS from April 2000 and increased stamp duty will also contribute to greater sustainability in housing and consumer demand. Policy will need to remain alert to the risks.

2.46   There is also an upside risk to the investment outlook. Incentives to invest are strong, not least because future growth will depend increasingly on securing an improved productivity performance. Although company borrowing has recently risen to high levels, firms' balance sheets remain healthy. This suggests that a return to much stronger rates of growth in capital spending is quite possible.

2.47   Moreover, in the global economy there is also clear evidence, following instabilities over the past two years, that growth is strengthening. Global pressures, including rising oil prices, mean that policymakers must remain vigilant and act decisively when necessary.

2.48   The downside risks mainly reflect imbalances in the world's two largest economies, the USA and Japan. In the US growth remains above trend, and the current account deficit has reached record levels. By contrast in Japan growth remains weak with the economy slipping back into recession in the second half of last year. A gradual rebalancing of global growth to a more sustainable pattern is expected this year as policy is tightened in the US and the recovery becomes more established in Japan. However, the risk remains of a sharp slowdown in the US and continued weakness in Japan with adverse effects on UK prospects.

2.49   Against this background, continued vigilance will be necessary if the MPC's successful track record is to be maintained. Responsible wage bargaining and price setting is key, as unsustainable wage and price rises would result in higher interest rates, with undesirable consequences for economic growth and unemployment. Continued fiscal prudence is also needed if stability is to be maintained. Low inflation and sound public finances are the best contribution the Government can make to securing a stable and competitive exchange rate over the medium term.

2.50   Potential for stronger sustainable output and productivity growth exists. The Government has taken significant steps to begin to close the productivity gap with its main competitors, described in Chapter 3. The share of business investment in GDP has already risen sharply, and within that growth in Information and Communications Technology (ICT) spending appears to have been particularly strong. Growth in e-commerce is also likely to provide an increasing spur to competition and productive efficiency. However, the Government is determined to adopt a prudent approach, erring on the side of caution where uncertainties exist. The upside possibilities are therefore illustrated by the upper ends of the GDP forecast ranges, based on $2^3/_4$ per cent trend output growth, and incorporating some modest improvement in underlying productivity performance not banked in the neutral case.

Fiscal outlook   **2.51**   Following a significant improvement in the public finances in 1999–2000, which is projected to persist, the large surpluses expected on the current budget would imply a fiscal tightening well in excess of that anticipated in Budget 99. While the golden rule helps ensure over time that current taxpayers pay for current goods and services it is also prudent to plan adequately to cover possible adverse shocks and ensure that the fiscal rules are met. It is against this background that the Budget decisions have been taken.

2.52   The economic forecast is based on a neutral estimate of $2^1/_2$ per cent a year trend growth. However, for the purposes of the public finance projections, a more cautious assumption of $2^1/_4$ per cent has been adopted. This assumption has been re-audited by the National Audit Office (NAO) as part of the rolling review of existing assumptions the Chancellor has asked the NAO to undertake[4]. For each of the three audited assumptions from the July 1997 Budget which were reviewed, the NAO concluded that they have "provided a reasonable basis for the elements of the fiscal projections to which they relate, and that they should continue to do so for future projections". In addition to the rolling review, the NAO has audited the methodology for forecasting tobacco revenues. The NAO concluded that the approach adopted is reasonably cautious.

BUDGET DECISIONS

Framework   **2.53**   The Budget represents a definitive statement of the Government's desired fiscal policy settings. As well as introducing new measures, this Budget sets the firm overall spending limits for the three year period covered by the 2000 Spending Review (2001–02 to 2003–04).

2.54   With the economy above trend and continuing to show momentum, it is vital that a clear distinction is made between the cyclical and structural strength of the economy. This approach helps to ensure that the Government remains on track to meet the fiscal rules over the economic cycle and takes account of the lessons of the past. It is also important that Budget decisions enable fiscal policy to continue supporting monetary policy. For these reasons, it is more important than ever that a cautious, forward-looking approach is taken towards fiscal policy settings.

2.55   Two key issues are considered before decisions are made about changes to the aggregate fiscal policy settings:

- the outcomes required to ensure that, over the economic cycle, the Government meets its fiscal rules and its broader medium-term fiscal objectives, including the need to maintain fairness between generations; and

- the path for the key fiscal aggregates that best ensures, over the economic cycle, fiscal policy supports monetary policy.

Decisions   **2.56**   The Government has taken both considerations into account in making its Budget decisions. In the face of substantially improved projections, the Government has been able to lock in the fiscal tightening over the next two years to an even greater extent than expected in Budget 99, while releasing substantial extra resources to its key public service priorities.

---

[4] See *Audit of Assumptions for the March 2000 Budget*, March 2000 (HC348).

2.57 The Government is:

- implementing a Budget package to promote enterprise and work and release extra resources to tackle child and pensioner poverty; and

- setting firm overall limits for public spending for the period of the 2000 Spending Review, allowing:

  - current spending to increase by $2\frac{1}{2}$ per cent a year in real terms in the three years to 2003–04, in line with the Government's neutral view of the economy's trend rate of growth; and

  - a more than doubling in net investment, rising to 1.8 per cent of GDP by 2003–04. This makes a significant further contribution to tackling the legacy of underfunding of Britain's public infrastructure while remaining consistent with the sustainable investment rule, with the debt to GDP ratio remaining well below 40 per cent in the medium term.

2.58 In implementing these measures, the Government remains well on track to meet the fiscal rules, including under the cautious case (see below). Maintaining a cautious approach is essential given the inherent uncertainties surrounding public finance projections.

2.59 Social security spending in 1999–2000 has been £2 billion lower than expected in Budget 99, and in 2000–01 is projected to be £2 billion lower than expected. The Government has decided that, in the light of the significantly improved fiscal position and its commitment to meeting the fiscal rules, it is able to allocate a further £4 billion to DEL in 2000–01, including the £1 billion DEL underspend, while locking in the fiscal tightening to a greater extent than projected in Budget 99. This provides:

- an additional £3 billion of current spending; and

- an additional £1 billion of capital spending for renewing public infrastructure.

This additional spending is being targeted at the Government's key public service priorities – education, health, law and order and transport. Further details of the allocations are given in Chapter 5.

2.60 A full explanation of the addition to DEL in 2000–01 and the firm spending limits for 2001–02 to 2003–04 within which the 2000 Spending Review will be completed is given in Chapter 5. These decisions allow spending on key public services to be sustained and increased, while at the same time ensuring that the Government's strict fiscal rules and objectives continue to be achieved. The Budget measures are set out in Chapter A.

Box 2.2: The 2000 Spending Review

The Government is currently conducting a Spending Review, to be completed by July 2000.

The aim of the Review is to determine how best departments' programmes can contribute to the achievement of the Government's objectives, in particular its aims of:

- opportunity for everyone to fulfil their potential through education and employment;

- a fair and inclusive society in which communities are healthy and secure; and

- higher productivity, sustainable economic growth and effective co-operation with our European and international partners.

The Review will roll forward the three-year planning cycle for public expenditure introduced in the 1998 Comprehensive Spending Review (CSR). The third year of the CSR plans (2001–02) will become the first year of the new three-year planning period. The Review will set new departmental spending plans for 2002–03 and 2003–04, with the firm overall limits for public spending announced in this Budget.

Besides setting new spending plans the Review will agree new Public Service Agreements with departments. These Agreements show Parliament and the public what they can expect to get for their money. They will set out the specific, measurable targets for service improvements which departments must deliver in return for investment.

The Review is taking a rigorous look at the effectiveness of existing programmes in considering the future path of spending in each area. For the first time the Review is being conducted on a resource budgeting basis, taking account of all the resources departments employ in delivering an objective, not just cash consumed.

One of the major innovations in the 2000 Review will be the inclusion of fifteen cross-departmental reviews. These will focus on key issues from crime reduction and intervention in deprived areas to science and research and the knowledge economy. The reviews will identify the best ways of improving inter-departmental co-operation and co-ordination.

MEDIUM-TERM FISCAL PROJECTIONS

2.61   Table 2.4 compares the revised medium-term projections for the current budget and public sector net borrowing with those published in Budget 99 and the Pre-Budget Report. Changes are decomposed into those explained by policy measures, and those due to forecasting and other changes.

Table 2.4: Changes in the surplus on current budget and net borrowing since Budget 99[1]

| | £ billion | | | | | | |
| | Outturn[3] | Estimate | Projections | | | | |
	1998-99	1999-00	2000-01	2001-02	2002-03	2003-04	2004-05
Surplus on current budget[1,2]							
Budget 99	4.1	2	4	8	9	11	–
Effect of revision/forecasting changes	3.1	7	8	6	4	1	–
Effect of policy measures	–	–	–1	–1	–1	–1	–
PBR 99	7.2	9.5	11	13	13	12	11
Effect of revision/forecasting changes	0.3	7.5	6	11	10	8	9
Effect of policy measures	–	–	–3	–9	–10	–11	–12
Budget 2000	7.5	17.1	14	16	13	8	8
Net borrowing[1,2]							
Budget 99	–1.0	3	3	1	3	4	–
Effect of revision/forecasting changes	–1.5	–6	–7	–5	–3	0	–
Effect of policy measures	–	–	1	1	1	1	–
PBR 99	–2.5	–3.5	–3	–3	1	4	6
Effect of revision/forecasting changes	–0.3	–8.4	–6	–11	–10	–8	–9
Effect of policy measures	–	–	4	11	13	16	15
Budget 2000	–2.8	–11.9	–6	–5	3	11	13

[1] Excluding windfall tax receipts and associated spending.

[2] Figures may not sum due to rounding

[3] The 1998-99 figures were estimates in Budget 99.

Fiscal stance   **2.62**   Table 2.5 compares the latest fiscal projections, including Budget decisions, with those presented in Budget 99. It shows that the fiscal stance, defined as cyclically-adjusted PSNB, is projected to be tighter over the next two years than in Budget 99. Thus the tightening in the fiscal stance has been locked in further, as compared with Budget 99, with fiscal policy doing more over this period to support monetary policy while the economy is above trend.

Table 2.5: Fiscal balances comparison with Budget 99[1]

| | Outturn[2] | Estimate | Projections | | | | |
	1998-99	1999-00	2000-01	2001-02	2002-03	2003-04	2004-05
Fiscal balances (£ billion)							
Surplus on current budget – Budget 99	4.1	2	4	8	9	11	–
Surplus on current budget – Budget 2000	7.5	17.1	14	16	13	8	8
Net borrowing – Budget 99	–1.0	3	3	1	3	4	–
Net borrowing – Budget 2000	–2.8	–11.9	–6	–5	3	11	13
Cyclically-adjusted budget balances (per cent of GDP)							
Surplus on current budget – Budget 99	0.2	0.6	1.0	1.1	0.9	1.0	–
Surplus on current budget – Budget 2000	0.6	1.8	1.3	1.3	1.0	0.7	0.7
Net borrowing – Budget 99	0.1	0.0	–0.2	–0.1	0.3	0.4	–
Net borrowing – Budget 2000	–0.1	–1.2	–0.5	–0.3	0.5	1.1	1.1

[1] Excluding windfall tax receipts and associated spending.

[2] The 1998–99 figures were estimates in Budget 99.

Adhering to key fiscal principles

2.63   Table 2.6 presents a summary of the key fiscal aggregates focused around five key themes: fairness and prudence, sustainability, economic impact, financing and meeting European commitments[5].

Table 2.6: Summary of public sector finances[1]

| | Outturn | Estimate | \multicolumn{5}{c}{Per cent of GDP} | | | | |
| | | | \multicolumn{5}{c}{Projections} | | | | |
	1998–99	1999–00	2000–01	2001–02	2002–03	2003–04	2004–05
Fairness and prudence							
Surplus on current budget	0.9	1.9	1.5	1.6	1.2	0.8	0.7
Cyclically-adjusted surplus on current budget	0.6	1.8	1.3	1.3	1.0	0.7	0.7
Average surplus since 1999–2000	–	1.9	1.7	1.7	1.5	1.4	1.3
Long-term sustainability							
Public sector net debt[2]	39.7	37.1	35.1	33.6	32.7	32.6	32.6
Net worth[2]	13.6	15.4	17.1	18.2	18.7	18.8	18.8
Primary balance	3.3	3.8	3.2	2.8	1.9	1.0	0.9
Economic impact							
Net investment	0.6	0.6	0.9	1.2	1.5	1.8	1.8
Public sector net borrowing (PSNB)	–0.3	–1.3	–0.7	–0.5	0.3	1.0	1.1
Cyclically-adjusted PSNB	–0.1	–1.2	–0.5	–0.3	0.5	1.1	1.1
Financing							
Central government net cash requirement[2]	–0.5	–0.6	–0.5	0.0	0.5	1.5	1.4
European commitments							
Maastricht deficit[3]	–0.6	–1.3	–0.6	–0.3	0.3	1.1	1.2
Maastricht debt ratio[4]	47.0	44.1	42.0	40.2	39.1	38.9	38.7
Memo: Output gap	*0.2*	*0.1*	*0.4*	*0.3*	*0.2*	*0.1*	*0.0*

[1] Excluding windfall tax receipts and associated spending.

[2] Including windfall tax receipts and associated spending.

[3] General government net borrowing on an ESA95 basis. The Maastricht definition includes windfall tax receipts and associated spending.

[4] General government gross debt.

Fairness and prudence

2.64   The golden rule is designed to achieve fairness between generations ensuring that, as far as possible, those generations who benefit from public spending meet the costs of the services they consume.

2.65   Since 1996–97, the Government has delivered a substantial improvement in the current budget, which has moved from a deficit of 3 per cent of GDP to an estimated surplus of 1.9 per cent in 1999–2000. Estimates of the cyclically-adjusted current budget suggest that much of this improvement has been structural.

2.66   The average current budget over the period 1997–98 to 1999–2000, which early indications suggest may constitute a complete economic cycle, is estimated to have been 0.7 per cent of GDP, indicating that the Government met the golden rule over the period.

2.67   Over the projection period, the surplus on the current budget is projected to fall gradually to 0.7 per cent of GDP by 2004–05. Consistent with the need to maintain a cautious approach, this profile shows that the Government is well on track to meet its golden rule over the projection period, with the average surplus on the current budget from 1999–2000 falling from 1.7 per cent GDP in 2000–01 to 1.3 per cent GDP in 2004–05.

[5] Based on the formulation introduced in *Analysing UK Fiscal Policy*, HM Treasury, November 1999.

2.68   It is also important to take into account the cyclical component of the surplus. The Government has maintained a prudent approach in its Budget decisions, and the cyclically-adjusted current budget remains comfortably positive throughout the projection period.

Long-term   **2.69**   Net debt has declined continuously as a proportion of GDP since 1996–97, when it **sustainability**   stood at 44 per cent of GDP. By the end of March 2000, it is projected to be 37.1 per cent of GDP. This is consistent with meeting the sustainable investment rule. The Budget 2000 projections show a decline in net debt, stabilising at 32.6 per cent of GDP by 2004–05 reflecting the sustained improvement in the position of the public finances. This is consistent with the projected more than doubling of net investment over the same period.

2.70   Net worth and the primary balance are alternative indicators of the sustainability of the public finances. Net worth, which is the difference between the total assets and liabilities of the Government, is projected to be 15.4 per cent of GDP by the end of 1999–2000, rising to almost 19 per cent of GDP by 2002–03. The primary balance, which is PSNB excluding debt interest payments, is forecast to be 3.8 per cent of GDP in 1999–2000, falling to 0.9 per cent of GDP in 2004–05.

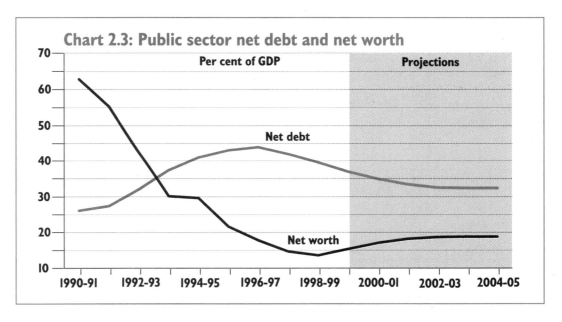

Chart 2.3: Public sector net debt and net worth

Economic impact   **2.71**   While the primary objective of fiscal policy is to ensure the medium-term sustainability of the public finances, fiscal policy also plays a role in supporting monetary policy[6].

2.72   The key indicator for assessing the overall fiscal impact is the change in PSNB. PSNB differs from the current budget because it includes net investment. Government investment will have an impact on economic activity and should therefore be included when assessing the economic impact of fiscal policy.

2.73   The overall fiscal impact is made up of changes in:

- the fiscal stance – that part of PSNB resulting from changes in cyclically-adjusted PSNB; and

- the automatic stabilisers – that part of PSNB resulting from cyclical movements in the economy.

[6] For a more detailed explanation of the Government's approach see *Analysing UK Fiscal Policy*, HM Treasury, November 1999.

2.74 The fiscal stance can change as a result of:

- a discretionary Budget measure to achieve the desired change in the fiscal stance; and

- a Budget decision to accommodate or offset the impact of non-discretionary factors (non-cyclical or structural changes to tax receipts or public spending) that are expected to affect the fiscal stance.

2.75 Table 2.7 explains how these concepts relate to the projections presented in this Budget. It shows the change in both the fiscal stance and the overall fiscal impact relative to the projections in Budget 99.

Table 2.7: The overall fiscal impact – change from Budget 99 projections

| | Percentage points of GDP | | | | |
| | Estimate | Projections | | | |
	1999–00	2000–01	2001–02	2002–03	2003–04
discretionary policy measures[1]	–	0.5	1.2	1.4	1.6
+					
non-discretionary factors	–1.2	–0.8	–1.4	–1.2	–0.9
=					
CHANGE IN FISCAL STANCE	–1.2	–0.3	–0.2	0.2	0.7
+					
automatic stabilisers	–0.4	–0.8	–0.4	–0.2	–0.1
=					
OVERALL FISCAL IMPACT	–1.6	–1.1	–0.6	0.0	0.6

[1] Includes measures announced in November 1999 Pre-Budget Report and Budget 2000.

2.76 In 1999–2000, there was a significant tightening of the fiscal stance, of 1.2 per cent of GDP relative to that anticipated at the time of Budget 99. This has occurred primarily through a more favourable composition of GDP, and lower than projected current expenditure. In addition to this large tightening of the fiscal stance, growth above that anticipated at the time of Budget 99 has meant that the automatic stabilisers have operated to a greater extent than anticipated (0.4 per cent of GDP). Taken together, the overall fiscal impact has supported monetary policy more than anticipated at Budget time, by 1.6 per cent of GDP.

2.77 Over the next two years the non-discretionary tightening of the fiscal stance is projected largely to persist. The package of measures announced in Budget 2000 partially offsets this. Overall, however, the fiscal stance is anticipated to be 0.3 percentage points of GDP tighter in 2000–01, and 0.2 percentage points of GDP tighter in 2001–02, than expected in Budget 99. The automatic stabilisers will also operate to a greater extent than previously allowed for, reflecting the stronger evolution of the economy now expected. The overall fiscal impact is therefore projected to support monetary policy more than anticipated in Budget 99, by 1.1 per cent of GDP in 2000–01, and by 0.6 per cent of GDP in 2001–02.

Financing   2.78   The financing requirement is primarily determined by two variables:

- refinancing redemptions of gilts, which are expected to be fairly stable over the projection period. From £19 billion in 2000–01 they are projected to fluctuate between £16 billion and £22 billion over the 2001–02 to 2004–05 period; and

- the central government net cash requirement, consistent with the rest of the fiscal projections, is forecast to rise over the period from minus £5 billion in 2000–01, to balance in 2001-02, and to £16 billion in 2003–04 and 2004–05.

2.79   The Debt Management Report[7], published at the time of the Budget, reviews developments in debt management over the past financial year, and sets out the details of the UK Government's borrowing programme for the forthcoming financial year.

European   2.80   The Maastricht Treaty and Stability and Growth Pact provide reference values for
commitments   general government net borrowing (3 per cent of GDP) and general government gross debt (60 per cent of GDP). The Budget 2000 projections show general government net borrowing (the Maastricht Deficit) at –1.3 per cent of GDP i.e. net lending, and general government gross debt at 44.1 per cent of GDP in 1999–2000. Both measures meet the reference values comfortably.

Dealing with   2.81   Forecasting the public finances involves a high degree of uncertainty. For this reason
uncertainty   the public finance projections are based on cautious assumptions audited by the NAO. The projections build in an additional surplus on the current budget over the economic cycle, providing a safety margin over what would be strictly necessary to meet the golden rule.

2.82   Chart 2.4 illustrates a more cautious case in which trend output is assumed to be 1 per cent lower than in the projection used for the medium-term public finance projections in Table 2.6. This scenario would imply that a greater degree of the projected surplus on the current budget is due to the cyclical strength of the economy. Even on this more cautious case the golden rule would be met, with the cyclically-adjusted current budget projected to be in surplus or balance over the forecast horizon.

---

[7] See *Debt Management Report*, HM Treasury, March 2000.

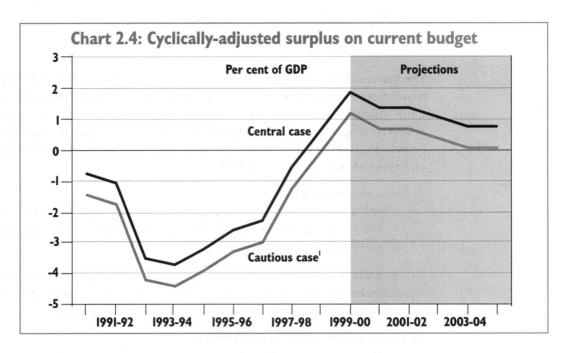

Chart 2.4: Cyclically-adjusted surplus on current budget

LONG-TERM FISCAL PROJECTIONS

2.83 In setting fiscal policy it is important that the Government ensures that its short-term decisions are consistent with a sustainable long-term framework. In line with this, the illustrative long-term fiscal projections for the UK (see Annex at the end of the EFSR) show a broadly sustainable fiscal position. Improvements in labour force participation or productivity would further strengthen this position.

2.84 The projections also show that if net investment is sustained at around $1^3/_4$ per cent of GDP, the debt ratio will stabilise at slightly below 40 per cent of GDP in the long-term, consistent with meeting the sustainable investment rule. The considerable uncertainty surrounding the long-term analysis of fiscal trends means that, despite the sound overall position, there is no scope for complacency.

2.85 In addition to the long-term sustainability of the public finances, the Government is focusing on how its wider economic, social and environmental policies impact on quality of life – both now and for future generations. The Government's strategy for sustainable development is summarised in Box 6.1.

3 MEETING THE PRODUCTIVITY CHALLENGE

The Government's long term economic ambition for the next decade is that Britain will have a faster rise in productivity than its main competitors as it closes the productivity gap. Since coming into office, the Government has taken significant steps to tackle the productivity gap through a range of measures in the areas of competition, enterprise, innovation, skills, investment and public sector productivity. Many of these measures will be implemented in Finance Bill 2000.

To promote competition:

- the Government has introduced a new Competition Act, which took effect on 1 March, giving tough new powers to the Office of Fair Trading to curb anti-competitive behaviour; and

- following the Banking Review by Don Cruickshank, the Government is bringing forward a package of measures designed to reduce prices and improve services for consumers and SMEs and promote innovation in banking.

To encourage enterprise and innovation:

- the Government is making capital gains tax changes to promote long term investment and entrepreneurship by shortening the business assets taper to four years and lowering the thresholds for qualification to allow all shareholdings in unquoted trading companies to qualify for the business assets taper. In quoted trading companies, all shareholdings by employees will qualify as will all other shareholdings above a 5 per cent threshold;

- the Government is introducing a package of enterprise tax measures, including permanent 40 per cent capital allowances for SMEs. Since 1997, the Government has cut the average corporation tax bill for small companies by nearly 25 per cent; and

- the Secretary of State for Trade and Industry will shortly announce a new clusters fund to enable RDAs to co-finance business incubators and small scale infrastructure to encourage innovation across the regions.

To raise the skills base in the UK the Government is:

- increasing resources to drive up educational standards further including the additional £1 billion education spending announced in Budget 2000; and changing the work permits rules to help address labour market shortages more effectively and to attract highly skilled overseas workers to the country.

To increase the levels of investment in the economy, the Government:

- is allocating an extra £100 million to support a £1 billion target umbrella fund to be taken forward by the SBS and RDAs levering in private finance to provide better access to venture capital for small, growth firms in the regions; and

- has asked Paul Myners, Chairman of Gartmore Investment Management, to look at whether there are factors discouraging institutional investors from investing in SMEs.

To improve productivity in the public sector:

- the Government is setting tough new targets in the 2000 Spending Review to ensure improved public sector service delivery with a particular focus on the impact that departmental policies have on the productivity of the wider economy.

INTRODUCTION

3.1   Since the election, the Government has been developing a strategy to increase productivity in the UK to help meet its central economic objective of achieving high and stable levels of growth and employment. This strategy started from a recognition of the UK's productivity gap compared to other major economies, and an understanding of our key weaknesses: a lack of domestic competition, insufficient incentives and opportunities for enterprise and innovation, poor skills and a history of under-investment. The 1999 Pre-Budget Report (PBR) set out these issues, and outlined the Government's strategy for tackling the UK's productivity challenge. This Budget sees the implementation of a number of key components of that strategy and sets out the next steps in an ongoing programme of reform.

3.2   It is now more important than ever that the UK is equipped to respond to the new opportunities provided by rapid globalisation, the growth of new technologies, associated with the internet and e-commerce in particular, and a European economy that is recovering and reforming. The Government needs to ensure that it is creating the right climate and incentives for entrepreneurial individuals and firms to seize these opportunities.

3.3   The Government's strategy is to build on the macroeconomic stability that it has created through making the Bank of England independent and adhering to the Fiscal Rules (see Chapter 2). That platform of stability has provided the essential underpinning for a structural reform programme aimed at promoting competition, encouraging enterprise and innovation, raising the skills base, creating the best conditions for investment, and improving public sector productivity.

3.4   The Government is continuing to consult widely on what more could be done to improve the productivity of the UK economy. In the run up to Budget 2000, the Chancellor has undertaken an enterprise tour to hear views about how to improve enterprise and employment in the regions and communities of Britain. In July, the Chancellor will host a major conference in London, bringing together leading UK and US entrepreneurs to discuss how to improve enterprise in the UK economy, and how Government and business can work together to help areas of deprivation reach their full potential.

THE PRODUCTIVITY CHALLENGE

3.5   It is widely accepted that UK productivity performance has been poor (see box 3.1). This is because of several key historic weaknesses (see charts 3.1-3.4). These are that:

- despite the UK being open to international trade, it has suffered from a lack of strong domestically generated competition;

- a weak enterprise culture – the number of people involved in starting businesses in the UK is about half that of the US, although we compare well with most of Europe.

- the UK has a weak record on innovation, with the lowest rate of business R&D in the G5;

- insufficient skills – we compare poorly with Germany on intermediate skills, and have fewer highly-skilled people than the US;

- before 1999 the UK invested less of its national income than the G7 average every year since at least 1965, leaving us with a lower capital stock than our major competitors.

Box 3.1: Productivity ambition

The Government's long-term economic ambition for the next decade is that Britain will have a faster rise in productivity than its main competitors as it closes the productivity gap. The UK's productivity gap with countries such as the US, France and Germany is substantial. On the frequently used measure of output per worker or labour productivity, the UK has a gap of 36 per cent with the US, around 25 per cent with France and almost 15 per cent with Germany. Matching the US performance would mean that the UK was around £5,000 better off per person.

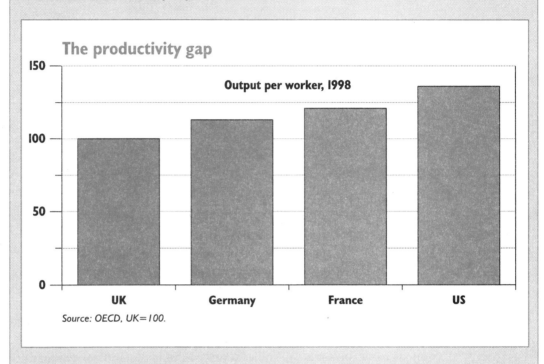

The productivity gap

Output per worker, 1998

Source: OECD, UK=100.

The Government aims to close this gap by creating the best economic environment for improving productivity in the UK. This is one:

- which is strongly competitive, so that businesses have to be innovative and entrepreneurial to stay ahead and markets are opened up for new entrants;

- which has a culture of enterprise with proper incentives for entrepreneurial, risk-taking individuals and businesses. This leads to innovation as new ideas and inventions are exploited successfully as new products and services;

- where all individuals have the skills to make the best use of new technologies that arise and can adapt in a fast–changing economy;

- where the resulting incentives promote more, and more productive, investment; and

- that is underpinned by improved public sector productivity delivered through better quality services and increased investment in infrastructure.

The productivity challenge

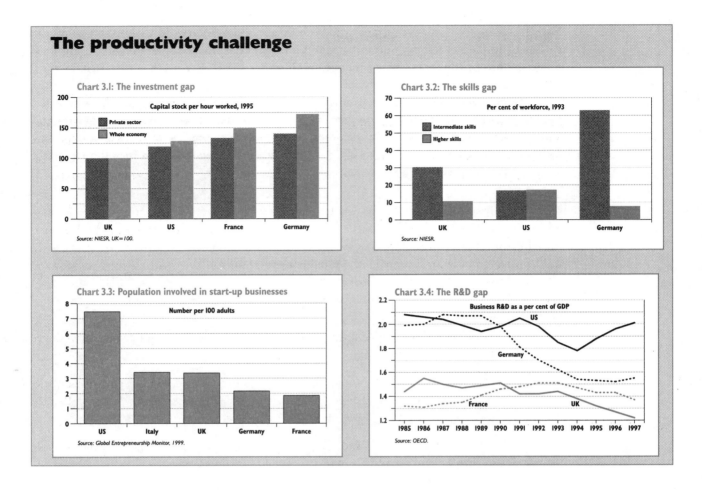

Chart 3.1: The investment gap
Capital stock per hour worked, 1995
Private sector
Whole economy
UK, US, France, Germany
Source: NIESR, UK=100.

Chart 3.2: The skills gap
Per cent of workforce, 1993
Intermediate skills
Higher skills
UK, US, Germany
Source: NIESR.

Chart 3.3: Population involved in start-up businesses
Number per 100 adults
US, Italy, UK, Germany, France
Source: Global Entrepreneurship Monitor, 1999.

Chart 3.4: The R&D gap
Business R&D as a per cent of GDP
US, Germany, France, UK
1985 1986 1987 1988 1989 1990 1991 1992 1993 1994 1995 1996 1997
Source: OECD.

3.6   The Government's strategy to address these weaknesses recognises that they are all inter–linked (PBR 1999 set out these arguments in detail). For example, R&D alone will not create new products and new wealth without the spur of competition and the vision of entrepreneurs. Equally, firms have put off past investment not only due to macroeconomic instability, but also because they could not find workers with the right skills. It is therefore only by dealing with all these weaknesses together, that the Government will meet its productivity ambition.

COMPETITION

3.7   A competitive economy will drive up productivity by setting firms a sharp incentive to improve the efficiency with which they produce goods and services, keeping prices down and quality up. Firms will know that if they fail to do these things, they will lose business to existing competitors or new entrants. At the same time, firms will be encouraged to innovate to ensure that they maintain an advantage in a fiercely competitive market, boosting productivity further.

Improving competition in the UK economy

The Competition   **3.8**   The new Competition Act 1998 came into force on 1 March. The Act revolutionises
Act   the enforcement of competition policy by enhancing the powers available to the Office of Fair Trading (OFT) to tackle anti-competitive practices and abuses of a dominant position. It also introduces strong penalties for transgressors – up to 10 per cent of UK turnover for each year of the infringement up to a maximum of three years – and ensures that the OFT is able to identify and pursue cases of anti-competitive behaviour entirely independently of

Ministers. The OFT will encourage whistle-blowers to come forward with information on cartels by implementing a leniency regime for companies that co-operate with them. This approach has been highly successful in the US.

3.9   To help ensure that the Act is implemented effectively, the OFT was awarded an extra £15.4 million over three years in the 1998 Comprehensive Spending Review. These funds have allowed the OFT to undertake an extensive programme to educate businesses in what the new Act means, and how it will be implemented. At the same time, the OFT has recruited additional experts to improve its capabilities, and organised additional training for its staff.

Review of competition in the professions   3.10   Certain professional rules are excluded from the prohibitions on anti-competitive agreements introduced by the Competition Act. The Chancellor announced in the PBR that the Director General for Fair Trading would provide advice to Ministers on the extent to which this can lead to distortions or restrictions in competition in the markets for professional services. These markets are worth over £25 billion.

3.11   The OFT has been considering how best to take forward this review. Its initial conclusions are that it should look at three generic types of restriction, between which there are likely to be significant interactions:

- rules which restrict entry to certain professions and legal restrictions on the ability of individuals who do not have specified qualifications from offering certain services;

- rules on the conduct of regulated professionals such as restrictions or prohibitions on advertising or price competition; and

- legal requirements which require third parties to use qualified professionals for certain transactions.

3.12   There may be linkages between the possible effects on competition of the way in which the professions are regulated and wider issues affecting these markets, such as the conduct of market participants. If so, the review will need to consider these as well.

3.13   The DGFT aims to put advice to Ministers later in the year. The Government will then need to balance any competition detriment identified by the review against other public policy objectives such as the protection of consumers from incompetent practitioners. In line with the recommendations made by Don Cruickshank last summer in his interim report on the regulation of the banking system, the Government will aim to ensure that any restrictions are proportionate and do not restrict competition more than is necessary. Following consideration by Ministers, the Government will consider whether the exclusion of certain professional rules from the Competition Act ought to be removed and whether other reforms to legislation are required, including to EC Single Market Directives.

3.14   In addition to improving the overall competition framework in the UK, the Government is:
- implementing the Utilities Bill, which will confer on the energy regulator a primary duty to advance the consumer interest through competition wherever possible and appropriate;
- planning to publish a Green Paper in the next month on competition in the water industry; and
- planning to publish a White Paper in the autumn on regulation of the communications industry.

Box 3.2 The Banking Review

In November 1998 the Chancellor asked Don Cruickshank to examine competition in banking (except for investment banking). The Cruickshank Report was published yesterday. The Government welcomes the Report and will act on its recommendations to improve competition in the industry and services to consumers.

Improving services for SMEs

- The Cruickshank Report found that banks are earning supernormal profits in providing banking services to SMEs. The Secretary of State for Trade and Industry and the Chancellor have referred the issue to the Competition Commission under the complex monopoly provisions of the 1973 Fair Trading Act.

- The Government agrees with the Cruickshank Report that greater effort should be made to improve access to risk capital for smaller growing businesses. A new Small Business Investment Task Force, jointly with the RDAs, will use a £1 billion target umbrella fund to develop the market in venture capital (see paragraph 3.43).

- The Government is cutting capital gains tax to encourage entrepreneurial investment, reward risk-taking, and promote wider share ownership amongst employees (see paragraph 3.34).

Lower prices and wider choice in money transmission

- The Cruickshank Report found barriers to entry and anti-competitive practices in the provision of money transmission services, which raise prices to consumers, add to business costs, and stifle innovation.

- The Chancellor is today announcing that the Government will legislate to open up access to payments systems and to oversee access charges.

- The Government in the meantime will expect banks to increase transparency in their charging, base charges on the economic cost of providing services, and to open up money transmission systems to new entrants.

More information for consumers and better redress for grievances

- The Government strongly supports the Cruickshank Report's view that to promote competition it is essential to educate consumers.

- When the Financial Services and Markets Bill is enacted the Financial Services Authority (FSA) will have a new statutory objective of promoting public understanding of the financial system. In the light of that objective the Chancellor has asked the FSA to report to him within three months, consulting widely, on how they propose to respond to the recommendations in this area.

Empowering consumers

3.15   To gain the full benefits of effective competition, individuals need to be well-informed consumers. This requires people to have access to easily understandable information comparing suppliers of similar products. This is why the Government is improving the information available to consumers on what are often complex products. For example, the FSA has set out proposals for publishing clear and helpful comparative information on products such as personal pensions, endowments, unit trust and ISA products (see Chapter 5). To meet its new remit to promote public understanding of the financial system, the FSA is also developing a customer focussed regime for regulating mortgages, majoring on disclosure.

ENTERPRISE AND INNOVATION

Enterprise

The ladder of opportunity for business

3.16   Enterprise is about using resources – knowledge, people and capital – to seize opportunities. Success depends on having access to resources and being aware of opportunities at every stage of the process of developing and growing a business. The Government's job is to create an environment in which enterprise can flourish. This requires an under-pinning of macroeconomic stability and vigorous competition. However, there is a positive role beyond this that the Government can play in encouraging an enterprise society. The aim of this Government is to help each firm raise and achieve its potential by creating a ladder of opportunity for business that starts before a firm is even created and stretches up to the largest companies in the country.

3.17   In practical terms, the Government has been working closely with business over the last eighteen months to identify the key barriers which can hold back enterprises from moving forward at each stage in their development: a lack of skills and ambition reducing the potential of start-ups; barriers and a lack of support when starting a business; and too few incentives to encourage existing businesses to aim for high-growth. The Government has designed and consulted on a large number of measures to help reduce these barriers, which will be introduced in this Finance Bill.

Pre start-up support

3.18   The Government's aim is to help create an environment which inspires and encourages entrepreneurial activity in all sections of society. To achieve this, it is important both to reduce cultural barriers which can stand in the way of individuals starting up or joining new enterprises, and to ensure that there is not an excessive fear of failure.

3.19   Raising the ambition and skills of young people will enable them to be successful in an enterprise economy, and is an important component in building an enterprise culture. From April, the Government will introduce measures announced in the 1999 PBR to boost enterprise skills in schools and to make young people more aware of business and the opportunities that it presents (see paragraph 3.72). The new National Curriculum will include a focus on enterprise and employment to improve the skills set of future entrepreneurs. This continues into higher education through the work of the Science Enterprise Centres.

3.20   Building on this, the Government is supporting the launch of the National Enterprise Campaign in May, spearheaded by the Confederation of British Industry, the British Chambers of Commerce and the Institute of Directors (see paragraph 3.73). The Campaign will include an initial focus on young people and boosting enterprise in high unemployment areas, including inner cities.

Reducing the fear of failure   3.21   Attitudes towards enterprise are affected by ability and the rewards for successful management and investment, and also by the penalties for not succeeding and the consequent fear of failure. Business failures are inevitable in a vibrant enterprise economy, but it is important to ensure that the process of failure does not unnecessarily deter the creation of new enterprises, nor hinder further access to finance. At the personal level, bankruptcy can stigmatise those individuals whose businesses have failed despite their honest endeavours. The Secretary of State for Trade and Industry will shortly issue a consultation document containing proposals for possible reform of the law relating to personal bankruptcy.

Table 3.1: The ladder of opportunity for business

PRE-START UP SUPPORT:

Raising ambition and improving skills	New National Curriculum. Enterprise skills in schools. National Enterprise Campaign.
Reducing the fear of failure	Proposed reforms to bankruptcy and insolvency law.

STARTING IN BUSINESS:

Easier compliance	New SBS gateway – online advice and call centre. New, bigger Inland Revenue Business Support Teams.
Better access to external finance	Phoenix Fund – new loan funds to help disadvantaged entrepreneurs. The Cruickshank Report on competition and efficiency in the banking sector.
More internal finance	Lower corporation tax rates. Permanent 40 per cent capital allowances for SMEs.
Improving skills	New Entrepreneur Scholarships. Phoenix Fund – supporting 1,000 business volunteer mentors.
Spreading ideas	Encouraging enterprise around universities.

ENCOURAGING HIGH GROWTH:

Better access to external finance	Capital gains tax reforms. Venture capital funds to help fill "equity gaps". Clusters fund for business incubators. Corporate venturing scheme. Improvements to Venture Capital Trusts and Enterprise Investment Scheme.
More internal finance	R&D tax credit.
Improving skills	Enterprise Management Incentives. All-employee share scheme. Encouraging business angel activity. Advice from Business Links.
Encouraging e-commerce	100 per cent capital allowance for spending by small enterprises on ICT equipment. Discounts for e-filing of tax returns. £60 million package to support SMEs on line.

3.22 A joint DTI/Treasury review is also currently underway into the corporate insolvency regime, with the assistance of a group of experts drawn from the private sector. The aim is to explore what more could be done to strengthen the "rescue culture" for businesses which may have longer term futures beyond their current financial difficulties. There will be further consultation on this issue in due course.

Starting in business

3.23 Starting in business requires access to resources including skills and finance. The Government's aim is to help all individuals gain access to the resources they need to turn their idea into a successful business. It is particularly important that no sections of society face unnecessary barriers to accessing any of this support.

Small Business Service **3.24** To give small firms easier access to the advice and support they need, the Government is setting up a new Small Business Service (SBS), which will be launched on 3 April. The SBS will act as a strong voice for small business at the heart of Government under the leadership of its Chief Executive David Irwin. The Chief Executive also has responsibility for ensuring that the SBS:

- simplifies and improves the quality and coherence of Government support for small businesses; and

- helps small firms deal with regulation and ensures small firms' interests are properly considered in future regulation. This will involve working with regulators and other Departments to minimise burdens on small business and ensure that clear guidance is available.

Payroll support **3.25** The Payroll subgroup of the Better Regulation Taskforce recently published a report which looked at the costs to business, and in particular small business, of complying with their payroll obligations. Firms taking on their first employees assume responsibilities as employers for collecting income tax and National Insurance payments.

3.26 The Budget contains substantial new measures which will help small firms with these costs. A central recommendation of the taskforce report was that small businesses needed to be encouraged to use online payroll support services. The Budget contains new 100 per cent allowances for investment in information and communications technology (ICT) equipment, new discounts for e–filing and using internet payroll services, and new resources to inform small businesses of the benefits of internet services and provide training and support to them (See 3.57–3.61).

3.27 To give further help to minimise the cost of complying with payroll obligations, the Government has been developing a range of other forms of support for new and small employers. From April 2000 the Inland Revenue will expand the range of help available on payroll issues by building on the success of the New Enterprise Support Initiative (NESI). The Inland Revenue:

- has today published a payroll software standard which will reassure small employers that accredited software will meet their payroll commitments;

- will increase both the size and scope of the work carried out by the NESI helpline for new employers and more than double the size of the Inland Revenue Business Support Teams. These will offer new employers a detailed visit by Business Support Team to take them through various payroll issues; and

- will, from April 2000, extend the quarterly PAYE scheme to benefit an additional 80,000 employers. Following the £400 rise in the last Budget, the threshold for quarterly payments will be raised from £1,000 to £1,500 a month, saving employers up to £150 a year.

Box 3.3: Women, work and enterprise

Women are playing a far more active role in the labour market than they did in the past:

- 70% of women are now economically active and this figure is rising; and

- 1.3 million of the 1.7 million new jobs the Government expects to be created by 2011 are forecast to be filled by women.

To further encourage women to work, the Government is working to narrow the pay gap between men and women, and to remove barriers to women's participation by:

- implementing the £470 million National Childcare Strategy to increase access to good quality affordable childcare to make it easier for women to get back to work (see paragraph 4.45);

- improving maternity and parental leave, and working with employers in the public and private sectors to promote flexible work arrangements;

- acting to end stereotyping in careers advice and work experience, to promote study and careers in science, technology and engineering.

- helping those women most in need of support through the Working Families' Tax Credit and its childcare tax credit component (see paragraph 4.46 and 4.58); and

- giving £140 million to provide extra support to allow carers to balance work and family responsibilities.

Women also play an important role in the enterprise economy, and are currently responsible for 25 per cent of new business start-ups. However, entrepreneurial activity among women is low in the UK relative to that of men. Compared to the UK, the US has twice as many men involved in trying to start a business, but 3$\frac{1}{2}$ times as many women.

This is in part because women can face problems obtaining access to suitable support, advice and finance. The Government wants to encourage more women to take up the opportunities of the new enterprise economy and is working through the Small Business Service and the Phoenix Fund to give further support to existing and potential women entrepreneurs, including those who are disadvantaged.

Enterprise open to all

3.28   To maximise the UK's enterprise potential, opportunities for growing businesses need to be available to everybody in the country. To ensure that enterprise is open to all and to encourage private investment in deprived, high unemployment areas the Government is supporting individuals and new businesses in such areas:

- the £30 million Phoenix Fund will establish a new network of 1,000 volunteer business mentors by April 2001; help to support new incubator workspaces; and support new and expanded loan funds;

- New Entrepreneur Scholarships will be offered to budding entrepreneurs in deprived areas from September 2001 to equip them with the management and business skills needed to turn their aspirations into successful businesses. Pilots will be run in London, Cornwall and Manchester later this year;

- the new Social Investment Taskforce – an initiative of the UK Social Investment Forum – chaired by Ronald Cohen of Apax Partners & Co., will consider a new strategic framework for social and community investment. This will include examining: tax incentives for investing in community development projects and social enterprises; a permanent investment fund to support a regular wave of new projects; and how to target more resources in venture capital funds at high unemployment areas;

- Kim Howells in the DTI has been appointed as Minister in charge of corporate social responsibility across Government. The Government sees corporate social responsibility as a key component of successful business strategies and is keen to see the practice become more widespread;

- the New Deal (see Chapter 4) will offer help for long term unemployed people to become self-employed and start their own business – for the over-50s, up to £3,000 each during their first year in business and in work; and

- the Government is looking at what lessons might be learned from the New Markets Initiative in the US, which is designed to stimulate major private investment in distressed areas.

Spreading ideas   **3.29**   In an enterprise economy, the rate of innovation will increase as people have the skills and incentives to turn ideas and technological developments into new products and services. Spreading ideas is key to encouraging new start up businesses in the economy and new production in existing firms. In this way innovation can act as a major source of growth in the economy.

3.30   The Government has a key role to play in ensuring that there are incentives to invest in R&D and to innovate as well as to exploit the results of that research. Encouraging both R&D and the commercial exploitation of intellectual property in the public sector and in universities will also support the formation of new businesses. To support these activities, the Government has:

- injected £1.4 billion in the 1998 Comprehensive Spending Review, including the £700 million Joint Infrastructure Fund endowed by the Government and the Wellcome Trust, towards ensuring the UK continues to generate leading-edge research;

- set up the £50 million University Challenge fund to provide seed funding for commercialising research;

- run the Science Enterprise Challenge. This provided £25 million for new centres to encourage enterprise in and around universities;

- committed up to £14 million a year on average from the Capital Modernisation Fund for the next five years towards the costs of establishing an Institute jointly between Cambridge University and Massachusetts Institute of Technology (MIT); and

- endorsed recommendations from the Baker Review to encourage the commercialisation of research from Public Sector Research Establishments.

Encouraging high growth

3.31   Too few businesses in the UK realise their growth potential. To do so, investment is crucial to capitalise on entrepreneurial talent and enable them to seize new opportunities for growth. This includes re-investment of the enterprise's own gains, external financial capital, and investment in building the enterprise's human capital through recruitment and training of skilled employees. The Government is introducing in this Finance Bill several measures to improve the fiscal incentives for companies and individuals to make this investment. Since 1997, the Government has cut the average corporation tax bill for small companies by nearly 25 per cent.

Capital allowances 3.32 To encourage all SMEs, manufacturing and services, companies and unincorporated, to invest from their own resources in capital stock, the Government introduced enhanced capital allowances for SMEs' plant and machinery investment in July 1997. This brings forward the tax relief for investing firms, providing a cashflow boost which is particularly helpful to smaller firms which are more reliant on cashflow to fund investment. The Government has maintained enhanced allowances at 40 per cent from July 1998 through to July 2000. In this Finance Bill, the Government will make these investment incentives permanent (see also paragraph 3.60 on capital allowances for ICT equipment).

3.33 SMEs' internal resources will often need to be supplemented by external finance and skills as the firm grows. The primary source of external finance for UK SMEs remains bank lending, and so it is important that this market is operating in as competitive and innovative a way as possible. This is one of the important aspects which the Banking Review chaired by Don Cruickshank examinined (see Box 3.2 above).

Capital gains tax 3.34 At early stages in their development, equity investments from individuals will often be a vital source of capital for SMEs. In recognition of this the Government introduced capital gains tax (CGT) taper relief in April 1998 to create incentives for long term investment in assets generating sustained growth, with particular support for entrepreneurial investment. The PBR in November stated that the Government was considering further change to the design of the business assets taper to ensure that the incentives it created had the maximum effect, and worked within the evolving risk capital market for smaller growth enterprises.

3.35 Following detailed consultation with business, the Government will shorten the business assets taper from ten to four years to bring the CGT incentives more into line with entrepreneurial investment patterns. The Government will also reduce the current percentage thresholds for equity shareholdings in trading companies to qualify for the lower rates from their current levels of 5 per cent for full-time employees and 25 per cent for others. In unquoted trading companies all shareholdings will qualify for the business assets taper. In quoted trading companies, all employee shareholdings will qualify as will other shareholdings above a 5 per cent threshold.

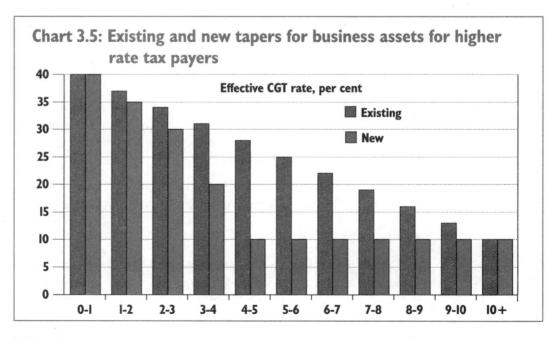

Chart 3.5: Existing and new tapers for business assets for higher rate tax payers

Effective CGT rate, per cent

■ Existing
■ New

3.36 For the 3 million or so enterprises in the economy which are reliant on private risk capital rather than public equity markets to fund their growth, this will encourage all those involved in the success of the business, be they directors, employees, owners or outside shareholders, to invest in the future of the business. It will also promote wider share ownership generally among employees in all companies. This will help support the Government's aim for more companies and their employees to have common incentives towards enterprise growth, and complement other measures which the Government has been developing.

Employee share ownership   **3.37**   As announced in Budget 1999, the Government is introducing in this year's Finance Bill a new comprehensive all-employee share plan to support firms' own efforts to foster a more enterprising and productive relationship with their employees. This will be the most tax-advantaged all-employee share scheme ever introduced in the UK. It will also provide greater flexibility than in current schemes, to meet the needs of companies and employees.

Enterprise Management Incentives   **3.38**   Enterprises often need to expand their management team to deliver their growth potential, and need to provide sufficient rewards to offset the extra risk entailed for individuals investing their time in less established businesses. Share options are one means for companies to attract the key personnel they need. In this year's Finance Bill, the Government will introduce Enterprise Management Incentives (EMIs), which will help recruitment and retention by small higher-risk companies of key employees, by offering access to tax-advantaged share options. Under this incentive, such companies will be able to offer options over shares worth up to £100,000 (at time of option grant). The options will be taxed on sale of the shares, rather than taxed as income at exercise of the options. Following consultation, the Government has decided to increase the maximum number of employees that can benefit from EMIs from 10 to 15 per company.

Employer NICs   **3.39**   Many e-commerce and high-tech companies offer their employees substantial share options as part of their remuneration package. Where options are exercised outside an Inland Revenue approved scheme and the shares are readily convertible into cash, companies are liable for employers' National Insurance contributions (NICs) on the gain. For companies with volatile share prices this creates an exposure to an unpredictable NICs liability and can put at risk their investment strategies and damage future growth. The Government has received suggestions that employers' exposure to these difficulties could be resolved, for example, by allowing a voluntary agreement between employer and employee that all or part of the employer's NICs liability will be met by the employee. The Government is seeking views on these suggestions. It is attracted to improving flexibility in this area and is considering legislation as part of its support for the employees of companies with high growth potential.

3.40   It is also important that leading, larger companies are in a position to offer competitive remuneration packages to attract world-class directors that can help them succeed and thrive in the modern, global market place. However, companies and ultimately shareholders have a key interest in ensuring that directors' pay is linked closely to their performance. Following last year's consultation on this issue, the DTI will shortly announce the Government's proposals in this area.

Corporate venturing   **3.41**   Growing enterprises can often benefit from closer linkages with established businesses in their technology sector. Corporate venturing investment by the larger business can help cement these links. To encourage this form of financing and business support, this year's Finance Bill will introduce tax incentives to encourage companies to undertake corporate venturing. Companies will be able to claim corporation tax relief at 20 per cent on investments in small higher risk trading companies as well as a deferral relief where they sell shares and reinvest the gain under the scheme.

3.42   These incentives will provide a further stimulus to the work the DTI has already undertaken to promote corporate venturing. The conclusions of a major research study undertaken jointly with the CBI and Nat West published last year showed the benefits of venturing. Further initiatives are planned to help companies understand how corporate venturing works including joint Treasury/DTI work with large companies to promote venturing, a rolling programme of regional events throughout this year and a practical guide for companies interested in establishing a corporate venturing relationship. The DTI will also be working with the National Business Angel Network to encourage them to promote corporate venturing by matching corporate investors with smaller companies.

Regional venture capital funds

3.43 As enterprises progress, and their financing needs grow, access to venture capital finance can become more important. The Government is already working with the Regional Development Agencies (RDAs) to establish the first wave of new regional venture capital funds. These will be public private partnerships, with Government support (via the DTI's Enterprise Fund) to lever in private risk capital for investment in small scale venture capital across the English regions, helping to meet a demand which is currently under-served by the commercial market. Along with the proposed UK High Tech Fund and the DETR's Coalfields Enterprise Fund, the Government is currently aiming to stimulate the creation of venture capital funds totalling nearly £500 million.

3.44 To build on this, and widen and deepen the venture capital provision for smaller enterprises, the Government will concentrate its resources and skills to develop this programme in a new £1 billion target umbrella fund, operated by the SBS with a new Small Business Investment Taskforce working closely in partnership with the RDAs. This activity will be led by an experienced business finance expert. The umbrella fund will encompass the venture funds totalling nearly £500 million currently in the process of creation. In order to lever in new private finance, the Government will commit a further £100 million of new resources over the period 2001–04. The European Investment Bank has also agreed to support this enhanced programme by investing further in the additional venture funds to be created under the new umbrella fund (subject to detailed assessment of individual proposals).

3.45 In taking forward this programme, the Taskforce and the SBS will work in strategic partnership with the RDAs to help create an environment where all enterprises with growth potential, wherever they are located, can access the finance they need to realise their potential. As part of this strategy, the SBS and RDAs will co-decide on regional priorities – the criteria for the funds and the allocation of Government support – to narrow the equity gaps for small scale venture capital across the UK. For example, relative to their SME sectors, the North of England, South West and Wales have 50 per cent or less early stage venture capital compared to the UK as a whole. The £1 billion target umbrella fund should go a substantial way towards narrowing regional disparities and moving the market forward over the next 3-5 years. The programme will also address the need for specific risk capital funds to finance business growth in deprived areas of the country.

Clusters

3.46 Clusters are geographically concentrated groups of firms and research institutions that combine intense competition with collaboration to stimulate innovation and productivity. Strong empirical support exists for the spill-over effects between firms and between firms and universities in R&D, innovation and knowledge sharing. Alongside this, the clustering of specialist service providers such as legal and financial advice as well as venture capital providers, can provide a strong stimulus to growth.

3.47 The Government is continuing to develop a clusters strategy for the UK. The 1999 PBR announced a cross-departmental Ministerial Group chaired by Lord Sainsbury to consider how the Government can promote and facilitate the growth of clusters. The PBR also announced changes to the planning system to strengthen the support for the growth and development of clusters of firms and research institutions. In the future, regional plans will proactively identify cluster areas and plan for their expansion.

3.48 The Secretary of State for Trade and Industry will shortly announce the next phase in the development of clusters. This will be a fund to enable RDAs to provide co-financing for business incubators, for example allied to universities, and small scale infrastructure in partnership with the private sector.

R&D tax credit **3.49** There is significant evidence from US companies that higher R&D intensity leads to better growth prospects over the next five years. Small firms in particular are less well-placed than large firms to raise finance for R&D programmes and to capture the potential spill-over benefits from their own R&D. Hence, SMEs tend to under-invest in R&D relative to larger firms. To address these issues, the Government has put in place the new R&D tax credit which will be introduced from April 2000 and be targeted on all small and medium-sized companies. As set out in the 1999 PBR, this tax credit will increase the 100 per cent relief for current spending on R&D to 150 per cent. So when added to the existing relief, the cost of R&D will be reduced by 30 per cent for a company benefiting from the small companies' corporation tax rate.

3.50 This tax credit and the introduction of permanent enhanced capital allowances (see paragraph 3.32) will help all small companies. As major contributors to the UK's R&D effort and because of their reliance on physical investment, these measures will be particularly beneficial for manufacturers, giving them extra resources to help them carry out the necessary investment and R&D to keep ahead of their competition and reap the potential benefits of the new enterprise economy.

Intellectual property rights **3.51** Following consultation, the Government will also be considering changes to the taxation of intellectual property rights. The aim of the reforms is to replace the separate and often out dated tax rules with a new and simpler treatment of intellectual property rights (IPR) transactions, based more closely on accounting practice.

Competitiveness of the tax system **3.52** One of the Government's aims is to make the UK a more competitive environment for entrepreneurs, investors in business and businesses themselves. It is therefore important that the UK tax system is competitive in the global arena, ensuring that the UK is seen as a productive place for businesses to operate, and a favourable base from which to invest abroad. To help achieve this, the Government is:

- giving companies greater flexibility in how they structure their business. This will give them more freedom to organise themselves in ways that suit their business rather than in ways driven by the tax system;

- abolishing the witholding tax on international bond interest. This deregulatory measure will abolish from April 2001 the current tax rules for financial institutions which act as Paying and Collecting Agents of international bonds and foreign dividends. Instead the Inland Revenue will collect routine information about the savings income of all individuals;

- extending the scope of the review of the taxation of intellectual property to include the possibility of tax relief for the costs of purchasing goodwill and some other intangibles. This reflects the increasing importance that intangible assets have to business;

- consulting with a view to improving business efficiency by providing rollover relief for gains arising on disposals of substantial shareholdings held by companies; and

- ensuring that the double taxation regime provides relief for all forms of business operating in the UK and does so equally across direct and indirect business structures.

E-commerce

The challenge to the UK economy

3.53   E-commerce has the potential to be of significant benefit to the UK economy and to both businesses and consumers. The sharpest spur to productivity, innovation and enterprise is competition. The internet intensifies competition by lowering barriers to entry, and increasing price transparency. As a new medium, the internet has sparked innovation, creating whole new markets and producing synergies between existing goods and services. Firms can benefit from shorter supply chains and reduced inventory costs. Consumers benefit from increased price transparency as a result of lower search costs; the ability to buy products direct rather than through intermediaries; and from higher quality services, available 24 hours a day, 7 days a week.

3.54   To ensure the UK economy benefits from the opportunities that the internet offers, the Government has set itself the goal of making the UK the best place in which to trade electronically by 2002. There are some key challenges that need to be met in order to achieve this goal. In terms of connectivity large and medium-sized UK companies are, on average, performing well compared to other G7 countries. But small and micro firms are lagging behind. The Government aims to get $1^1/_2$ million SMEs online by 2002; with 1 million actually trading online.

3.55   Another key challenge facing the UK today is to ensure that the internet does not result in a digital divide – a country of IT-haves and IT-have nots. The Government has set a goal of universal access to the internet by 2005.

3.56   Finally, Government itself must modernise so that it benefits from the opportunities presented by new technologies. The cross-cutting review of the knowledge economy being carried out as part of the 2000 Spending Review is looking at all aspects of Government and e-commerce. It is being headed by the Chief Secretary to the Treasury and Patricia Hewitt, the DTI minister for small firms and e-commerce.

Getting SMEs online

Discounts for e-filing   **3.57**   To encourage firms to take up the challenge to get online, the Chancellor announced on 16 February that firms will be eligible for discounts for electronic filing and payment of tax returns. During 2001–02 small businesses that file their VAT quarterly returns or PAYE end of year returns via the internet and pay the tax due electronically will receive a one-off discount of £50 (or £100 for both PAYE and VAT). Similarly, Self Assessment taxpayers who file their return over the internet and pay electronically will receive a one-off discount of £10. There will be an extra one-off discount of £50 for small employers who pay tax credits to employees and qualify for the £50 PAYE discount. The PAYE and tax credits discounts will also be available to small employers using an internet payroll service.

Support package for SMEs   **3.58**   The Government recognises that getting on-line means more than simply setting up a website. It is important that all firms, and especially SMEs, understand that new technology is crucial to their business. The Government is investing £60 million to help SMEs understand what getting online means for their business; to help SMEs get online; and to help them get the right services once they are online. This will include:

- £10 million for a major boost to awareness, advice and training for small firms on using IT, through an expansion of the DTI's Information Society Initiative;

- £20 million for a new call centre and web–based advice and information services, to help answer the basic questions people have when starting or running a small firm and give value–added support; and

- £30 million to build a comprehensive infrastructure for a secure electronic interface with government, businesses and citizens.

3.59   Key elements in this package of support will be delivered in the coming year. A lead role will be taken by the SBS, with regular enhancements to the SBS website and a fully functional information service up and running by the end of the year. It is crucial that the website and call-centre provide exactly what small businesses want and need, and so their help in designing it will be vital.

Capital allowances for ICT equipment

3.60   ICT equipment is at the heart of the new internet revolution. In the new knowledge economy, it is investment in ICT that will be a driver of future business success and productivity growth. E-commerce is opening up global markets to small firms that were once closed due to their size. The internet is not only radically reshaping relationships with consumers but also transforming relationships along the supply chain. Small firms cannot be left behind in this process which is as significant as the industrial revolution, so the Government needs to do even more to get UK small firms prepared for the new challenges of the knowledge economy.

3.61   For the UK to lead the knowledge economy, there needs to be a step change in the use of ICT technologies by small enterprises. This is why from April this year, the Government will introduce 100 per cent first year capital allowances for small enterprises investing in ICT equipment for the next three years, to help them gear up and succeed in the knowledge economy.

Promoting universal access

3.62   Everyone must have the opportunity to reap the benefits the internet offers. Transforming education and widening access will ensure the opportunities of new technologies are shared by everyone. To this end, the Government is:

- providing £1.7 billion for the national IT strategy;

- enabling employees to borrow computers from their companies as a tax-free benefit. About 300,000 people are expected to borrow computers in this way by 2002–03;

- developing a system under which poorer individuals – sometimes through local partnerships – will be able to lease or own recycled computers. Around 100,000 computers should be available by the end of 2001;

- linking all schools, libraries, colleges and universities via the internet through the National Grid for Learning by 2002; and

- establishing up to 1,000 ICT learning centres across the UK to improve access to ICT for all.

3.63   Using the internet must be affordable. One of the key inhibitors to greater use of the internet in the UK has been expensive local telephone charges. The telecoms regulator, OFTEL, has already taken a number of steps designed to increase competition in the telecoms market and drive down the cost of internet access. And the Chancellor has challenged the telecoms industry to reduce the cost of using the internet to US levels. The Government welcomes the recent developments in this area but there is a great deal still to be done. Our goal must be to see prices – for both traditional (narrowband) and high-speed (broadband) access – comparable with the lowest in the world.

Box 3.4: The Government's regional enterprise policy

The Government is acting at a national, regional and local level to raise productivity. To encourage balanced economic growth across all regions and to enable each region to make the most of its comparative advantages, the Government has developed policies to focus on innovation, investment, infrastructure and employment. The RDAs and the SBS will be crucial in delivering these initiatives.

Innovation: To encourage innovation and knowledge sharing among different firms and with universities, the Government is continuing to develop a clusters strategy for the UK. The Secretary of State for Trade and Industry will shortly announce a fund to enable RDAs to provide co-financing for business incubators and small infrastructure projects in partnership with the private sector in all regions of the country (see para 3.46).

Investment: To improve the level of investment in small scale venture capital across the regions, the Government will promote a new £1 billion target umbrella fund levering in significant additional private finance. The SBS and RDAs will together decide on regional priorities – the criteria for the funds and the allocation of Government support – to narrow the equity gaps for small scale venture capital across the UK. The Government will commit a further £100 million of new resources for the UK as a whole to support this over the period 2001–04 in order to leverage in private investment and reach the £1 billion target. (see para 3.43).

Infrastructure: The potential represented by innovation and venture capital will only be turned into reality if it is complemented by policies designed to upgrade regional infrastructure through improved transport links and educational facilities. The PFI is a major contributor to this across every region. For example

- the link up of all Dudley's schools to the **National Grid for Learning**;

- **£180 million of transport investment in Tyne & Wear**; and

- urban rapid transit projects in **Leeds, Edinburgh and Nottingham**.

Employment: To encourage employment in all regions of the country:

- the **New Deal** (see Chapter 4) is helping people move from welfare to work. Over 25,000 young people have found jobs through the **New Deal in the North West**, over 20,000 in **Scotland**, over 20,000 in **Yorkshire and Humberside** and over 12,500 in **Wales**; and

- the **Working Families Tax Credit** (see paragraph 4.58) will boost the incomes of around 1.4 million working families, making work pay and increasing employment opportunities. These benefits flow to all regions: 170,000 households will benefit in the **North West and Merseyside**, 160,000 in the **West Midlands** and 110,000 in the **South West**. Reflecting the fact that poverty exists in all regions, 150,000 households are eligible in the **South East**.

SKILLS

3.64 To create and to benefit from an enterprise economy, the workforce has to have a high level of basic skills, and the ability to adapt to changing working practices. The lack of a sufficiently skilled workforce can prevent businesses from using new technologies and innovating, hence holding back their potential growth. Standards are now rising in both primary and secondary education, but the UK has further to go to deliver the levels of educational attainment that will support productivity growth and a more enterprising economy.

3.65 The Government has begun to address the numbers of people without basic skills both at primary and secondary stages, and through improving the facilities available for life-long learning (see box 5.2 on the Government's education ambition).

National Curriculum

3.66 In primary and secondary education, the Government has:

- revised the National Curriculum to include a new focus on enterprise skills at both primary and secondary level. From September 2000, the National Curriculum will make more explicit the links between education, employment and enterprise; and it will also include financial literacy and consumer education. Guidance, schemes of work and materials for schools are now being developed in time for September 2000; and

- introduced literacy and numeracy strategies in primary schools: those aged 11 who meet the required standard in English and mathematics rose five and ten percentage points respectively in 1999 compared to 1998.

Individual learning accounts

3.67 To allow members of the workforce to adapt their skills so that they can continue to fulfil their potential in a changing working environment, the Government is now implementing a national framework under which everybody 19 or over can apply for an individual learning account. People in England with an individual learning account will be eligible for 80 per cent discounts on computer literacy courses and some other specific types of learning, or 20 per cent discounts on a wide range of other eligible activities. (Scotland and Northern Ireland will decide their own priorities for what will be eligible for receipt of the discounts). These discounts will be available from September 2000 when vocational training relief will be withdrawn.

3.68 As announced in Budget 1999, a new relief will ensure that employees who hold individual learning accounts pay no tax or NICs on their employers' contributions towards their learning, provided the employers make available such help to their entire workforce on similar terms.

learndirect

3.69 UfI limited (the company taking forward the University for Industry concept) will also seek to drive up demand for learning through the development of its consumer brand learndirect. The learndirect helpline (0800 100 900) has already helped over a million people looking for impartial information about opportunities, including many who have been discouraged from taking part in education in the past. From Autumn 2000, learndirect will also provide a portfolio of high-quality, online learning materials. These will offer individuals the opportunity to acquire new skills and knowledge, at a pace that suits them, from their home, work or one of up to 1,000 learndirect centres in all regions of the country.

3.70 A further help for workers faced with the consequences of change is the Rapid Response Fund. It provides intensive support when a large scale redundancy is announced. RDAs bid for resources from this fund to promote fast retraining where there is no alternative provision available.

3.71   Addressing the basic skills of people in the UK will not be enough on its own. The Government also needs to ensure that young people have the mind-set to be successful in an enterprising economy, and that they are inspired and encouraged to do so. For example, young people need to understand and believe in self employment as a career option, and be ready to do several jobs in the course of their working lives.

Education business links   **3.72**   To begin to foster a spirit of enterprise among young people in the UK, the Government is providing £10 million to enhance education-business links from April 2000. As announced in the 1999 PBR, this money will:

- improve the quality of the existing infrastructure of education business link organisations;

- enhance teachers' professional development and improve the quality of work experience for pupils; and

- help to double the scale of enterprise programmes with a proven track-record of success, such as those provided by Understanding Industry and Young Enterprise (including Junior Achievement in primary schools).

National Enterprise Campaign   **3.73**   The Government is also supporting the National Enterprise Campaign which will initially aim to encourage more entrepreneurial attitudes among young people by using entrepreneurial ambassadors as role models and mentors. Sir Alan Sugar and Sir Richard Branson will both add their weight to the Campaign alongside several other well-known entrepreneurs including Martha Lane Fox and James Dyson. To complement the work of the Campaign, the Chancellor will publish a book later this year showcasing successful entrepreneurs and containing examples of how they got started in business. Its aim will be to inspire young people to follow similar routes into business.

Management education   **3.74**   To make businesses successful, however, the UK requires a considerable pool of people with management expertise. Managers and management teams play a key role in whether a business will be a success or failure. The latest survey by the Society of Insolvency Practitioners showed that over half of all company failures in the UK are directly attributable to poor management and leadership.

3.75   To address these problems, and to help more companies survive and flourish, the Government aims to improve the quality of management education available. To this end:

- the Government will create the new Council for Excellence in Management and Leadership under the leadership of Sir Anthony Cleaver, Chairman of AEA Technology plc. The Council will develop a strategy for improving levels of leadership and management competence, reporting in March 2001; and

- the Business Schools Small Firms Advisory Group will shortly report to the Council identifying how Business Schools can more effectively meet the needs of SMEs and entrepreneurs.

Work permits   **3.76**   Although skills levels in the national population are rising, skills shortages are emerging in our increasingly tight labour market. Failing to fill these vacancies with skilled workers will retard productivity and growth and mean fewer employment opportunities in the longer term. Developing people in the UK through education and training is key in achieving this, but access to skilled people from overseas is also part of the answer. Equally important is to enhance the UK's image as an attractive location for talented overseas students and entrepreneurs.

3.77 Following the announcement in November's PBR the Government has carried out a thorough review of the work permits system. The UK has always benefited from a market-driven work permits system, so that employers can recruit skilled people from abroad without any artificial limits or quotas on the number of work permits that can be issued. This rationale will remain the same, but to enhance the effectiveness of the work permits rules, both to meet skills shortages and to attract more highly skilled workers and entrepreneurs from abroad who can benefit the UK economy, the Government has decided to:

- ensure that the work permit and immigration arrangements help attract overseas students to the UK, and enable employers to recruit talented foreign graduates by: providing a more transparent path for those students whose skills are needed to be able to switch to work permits without leaving the country; reviewing the Training and Work Experience Scheme; and exploring other ways of making it easier for students with valuable skills to get permission to work;

- make the shortage category list, which allows for streamlined applications, more responsive to emerging skills shortages by: implementing today new shortage categories for IT workers; and, for the future, by improving sectoral labour market analysis by the Overseas Labour Service (OLS) to more rapidly identify skills shortages;

- reduce the burdens on business by: eliminating the labour market test for extensions and changes of employment for work permit holders; eliminate the need for permits for supplementary work; increase the maximum period for a work permit to 5 years; and introduce season tickets for workers who enter for short periods on a regular basis and explore the scope for more permit-free categories;

- ensure the system reflects current UK and global labour markets by: revising the skills criteria for business and commercial work permits; reviewing the current Keyworker category for less skilled workers; and redesigning the arrangements for entertainers; and

- maximise the benefit to the UK economy of our flexible and modernised UK work permits system by: marketing it more effectively at home and abroad; introducing electronic filing of applications; and, improving the interface between the OLS and the Home Office, including providing a one-stop shop for applications and extensions from people already in the UK.

3.78 The Government will also run a number of pilots with appropriate safeguards to establish whether they offer genuine advantages:

- allowing multinational companies to self-certify entry clearance for intra-company transfers;

- enabling people of outstanding ability to gain entry clearance to seek work in the UK; and

- introducing a new category of "innovators", relaxing the capital requirements for entrepreneurs offering exceptional economic benefit, to come to the UK to set up high-tech businesses.

INVESTMENT

3.79   The Government's new macroeconomic framework (see Chapter 2) combined with the structural reforms designed to raise the productivity of the economy, together create the very best environment for investment. The sharper stimulus provided by the measures to create a more enterprising economy should help Britain to reduce its history of under-investment. The Government can also have a more direct influence on investment both through the tax system and through the institutional structures it creates.

3.80   There are early indications that greater macroeconomic stability, the Government's swift action to remove distortions and enhance incentives through the corporate tax system and confidence in the UK's future are beginning to have a beneficial effect. Business investment as a share of GDP has increased in recent years and should reach $14^{1}/_{2}$ per cent for 1999. This is its highest share since at least 1965 and means that for the first time since that date it is on course to exceed the G7 average. As the Government's structural reforms take effect they will help to reinforce this investment performance, and help to reverse the UK's poor record.

The tax system

Corporation tax

3.81   The Government has cut corporation tax rates to 30, 20 and 10 per cent, their lowest ever levels, and the lowest among major industrialised countries. The 10 per cent rate will take effect in April 2000 and enable 270,000 small and growing companies to retain more of their profits for re-investment and growth. Moreover, the Government has provided added certainty for firms taking long-term investment decisions by committing to keep corporation tax rates at this level or lower for the rest of this Parliament.

3.82   To further boost investment in manufacturing and services, the Government will make permanent the current 40 per cent first year allowances for SME capital investment in plant and machinery. Moreover, the Government will be giving special priority to small business capital investment in computers and other e-commerce equipment. These small businesses will be able to write off in the first year all of the cost of investments in ICT equipment until 2003 (see paragraphs 3.32 and 3.60).

Capital markets

Institutional investors

3.83   The UK has long benefited from deep and sophisticated equity markets, enabling a wide range of companies to raise capital efficiently. Institutional investors – pension funds and life assurance companies – are key players in those markets, controlling around 45 per cent of quoted equity investments. The Government is concerned that there may be factors encouraging institutional investors to follow industry–standard investment patterns which focus overwhelmingly on quoted equities and gilts and avoid investing in SMEs and other smaller companies.

3.84   The Government has asked Paul Myners, Chairman of Gartmore Investment Management, to look at these issues. He will shortly be launching a consultation exercise, which will consider a number of issues in this area including:

- whether regulatory provisions have unintended effects on investment decision–making;

- how pension funds make their investment decisions, and the role of professional advisers;

- how institutional investors' results and charges are reported; and

- the incentive effects of the methods used to assess fund performance.

He will consider the implications of these and other issues and report back with recommendations by the next Budget.

3.85   The Financial Service and Markets Bill establishes the Financial Services Authority (FSA) as a single regulator to meet the challenges of evolving markets. Its aim is regulation that has a light touch where possible, and provides protection where necessary. Under the Bill, the competent authority for listing will be transferred from the London Stock Exchange to the FSA to avoid any conflicts of interest and to facilitate competition.

PUBLIC SECTOR PRODUCTIVITY

3.86   As well as setting macroeconomic and microeconomic polices to create the right climate for productivity improvements, the Government is also a major agent in the economy in its own right. To improve productivity in the public sector, the Government is focussing on service delivery in the 2000 Spending Review, as well as continuing to make best use of its assets and creating partnerships with the private sector through both the Private Finance Initiative (PFI) and Public Private Partnerships (PPPs).

Improving public sector service delivery

Spending Review 2000   3.87   The Spending Review 2000 to be announced in July will produce spending plans that will ensure that Departments can deliver effective and responsive services, improve efficiency and manage their assets over the following three years. In setting the plans, the review is scrutinising departments' current performances in these areas against the targets that were set in Public Service Agreements following the Comprehensive Spending Review in 1998.

3.88   One of the key common themes of the Spending Review this year is productivity. Departments' plans for the review period are therefore being examined to assess how they will contribute to higher productivity and sustainable economic growth. This work will ensure that in delivering public services, the Government is encouraging productivity growth throughout the economy.

Public Services Productivity Panel   3.89   In its drive to improve productivity in the public sector the Government continues to be advised by the Public Services Productivity Panel, a small group of senior business people and public sector managers. The Panel, chaired by the Chief Secretary to the Treasury, was established for a year in the first instance. The Government is now renewing the Panel for a minimum of a further two years. The Panel's advice is based on the detailed studies that it carries out into different areas of government, working closely with the departments concerned. The studies are aimed at identifying and tackling key areas for improvement and at sharing good practice within the public sector.

3.90   Recent Panel studies have led to:

- proposals to reform incentives for the front-line office staff working in the Government's large office networks such as the Benefits Agency and the Inland Revenue;

- a comprehensive overhaul of arrangements for booking and managing NHS outpatient appointments to reduce waiting times; and

- an action plan for continuous improvement to customer service in the large transport agencies such as the Driver & Vehicle Licensing Agency and the Driving Standards Agency.

Partnerships

3.91   Partnerships between the public and private sectors are central to the Government's programme for modernising public services. By drawing on the best of both sectors, PPPs can help the public sector to deliver modern, high-quality public services.

3.92   The Government set out its approach to PPPs in a policy paper, "Public Private Partnerships: The Government's approach", launched on 15 March. This paper sets out in detail, for the first time, the Government's objectives for PPPs and the underlying principles which are central to the way in which Government goes about developing new partnerships with the private sector. It presents the opportunities associated with different types of partnership arrangements and demonstrates how PPPs will deliver real improvements to public services, for the benefit of customers, local communities and the country as a whole.

Partnerships UK and Office of Government Commerce

3.93   PPPs also bring with them new challenges for the public sector. It needs to learn to be a better and more effective partner, client and procurer of private sector services. Partnerships UK will be a new company jointly owned by the public and private sectors which will help the public sector build more effective, value for money partnerships with the private sector, continuing and building upon the work of the Treasury Taskforce. The development of Partnerships UK's business plan is now well advanced and the business will begin operations later in the spring.

3.94   The Government is also taking action to raise its game in the way it procures goods and services across the board. The creation of the Office of Government Commerce (OGC) is central to this agenda. By drawing together central government procurement agencies into a single organisation and providing a new drive to improve performance, OGC will help deliver a step change in public sector procurement practice. Peter Gershon has recently been appointed as Chief Executive to the OGC which will be up and running from April 2000.

4 INCREASING EMPLOYMENT OPPORTUNITY FOR ALL

The Government's aim is employment opportunity for all – the modern definition of full employment. Macroeconomic stability is a prerequisite to achieving this aim. But it needs to be backed up by microeconomic policies to ensure that individuals throughout the country are able to compete effectively for jobs, that there is a secure transition from welfare to work and that employment is financially rewarding. The Government's long-term employment ambition is that a greater proportion of people should be in work than ever before. To deliver employment opportunity for all, the Government has introduced an ambitious set of reforms building on the evidence of what works: helping people to move from welfare to work; easing the transition into work; helping make work pay; and helping people to secure progression up the earnings ladder. Budget 2000 builds on the success of these reforms to date.

Building on the success of the New Deal by:

- strengthening the New Deal for 18–24s by introducing nationally an Intensive Gateway for all young people on the New Deal from June 2000;

- extending the New Deal for 25 plus to provide a more intensive programme based on the principles of the New Deal for 18–24s on a national basis from April 2001;

- introducing Action Teams in areas with the highest unemployment, to help match unemployed people to vacancies;

- providing more choices for lone parents who are considering work; and

- developing plans for extending the New Deal for disabled people nationwide and introducing rehabilitation and retention pilots to test different ways to help disabled people move into, and remain in, work.

Helping people to move into work through:

- a Job Grant to help people to make the transition from welfare to work; and

- extended payments of Income Support for Mortgage Interest when moving into work, to match the Housing Benefit run-on already available.

Making work pay through:

- a guaranteed minimum income of £214 per week, over £11,000 a year from April 2001 for all families with children where someone is in full-time work; and

- a proposed employment tax credit to extend the principle of the Working Families' Tax Credit to people without children from 2003.

INTRODUCTION

4.1   The Government's aim is employment opportunity for all – the modern definition of full employment. Macroeconomic stability is a prerequisite to achieving this aim. But macroeconomic stability is not enough to secure job opportunities for all. It needs to be backed up at the microeconomic level to ensure that individuals throughout the country are able to compete effectively for jobs, that there is a secure transition from welfare into work, that employment is financially rewarding and that people are able to secure progression in work. The Government has introduced radical reforms of the tax and benefit system backed up by active labour market policies to achieve this aim.

Achieving high and stable levels of employment across Britain

4.2   The past few years have seen a substantial improvement in Britain's labour market. Employment currently stands at a record level, with 800,000 more people in work than in spring 1997. As Chart 4.1 illustrates, employment in the UK is also high by international standards. This reflects a combination of stable economic growth, successful employment policies such as the New Deal and the rapid rise in female employment over the last few decades. Chapter 2 set out how macroeconomic stability is being achieved through a credible monetary and fiscal policy framework, which includes discipline and responsibility in wage bargaining. The Government's long-term employment ambition is that a greater proportion of people should be in work than ever before. Box 4.1 sets out this ambition.

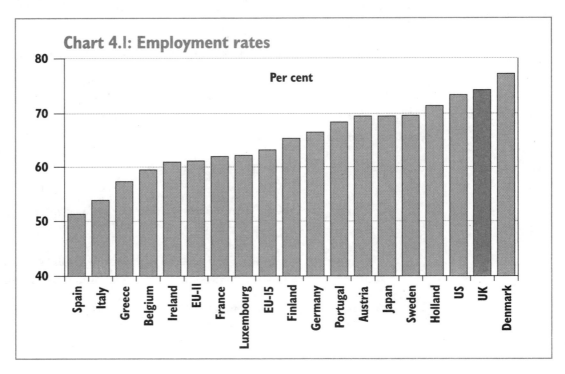

Chart 4.1: Employment rates

Per cent

Box 4.1 Employment ambition

The Pre-Budget Report set out the Government's long-term economic ambition that by the end of the decade there will be a higher percentage of people in employment than ever before.

The Government believes that work is the best route out of poverty and that helping people to move from welfare to work can tackle the underlying causes of deprivation and break the intergenerational cycle of poverty. Expanding the effective supply of labour will also allow the economy to grow more rapidly without running into skills shortages and inflationary pressures.

The Government's employment ambition is to deliver high and stable levels of employment, taking account of the economic cycle, so that at least three quarters of the working age population are in work by the end of the decade. The Government will measure the employment rate using the Labour Force Survey. Since 1959, the highest employment rates were achieved at the peaks of the employment cycles in 1974, at 75.7 per cent, and in spring 1990, at 75 per cent, but these employment rates were not sustained and fell soon afterwards. In comparison, the employment rate over the 1960s was more stable at around 73–74 per cent. Economic stability is the first condition which must be achieved for the Government to meet its objectives of high and stable levels of growth and employment. The ambition must be met not through an unsustainable boom, but through sustained policies for macroeconomic stability.

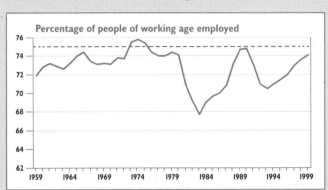

Percentage of people of working age employed

But macroeconomic stability is not enough to ensure employment opportunity for all. The Government's strategy for achieving its employment ambition includes welfare to work policies as the key to delivering employment opportunities; tax and benefit reform to make work pay; easing the return to work and enabling people to move up the earnings ladder.

According to the Labour Force Survey, more people are in employment today than ever before. Since spring 1997, employment in the UK has risen by 800,000 and the employment rate currently stands at 74.3 per cent.

4.3   Unemployment is currently at a 20-year low. At 5.9%, ILO unemployment is at its lowest level since the series began in 1984. The claimant count currently stands at 1.15 million, down by half a million since spring 1997. Alongside these falls in unemployment, the stock of unfilled vacancies at Jobcentres is also at record levels: the ratio of jobseekers to vacancies currently stands at just over 3 claimant unemployed people to each Jobcentre vacancy, compared to around 10 people to each vacancy a decade ago.

4.4   Whereas the recovery of the late 1980s was largely confined to the South of England, this time every region of Britain has seen falling unemployment and rising levels of vacancies, creating a more balanced and sustainable recovery. Unemployment has fallen fastest, and vacancies have risen fastest, in those regions that were hit the hardest in the 1980s. Within regions, however, there remain pockets of high unemployment and inactivity. But the problems of Britain's most deprived areas are not necessarily a lack of jobs – in almost every case, these areas sit alongside, and within travelling distance of, labour markets with high levels of vacancies. People need to be equipped to take advantage of these opportunities.

Tackling the underlying causes of deprivation and increasing opportunity

4.5   While unemployment is at its lowest level since the 1980s, and is low in comparison to most other European countries, the UK continues to have a high proportion of workless households. Although the number of households with no-one in work has fallen by 106,000 since spring 1997, many groups remain excluded from the labour force in large numbers – lone parents, disabled people and partners of unemployed people all have high rates of inactivity. Around 6.7 million people below pensionable age – 4.5 million adults and 2.2 million children – live in households where no-one is in work: twice as many as 20 years ago. This combination of high employment and large numbers of workless households has come about because worklessness has become increasingly concentrated within households. These concentrations of worklessness are now the most important cause of poverty among working-age people and their children. Two-thirds of working age households on low incomes have no-one in work, and about half of all children in poverty are in households where no-one is in work.

4.6   Long periods of unemployment, or inactivity, can have long-term damaging effects on future employment prospects and earnings potential. Getting a job, keeping a job and progressing up the earnings ladder are the key to improving opportunities. For 8 out of 10 people in the bottom fifth of the income distribution between 1991 and 1995, getting a job moved them out of low income. By ensuring that employment opportunities are open to all, the Government is tackling one of the most important underlying causes of poverty.

A strategy for achieving employment opportunity for all

4.7   The Government's strategy for ensuring employment opportunity for all comprises the following key elements:

- helping people to move from welfare to work, through the New Deal;

- easing the transition into work, by removing barriers to working and ensuring that people are financially secure when moving from welfare to work;

- making work pay, through reform of the tax and benefit system; and

- securing progression in work, through lifelong learning.

WELFARE TO WORK

4.8   There are currently 1.15 million unemployed people claiming Jobseekers' Allowance (JSA), but every year there are over 3 million new claims for JSA. The labour market is dynamic and most of these claims end relatively quickly, with over 50 per cent of people moving off JSA within 13 weeks. There are a further 3.8 million people of working age receiving other out of work benefits, including sick and disabled people and lone parents. Disabled people are more than three times as likely to be inactive as people without a disability. Over 50 per cent of lone parent households have no-one in work, compared to only 7 per cent of couples with children. But many of the economically inactive say that they would like to work. That is why the Government is providing intensive support – combining rights with responsibilities – to help people to move from welfare into work through policies including ONE and the New Deal. The Government wants to ensure that there is work for those who can, and security for those who cannot work.

Forging a new culture – putting work first

4.9   The Government's new ONE service combines a one-stop shop for benefits and employment advice, a personal adviser service to help people back into work, and work-focused interviews for all new benefit claimants: one place for work and benefits. It aims to forge an entirely new culture which puts work first, and provides a modern, integrated and flexible service for all. ONE is currently running in 12 pilot areas, including 4 using call centre technology and 4 led by the private and voluntary sectors.

4.10   ONE represents a fundamental shift in the way that the Government supports people – away from a system that asks simply "what money can we pay you?" to one that says "how can we help you become more independent?". While it is too early to draw any firm conclusions, the early signs in the ONE pilot areas are encouraging. From April 2000, new claimants in ONE pilot areas will be required to take part in an interview to talk about their prospects of finding work and about the help that is available both to move into work, and to ensure that work pays.

4.11   To deliver support for people of working age, during 2001 a brand new, modern agency will be established with a clear focus on work. The new agency will draw together the Employment Service and the parts of the Benefits Agency which support people of working age. It will deliver a single, integrated service to benefit claimants of working age and employers. The agency will continue to develop the partnership approach to working with the private and voluntary sectors which the Government has adopted in implementing its welfare to work policies.

The New Deal

4.12   Through the New Deal, the Government is ensuring that people do not become detached from the labour market. The New Deal provides help and support for people moving into work to ensure that they are well equipped to compete effectively in the modern labour market. Over 750,000 people have participated in the New Deal and around 260,000 of them have already moved into work. Budget 2000 builds on the success of the New Deal to date, by:

- strengthening the New Deal for 18–24s by introducing nationally an Intensive Gateway for young people on the New Deal from June 2000;

- extending the New Deal for 25 plus to provide a more intensive programme based on the principles of the New Deal for 18–24s on a national basis from April 2001;

- introducing Action Teams in areas with the highest unemployment, to help match unemployed people to vacancies;

- providing more choices for lone parents who are considering work; and

- developing plans for extending the New Deal for disabled people nationwide and introducing rehabilitation and retention pilots to test different ways to help disabled people move into and remain in work.

New Deal for 18–24 year olds

4.13 Long-term youth unemployment has fallen by 70 per cent since May 1997. The New Deal for 18–24 year olds helps young unemployed people to secure jobs as the most effective way of enhancing their earnings, increasing their skills and securing their future economic independence. The New Deal for 18–24 year olds includes:

- a Gateway of up to 4 months, including help with job search, careers advice and guidance from a personal adviser;

- for those who do not find unsubsidised employment, a period of mandatory full-time activity through one of four options (subsidised employment, full-time education and training, work on the environmental task force or work with the voluntary sector), to help improve their employment prospects; and

- follow-through to ensure that clients are helped to build on their experience and move into employment.

4.14 Over 400,000 young people have joined the New Deal since it was launched nationally in April 1998 and over 185,000 have found jobs. In addition, over 116,000 young people have gained work experience and training through the other New Deal options. Independent analysis by the National Institute of Economic and Social Research estimates that the New Deal for 18–24 year olds has reduced long-term youth unemployment by nearly 40 per cent relative to what it would otherwise have been. Box 4.4 presents some of the evaluation results to date.

4.15 As set out in the Pre-Budget Report, the Government plans to expand an Intensive Gateway approach from June 2000, building on the lessons learnt from the 12 pilots launched last year. The Gateway is designed to prepare young people more effectively for work and provide them with a greater impetus for their jobseeking activity. It will include:

- a full-time course involving job-search activity and addressing "soft" skills, such as punctuality, team working and communication skills; and

- more intensive personal adviser help with job search before and after the course.

4.16 The Intensive Gateway will benefit those young people whose job search activity would gain from an injection of further pace and purpose. As announced in Budget 99, the final month of the Gateway has been intensified for all New Deal for 18–24 year old participants to prepare them for the New Deal options and to emphasise that remaining on benefits is not an option.

4.17 The Government's New Deal Innovation Fund backs good ideas generated at the local level for improving the effectiveness of the New Deal. The Pre-Budget Report outlined the Government's intention to provide further funds from the receipts of the Windfall Tax to extend the Innovation Fund beyond 2000. £9.5 million will be allocated to extend the Innovation Fund over the next three years – £5 million of which will be ring-fenced for measures within inner cities to explore the use of intermediaries in getting disadvantaged people into jobs.

Box 4.2: Preparing people for work

As set out in the Pre-Budget Report, the Government will be offering support to intermediary organisations who, working closely with employers, will help long-term unemployed people move into and remain in employment. As part of an extended New Deal Innovation Fund, proposals will be invited from intermediary organisations working in 11 inner city areas to achieve this aim. Help will reflect local needs and be focused within the context of the New Deal. Public money will be linked to matched funding from the private sector, and employers in particular.

The Innovation Fund is also being used to explore the role that sector-based intermediary organisations can play in supporting employers – particularly small businesses – and unemployed people to take full advantage of the opportunities offered by the New Deal. As an initial step, a workshop was held at No. 11 Downing Street to explore and discuss how intermediaries might support disadvantaged unemployed people from London to find and keep financial-sector jobs in the City. This workshop brought together business leaders, and voluntary and community groups to explore the lessons to be learnt from both US and UK experience to see how this can be taken forward. Since then, 10 major financial companies have agreed to review their human resource requirements and the vacancies which New Deal participants could be trained for, support the development of intermediaries in order to meet the sector's requirements, and contribute towards the cost of the project.

The workshop provided an excellent launch for this initiative and facilitated a significant level of commitment, which has now been secured. A similar workshop is now being planned for the IT sector, and it is hoped that this will provide a foundation for equivalent results. The Government is exploring how this approach can be extended to other sectors.

New Deal for 25 plus

4.18   Since June 1998, people aged 25 and over who have been unemployed for two years or more have been eligible for the New Deal for 25 plus. This includes access to a personal adviser service and, alongside a range of options for long-term unemployed people, a £75 per week wage subsidy and opportunities to undertake full-time education and training. By December 1999, around 216,000 long-term unemployed people had started on the programme and over 34,000 had found jobs. Since November 1998, a more intensive approach has been tested in some areas, and at earlier durations of unemployment, building on the principles of the New Deal for 18–24s.

4.19   As announced in the Pre Budget Report, from April 2000, participants in the New Deal for 25 plus will benefit from enhanced gateway provision with more intensive contact with their New Deal personal adviser and greater access to support services, as well as improved job search facilities being put in place across the Employment Service this year.

4.20   The Pre-Budget Report also set out plans to intensify and extend the New Deal for 25 plus on a national basis from April 2001 – along the lines of the New Deal for 18–24s – incorporating lessons learned from the innovative New Deal 25 plus pilots. A comprehensive set of measures aimed at helping all unemployed people aged over 25 will come into effect nationally from April 2001. For people aged over 25 who have been unemployed for 18 months, there will be a step change in New Deal provision, heralding a stronger emphasis on rights and responsibilities, similar to the approach pioneered in the New Deal for 18–24s, comprising:

- a structured gateway provision, including help with job search, careers advice and guidance;

- for those who do not find unsubsidised employment during the Gateway, full-time activity including flexible access to a period of subsidised employment, support for self-employment, work-focused training, or a programme to improve key work skills to enhance their employment prospects, which could include work trials with an employer or work with the voluntary sector; and

- follow-through to ensure clients are helped to build on their experience and move into employment.

Box 4.3: Self-employment

The Government's aim is to help create a supportive environment for entrepreneurial activity in all sections of society. Long-term unemployed people who want to move into self-employment can face particular difficulties getting their businesses off the ground. The Pre-Budget Report announced that the Government was considering the case for a start up grant to act as an income bridge between benefits and business. Budget 2000 includes a number of measures to help unemployed people move into self-employment.

From April 2001, the New Deal for 25 plus will provide specialised help and financial support for people wanting to move into self-employment, building on the self-employment option in the New Deal for 18-24 year olds. This allows a period of test-trading for up to 6 months during which people can remain on Jobseekers' Allowance, whilst their profits are put into a special account which can be accessed once they leave benefit. People moving into self-employment will also be eligible for the new £100 Job Grant, as well as the enhanced Housing Benefit run-on and the new Income Support for Mortgage Interest run-on, providing a secure income in the crucial first weeks of trading.

For self-employed people with children, the Working Families' Tax Credit provides an income bridge. And for those over 50, who are more likely to move into self-employment than younger workers, the Employment Credit offers up to £3,000 in the first year. The Government is considering how to extend this principle to other people without children through an employment tax credit, which would offer further help to those moving into self-employment. The Employment Service will work with the Small Business Service to ensure high quality support is available for those who wish to take the self-employment option.

Enhanced provision for jobseekers

4.21 The Government has also announced that more resources will be provided to intensify contact between the Employment Service (ES) and jobseekers aged 25 and over who have been on Jobseekers' Allowance for 6 months or more. From April 2000, the Employment Service will:

- introduce an extended and more intensive Restart interview for jobseekers to provide more support, encouragement and help with job search, thereby improving their chances of finding work;

- provide more intensive Fortnightly Jobsearch Reviews around the 6 and 12 months of unemployment points, to check progress and discuss the jobs available; and

- introduce pilots to explore how best to match jobseekers to vacancies, and telephone them regularly through ES Direct to offer them jobs.

4.22 The Pre-Budget Report announced a significant new programme of investment to modernise the Employment Service. This involves harnessing the full potential of new technologies to bring about a radical improvement in its services to employers and to jobseekers. During 2000, the Government will:

- launch a new jobs and learning bank, accessible through the internet;

- begin to expand access to the jobs and learning bank from public places and through a network of touch-screen jobpoints in Jobcentres;

- enhance and deepen its links with the BBC and other potential partners to ensure that the full potential of interactive digital television is used to help bring together jobseekers and employers; and

- put in place a nationwide network of job-broking call centres which, as well as providing a single point of contact for employers and jobseekers, will enable jobseekers to be informed of vacancies for which they might be suitable.

New Deal for 50 plus **4.23** The employment rate of men aged over 50 has fallen dramatically in the last 20 years. At the same time, women over 50 have not experienced the marked increases in labour market participation that younger women have enjoyed. Budget 99 announced the New Deal for 50 plus, which was launched in nine Pathfinder Areas in October 1999. The New Deal for 50 plus will be rolled out nationally in April 2000 and provides: personal advice; help with job search; an employment credit of £60 a week for full-time and self-employment and £40 for part-time employment for one year; and training support. This support is available on a voluntary basis to people aged over 50, where they or their partner have been on benefits for more than six months, to help them return to work.

Box 4.4 Evaluating the New Deal

The design of the New Deal is built on the evidence of what works. International evidence has suggested that active labour market policies that help to move people back into work as quickly as possible are the most successful. The Government has already started to implement a rigorous programme of evaluation, including the use of random assignment in some key areas, to assess how well the New Deal is performing and to ensure that future developments can build on the success of the New Deal. Early evaluation findings are now emerging.

Independent evaluation of the New Deal for 18–24s which has now been published[1] suggests that only half of the young people leaving unemployment through the New Deal would have done so without the programme. All active labour market policies will experience some deadweight (people who would have moved into work even without the programme) but these results compare favourably with results from other active labour market policies.

The evaluation also estimates that:

- approximately 10,000 young people leave unemployment each month from the New Deal;

- over a four year period, over 500,000 young people will leave unemployment via the New Deal;

- the New Deal for 18–24s will be close to self-financing as the extra activity it generates leads to higher Government revenue; and

- overall, the New Deal for 18–24s is estimated to have reduced long-term youth unemployment in Britain by almost 40 per cent relative to what it might otherwise have been.

Prior to its national launch, the New Deal for lone parents ran in eight pilot areas. The full evaluation of the pilot stages of the New Deal for lone parents is now available[2]. The evaluation suggests that the New Deal for lone parents is having a real and positive effect. After 18 months, over 3 per cent more lone parents had left Income Support in the New Deal pilot areas than in the comparison areas. This estimate also compares favourably with international evidence of welfare to work programmes. A cost-benefit analysis of the pilot stages showed that the New Deal for lone parents produced public finance returns which covered its operational costs, while it produced significant positive benefits in terms of its wider economic value.

[1] B. Anderton, R. Riley and G. Young (1999) "The New Deal for Young People: First Year Analysis of Implications for the Macroeconomy", National Institute of Economic and Social Research, Employment Service Research and Development Report.
[2] J. Hales et al "Evaluation of the New Deal for Lone Parents: Early lessons from the Phase One Prototype – Synthesis Report", Department of Social Security Research Report, March 2000.

Worklessness in deprived areas   4.24   While the aggregate labour market is stronger than at any time in the last 20 years, pockets of low employment and high unemployment remain across the country, especially in Britain's inner cities. Meeting these challenges requires a multi-faceted strategy. Following the Social Exclusion Unit's September 1998 report on neighbourhood renewal[1], the Government

[1] Bringing Britain Together: a national strategy for neighbourhood renewal, report by The Social Exclusion Unit, 1998

established 18 Policy Action Teams to help to develop a coherent national strategy. The Policy Action Team on Jobs[2] identified four principal reasons why people living in the most deprived neighbourhoods might fail to obtain the jobs on offer nearby:

- lack of skills and aptitudes, especially self-confidence and inter-personal skills;

- inadequate matching between employers and jobless people;

- worries about making the transition from benefits into work; and

- racial discrimination against ethnic minorities.

4.25   A separate Treasury paper, *The Goal of Full Employment: Employment Opportunity for all Throughout Britain*, published on 29 February, describes this patchwork of areas of prosperity and deprivation. The paper shows how Britain's most deprived areas sit alongside, and within travelling distance of, labour markets where vacancies are going unfilled. It is not enough just to ensure that there are job opportunities everywhere – the challenge is to ensure that people in Britain's most deprived communities are equipped to take advantage of vacancies arising in nearby areas.

4.26   The New Deal for 18–24s is already addressing this challenge for young unemployed people throughout the country. The Pre-Budget Report announced that through the New Deal Innovation Fund, money would be made available to provide additional support for private and voluntary sector intermediaries in around 11 inner-city areas which can add value by linking long-term unemployed people to employers with vacancies to offer. The Pre-Budget Report also announced enhancements to job matching services for unemployed people over the age of 25, as set out in paragraph 4.21. Budget 2000 announces further enhancements to the New Deal to ensure that people can compete effectively for the jobs created in Britain's dynamic labour market, and to support this it also announces more targeted support to tackle barriers to employment in areas of deprivation.

Employment Zones   **4.27**   From April 2000, Employment Zones will be introduced in 15 areas in England, Scotland and Wales that suffer from particularly high levels of unemployment. Employment Zones are a new and innovative approach that aim to help around 50,000 long-term unemployed people aged over 25 back into work. They will offer the opportunity of tailoring programmes specifically to people's needs, with jobseekers and their personal advisers being able to set up Personal Job Accounts to use, more flexibly, funds that are available for support. Employment Zones will be provided by a combination of public, private and voluntary sector organisations. Like other welfare to work policies, they will be evaluated to discover best practice that can be shared in future developments.

Action Teams   **4.28**   Action Teams will be set up in 20 of Britain's communities with the highest unemployment and lowest employment, along with additional support in the 15 Employment Zone areas. They will have access to a £40 million fund to work with long-term unemployed people in the most deprived areas, to identify suitable vacancies in neighbouring areas and to bring the two together. These Action Teams, bringing together the Employment Service and private and voluntary sectors, will use this additional funding to tackle barriers to employment, including funding for transport to enable people to access nearby vacancies. The Action Teams will operate initially for one year from autumn 2000 and will be extended on the basis of their effectiveness at getting people into work.

New Deal for lone parents   **4.29**   The Government is determined to help into work both those who are unemployed, and those who are outside the labour market but who would like to find work. Balancing work and family responsibilities is often difficult for parents, particularly when they are the sole carer of a child. But taking long periods out of the labour market while caring for children can put

---

[2] *Jobs for all, national strategy for neighbourhood renewal*, Department for Education and Employment, 1999

families at greater risk of poverty and can be damaging to long-term earnings potential. Lone parent households are far less likely to work than married or cohabiting couple households. This lower labour market participation puts lone parent families at greater risk of low income and a lack of opportunity – 1 in 4 children live in families headed by a lone parent, yet children in lone parent households make up almost half of all children in poverty. But most – 9 out of 10 – lone parents say that they would like to work at some point. The Government wants to provide genuine choices for lone parents, to help them to balance work and family life, and to tackle the barriers to work that they face.

4.30   The New Deal for lone parents (NDLP) was launched nationally in October 1998. It provides the opportunity for all lone parents to meet a personal adviser and receive help and support to improve their prospects and living standards by taking up, and increasing, paid work. From the national roll-out of the NDLP to the end of December 1999, over 103,500 lone parents had participated and more than 35,000 had already moved into employment.

4.31   Building on the success of the NDLP to date, a package of improvements was outlined in the Pre-Budget Report, increasing the choices and opportunities available to lone parents considering work. The package, which will be introduced this year, includes more intensive support for lone parents soon to move onto JSA as their children reach age 16, access to specialised resource centres to help with preparation for work and job search, and an extension of invitations to participate in the New Deal to lone parents on Income Support with children from the age of three. Innovative pilots, run by private and voluntary sector organisations, have begun testing new approaches to help lone parents into work, including mentoring, work experience and training. An in-work training grant will also be piloted later this year, helping lone parents to gain qualifications once they move into work through the New Deal.

4.32   From April 2000 in the 12 pilot areas of ONE, all lone parents making a new benefit claim will be required to meet with a personal adviser to discuss options for work and training. To ensure that lone parents are able to consider all of the choices available to them, starting this autumn in pathfinder areas and nationally from April 2001, lone parents on Income Support with children over the age of five will be required to meet with a specialist lone parent personal adviser to guide them through these choices. The Government recognises that for some lone parents, particularly those with young children, choices are constrained. Providing information about opportunities to work, study or care for their children full time, will help lone parents to plan for their future. The choices on offer to lone parents will include:

- work of 16 hours or more, to move lone parents onto the Working Families' Tax Credit;

- the choice to try some work under 16 hours; and

- the opportunity to undertake education and training.

These choices will be offered on a voluntary basis. Chapter 5 sets out in more detail the overall strategy for abolishing child poverty and for ensuring security for lone parents and their children, particularly when their children are young.

4.33   A personal adviser will be able to guide lone parents through these choices, and help them to prepare for their future as their children get older. Lone parents who would like to move into work of 16 hours or more, and onto the Working Families' Tax Credit, from April 2001, will receive a guaranteed minimum income of £155, or £214 at 35 hours a week, and help with childcare costs through the childcare tax credit. They will also receive help to make the transition into work through the Income Support run-on and from April 2001, lone parents with mortgages who are moving into work will be eligible for a 4 week Income

Support for Mortgage Interest (ISMI) run-on and a 1 year linking rule to help them to feel and be more secure when making the transition into work (see paragraph 4.44). Lone parents will also be provided with help to prepare for, and to move into, work through NDLP.

4.34 For those lone parents who want to work for less than 16 hours, the first £20 of their earnings will be disregarded against their Income Support or JSA. Lone parents who are childminders can gain even more – two-thirds of their earnings from childminding are ignored, with the remaining third subject to the £20 disregard. From April 2002 lone parents on Income Support will see up to £10 a week extra of any maintenance paid to them, through a new maintenance premium introduced under the reformed Child Support Agency. Personal advisers will also be given access to resources to provide help with childcare for lone parents in jobs of less than 16 hours.

4.35 Those lone parents who would like the opportunity to prepare for some work in the future will be eligible for free access to Further Education courses and help with childcare through access funds. They will also be eligible to apply for a means-tested Childcare Grant for lone parents in Higher Education which will be fully disregarded for benefits purposes. Help to train for work through the New Deal for lone parents will also be provided and from April 2001, lone parents undertaking training and education will be eligible for a £15 per week premium on top of their Income Support to help them cover the additional costs of studying.

New Deal for partners of unemployed people

4.36 Where one partner is unemployed, the chances of the other partner being in work are much lower. This is especially the case for women: where the male partner is unemployed, only 40 per cent of female partners are employed. In contrast, where the male is employed, 75 per cent of female partners are employed. The large increases in female employment over the past 20 years have come in households where the partner is already in work. The New Deal for partners of unemployed people was launched in three pathfinder areas in February 1999 and was rolled out nationally in April 1999. It provides a personal adviser service aimed at helping partners of unemployed people to move into work. Partners aged 18–24 are eligible to receive help through the New Deal for 18–24s.

New Deal for disabled people

4.37 Disabled people are among the most disadvantaged in the labour force: in any year, only 5 per cent of those receiving incapacity benefits return to work. The Government has therefore set aside £195 million from the receipts of the Windfall Tax specifically to assist this group. The New Deal for disabled people has been testing a range of approaches – a personal adviser service, innovative schemes and benefit changes to find out what really works. To date, over 2,500 people have been helped into work by the New Deal for disabled people pilots.

4.38 Budget 2000 announces the first stage of work in developing a nationwide service to help disabled people find work. The service will continue to be exploratory, testing and evaluating different approaches in order to develop the most effective policies for disabled people.

4.39 Budget 2000 also announces that the Government intends to test the effectiveness of helping people when they become ill in work, with job retention and rehabilitation pilots. These pilots, beginning from 2001, will test the effectiveness of early work-focused help with health, employment and other services.

Funding Welfare to Work

4.40 The Welfare to Work programme is funded from the receipts of the one-off Windfall Tax on the excess profits of the privatised utilities. The Windfall Tax raised a total of £5.2 billion. Table 4.1 sets out the latest estimates of the allocation of Windfall Tax receipts between programmes.

Table 4.1 Allocation of the Windfall Tax receipts

£million	1997-98	1998-99	1999-00	2000-01	2001-02	1997-02
Spending by programme[1]						
New Deal for 18–24 year olds[2]	50	210	320	440	460	1480
New Deal for the over 25s[3]	0	10	110	160	320	600
New Deal for 50 plus	0	0	0	20	20	40
New Deal for lone parents	0	20	40	60	90	220
New Deal for disabled people[4]	0	10	30	90	80	210
New Deal for partners of unemployed people	0	0	10	20	20	50
New Deal for schools[5]	90	270	330	580	310	1590
Childcare[6]	0	20	10	0	0	40
University for Industry[7]	0	5	0	0	0	5
ONE pilots[8]	0	0	0	5	5	10
Action Teams				20	20	40
Enterprise development	0	0	0	20	10	30
Total Expenditure	**140**	**550**	**850**	**1420**	**1340**	**4300**
Unallocated						900
Windfall Tax receipts	**2600**	**2600**				**5200**

[1] Rounded to the nearest £10 million (except for UfI and ONE). Constituent elements may not sum to totals because of rounding. Outturns for 1997–98 and 1998–99, projected outturns for 1999–00 and allocations for 2000–01 onwards.

[2] Includes £20 million for 18–24 year old childless partners of unemployed people.

[3] Includes £10 million for skills development fund. Includes an indicative allocation for enhancements from April 2001, yet to be finalised.

[4] Includes £10 million in 1999–00, an element of the November 1998 announcements on Welfare Reform.

[5] Capital spending on renewal of school infrastructure, to help raise standards – announced in the 1997 Budget.

[6] Includes £30 million for out-of-school childcare. The costs of the 1997 Budget improvements in childcare support through Family Credit are included from April 1998 until October 1999, when the measures were incorporated in the childcare tax credit within the Working Families' Tax Credit.

[7] Start-up and development costs. Other costs of the UfI are funded from within departmental expenditure limits.

[8] Funding for repeat interviews. Other funding comes from the Invest to Save budget.

EASING THE TRANSITION TO WORK

4.41 For many people, especially those who have been out of work for long periods, the transition back into work can be a difficult period. Although they would be better off in work, the associated risks, especially managing until the first pay cheque, can make many people prefer certain, but lower, benefit levels. The problems of dealing with a short-term transition into work can leave people trapped for long periods on benefits. There are currently a number of schemes intended to ease the move into work, but each is narrowly targeted, often discretionary and with complex rules. Evidence suggests that the system is little understood, with schemes simply providing an unexpected windfall rather than giving people the security to make the move into work. To provide that security, the system needs to be made simpler and more automatic. The Government also recognises that some groups require additional support to overcome specific barriers to work. In particular, families with children can be constrained by the cost and availability of childcare. The Government has therefore implemented a number of reforms to help families with children to make the transition into work.

Job Grant 4.42 The Government will introduce from spring 2001, a Job Grant of £100 for people who move from welfare into work. This builds on the Income Support run-on for lone parents announced in Budget 99 which lone parents will continue to receive. All others who move into work of more than 16 hours a week, expected to last 5 weeks or more, and who have been claiming Jobseekers' Allowance, Income Support, Severe Disablement Allowance or Incapacity Benefit for at least 52 weeks will be eligible. The Job Grant will replace the discretionary and narrowly-targeted Jobfinder's Grant and Jobmatch, providing a single transitional payment, available much more widely, and without the complex eligibility criteria of previous schemes.

Simplifying extended payments in Housing Benefit

4.43 Housing costs are a particular concern to many people moving back into work. Although Housing Benefit can be paid in work, the time taken to process claims can lead to rent arrears building up. Housing Benefit can already be paid, at out-of-work rates, for the first four weeks in work under the Housing Benefit Extended Payments scheme for recipients of Income Support and JSA. But again, complex rules mean that take-up is low. To address this, the Government will simplify the rules of the Housing Benefit Extended Payments scheme from April 2001 to ensure that payments are as near-automatic as possible.

Income Support for Mortgage Interest run-on

4.44 The Government also intends to provide help with housing costs for homeowners going back to work. Homeowners who have been out of work and on Income Support or Jobseekers' Allowance for nine months or more receive help in paying the interest on their mortgage through Income Support for Mortgage Interest (ISMI). This support currently stops as soon as they take a job, at just the point where they may also need to start paying back built-up arrears. Alongside the extended payment of Housing Benefit, from spring 2001 the Government will provide a four week ISMI run-on for those entering work. It will also improve the existing linking rules so that everyone getting ISMI will be able to requalify for it directly if they return to benefits within 1 year of taking a job.

National Childcare Strategy

4.45 The £470 million National Childcare Strategy was launched in 1998. It has three key strands: to make childcare more accessible and available to every community; to improve and maintain the quality of childcare; and to make childcare more affordable.

- by the end of December 1999, 62,000 more childcare places had been created, on top of the nursery places for 3 and 4 year olds;

- from September 2001, the registration and inspection of childcare providers will be unified under OFSTED to ensure a single quality standard. The Qualifications and Curriculum Authority have already completed the first stage of the review of the early education and childcare qualifications framework; and

- the new childcare tax credit in the Working Families' Tax Credit is already making childcare more affordable: there are nearly twice as many families benefiting from the childcare tax credit than were benefiting under Family Credit.

Childcare tax credit

4.46 The childcare tax credit component within the Working Families' Tax Credit and the Disabled Person's Tax Credit provides generous and direct support for childcare costs for the first time. The credit is worth 70 per cent of eligible childcare costs up to a limit of £100 a week for a family with one child and £150 a week for families with two or more children. It is particularly beneficial to low earners compared with the childcare disregard within Family Credit and Disability Working Allowance. This extra financial support tackles another barrier to work and underpins the increase in childcare places being delivered by the National Childcare Strategy.

Encouraging employers to provide childcare

4.47 To encourage employers to help employees with childcare, all provision in kind will remain exempt from employer Class 1A national insurance contributions (NICs) when these are extended to other employee benefits from April 2000. This employer NICs exemption will apply to direct provision, childcare vouchers and payments under contracts between employers and third party providers.

Box 4.5: The informal economy

The Pre-Budget Report announced that Lord Grabiner QC would conduct a review of the hidden economy and report back in time for the Budget. Lord Grabiner's report, *The Informal Economy*, published on 9 March, reviews the problems of unregistered businesses, and self-employed people and employees in the hidden economy, and makes a number of recommendations. The report suggests that people can become trapped in the hidden economy because they are not aware of the legitimate opportunities that are available. Following Lord Grabiner's proposals, the Government is introducing a number of new incentives for people to leave the informal economy and take up legitimate work. The Government will:

- set up a confidential telephone line to advise people in the hidden economy about how to put their affairs in order, and about how the tax and benefit rules apply to them;

- extend the help which is given to people who start out in self-employment;

- introduce a requirement for new businesses to tell the Inland Revenue as soon as they start up, so that they can be offered early help and advice;

- make further changes to simplify the transition from benefits into work; and

- launch a campaign to publicise the existing incentives to join the legitimate economy, such as the Working Families' Tax Credit.

Lord Grabiner also recommended new measures to take action against those who persist in the hidden economy, especially employers who commit multiple tax offences and collude in benefit fraud. The Government will:

- legislate for a statutory offence of fraudulently evading income tax, to be tried in the magistrates' court;

- require people suspected of doing undeclared work while signing on as unemployed to attend the Jobcentre more frequently, at unpredictable times;

- legislate to give investigators the power to trace suspects by making "reverse searches" of the telephone directory; and

- prepare to implement a "two strikes and you are out" approach for benefit fraud – removing people's right to claim for a specified time if they have been caught twice.

Moving people into the formal economy

4.48 Some people who are unable to manage the transition into work choose to take the short cut and undertake work in the informal economy which they do not declare. The informal, or hidden economy, is estimated to cost taxpayers billions of pounds each year in unpaid taxes, and around half a billion pounds in benefits fraudulently claimed by people who are carrying out work which they do not declare. Following a report by Lord Grabiner QC (see Box 4.5), the Government is introducing a number of new measures to encourage people to make the transition into legitimate jobs and to tackle those who persist in the hidden economy.

4.49 The Government will make it easier for those in the benefits system to try out work. From April 2001, it will increase the amount of earnings disregarded in Income Support and JSA by £5 to £20 for those groups facing restricted work choices, such as lone parents, carers or disabled people. In future these groups will be able to keep £20 per week of any earnings without losing any benefit. This will boost their income and help them progress in work and move off benefits. From April 2002, the Government will also suspend Income Support and JSA claims for 12 weeks rather than close them when people leave benefit, to streamline the process of re-claiming if a job falls through within that period. The Government will also consider the case for introducing a similar arrangement in Housing Benefit. This should encourage benefit recipients to report starting work which may be temporary or insecure and help ensure that they are not deterred by the normal claim procedure. Together, these measures will reduce the barriers to trying legitimate work.

MAKING WORK PAY

4.50   For the vast majority of people, there are clear financial rewards to work. But people are often understandably reluctant to move into jobs where the financial gain is small or non-existent – the unemployment trap. Evidence also suggests that some individuals can experience repeated short spells of low paid work and non-employment without ever moving up the earnings ladder – the low pay, no pay cycle.

4.51   Moreover, people in employment are often discouraged from working longer hours or taking a better job because their work is penalised by high marginal deduction rates[3] – the poverty trap.

4.52   Policies aimed at re-attaching individuals to the labour market, such as the New Deal, therefore need to be complemented by measures that reward work, reduce in-work poverty and provide incentives to move up the earnings ladder. It is against this background that the Government has undertaken a number of reforms to ensure that work pays.

National Minimum Wage   **4.53**   The National Minimum Wage, introduced in April 1999, ensures fair minimum standards of pay and underpins the Government's tax and benefit reforms. The introductory rates were:

- £3.60 an hour for adult workers aged 22 and over;

- £3.20 an hour for trainees (workers aged 22 and over in the first six months of employment and receiving training leading to a recognised qualification); and

- £3.00 an hour for workers aged 18-21 inclusive, rising to £3.20 in June 2000.

4.54   In February 2000 the Government published the Low Pay Commission's Second Report, which assessed the initial impact of the National Minimum Wage. The Report found that the National Minimum Wage had been a success, and has not had any adverse effects on employment or the wider economy. In the light of this assessment, the Government has announced that it will increase the rate for adult workers aged 22 or over to £3.70 an hour from October 2000. The Government has asked the Low Pay Commission to continue to monitor the impact of the National Minimum Wage, and to report its findings by July 2001.

Income tax   **4.55**   Budget 99 introduced a 10p starting rate of income tax from April 1999. The 10p rate has halved the marginal tax rate for 1.9 million low paid workers. As also announced in Budget 99, from April 2000 the basic rate of income tax will be reduced to 22p – the lowest level for 70 years.

---

[3] Marginal deduction rates measure the proportion of any marginal increase in income lost through reduced benefit entitlement and increased taxation.

National 4.56   Jobs at the lower end of the earnings distribution now pay following the Government's
Insurance reforms to national insurance:
Contributions

- the entry fee on employee NICs was abolished in April 1999; and

- as announced in Budget 99, the threshold above which employees pay NICs
  will be increased to £76 a week in April 2000 and will be aligned with the
  income tax personal allowance in April 2001. This will move around 1 million
  people on earnings of less than £87 out of NICs altogether, while maintaining
  their entitlement to contributory benefits.

4.57   The Government has also reduced the NICs burden on employers through the
introduction of a single employer rate. In April 1999, the point at which employers began to
pay NICs was aligned with the personal tax allowance. In addition, as set out in the Pre-
Budget Report, employer NICs will be reduced by 0.3 percentage points from April 2001,
thereby ensuring that all revenue from the climate change levy is recycled back to business.
This Budget announces that the revenues from the aggregates levy will be recycled through
a further reduction in the rate of employer national insurance contributions of 0.1
percentage points from April 2002 (see Chapter 6 for details of the climate change levy
package and the aggregates levy).

Working 4.58   The Working Families' Tax Credit was introduced in October 1999. It will make work pay
Families' Tax for up to 1.4 million low and middle income working families with children, half a million more
Credit than would have received Family Credit. Payment through the wage packet, from April 2000, will
underline the message that work pays and for many will end the need to pay tax and receive in
work support separately. The childcare tax credit component of WFTC, as detailed in paragraph
4.46, will help many families to whom the costs of childcare are a barrier to employment.

4.59   Chapter 5 describes further increases to the WFTC credits for children under 16 from
June 2000. These, combined with the increase in the minimum wage to £3.70, will guarantee
a minimum income of £208 from October 2000 and £214 from April 2001 for a family with
children, with someone in full-time work.

4.60   Together these tax and benefit reforms mean that by 2001 the tax burden on a family
on average earnings with two children will be the lowest since 1972. As Chart 4.2 shows, the
net tax rate on a family with two children will be negative (they will pay less in income tax and

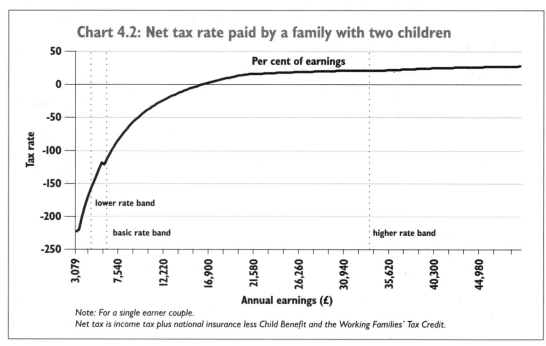

Chart 4.2: Net tax rate paid by a family with two children

Note: For a single earner couple.
Net tax is income tax plus national insurance less Child Benefit and the Working Families' Tax Credit.

Box 4.6 The launch of the Working Families' Tax Credit

In October last year the Government introduced the **Working Families' Tax Credit**, increasing financial support and making work pay for around 1.4 million families with almost 2.8 million children. At the end of February 2000, only five months after the launch of the new policy, already:

- over 3 million calls have been received enquiring about the Working Families' Tax Credit, and over 1 million new applications have been received;

- over 1 million families are now receiving the Working Families' Tax Credit or are in the transition period from Family Credit. This is over 200,000 more than received Family Credit at its peak; and

- the childcare tax credit component of the Working Families' Tax Credit has been particularly successful with over 90,000 recipients. At its peak, in August 1999, 47,000 families claimed the childcare disregard in Family Credit.

The 12 week advertising campaign to raise awareness and encourage take-up of the new Tax Credit has proved a success. Recent tracking data showed that nearly nine out of ten of those likely to be eligible for the Working Families' Tax Credit recognised or were aware of the advertisements. This level of awareness compares very favourably with other Government and non-Government advertising campaigns. Among those to be helped by the Better Deal are:

Tim, a 41 year old widower, has two children. Having spoken to a New Deal for Lone Parent's Adviser in January after nine years out of employment, Tim successfully found a new job. Receipt of the Working Families' Tax Credit made him £84 a week better off in work than on Income Support.

Mr and Mrs Wilkinson have three children under five and both work, he full time and she part time. They applied for Working Families' Tax Credit in October and their claim was turned round in one day. Their net weekly income was £270.50 and their award over £23 per week.

The Working Families' Tax Credit meant that Joy could afford full time childcare enabling her to start a small business. She now says "Without the tax credit my business would not have been possible and although I have only begun trading it is going extremely well. I have secured some orders and am in the process of advertising on the internet."

NICs than they receive in tax credits and child benefit) until their income reaches nearly £16,000 a year. A family on the minimum wage with two children will have their income topped up by 90 per cent.

Disabled Person's Tax Credit 4.61   The Disabled Person's Tax Credit (DPTC) was also launched in October 1999 to give disabled workers a better deal. By October 2000, the Disabled Person's Tax Credit will boost the incomes of 32,000 working people, nearly twice as many as were receiving the Disability Working Allowance (DWA), by on average £25 a week. The Disabled Person's Tax Credit is open to people who work for 16 hours or more a week, have an illness or disability which puts them at a disadvantage in getting a job, and who are either receiving one of a range of incapacity or disability benefits at the time of their application, or have been receiving certain benefits within the previous 6 months. From October 2000 a new fast-track to DPTC will be introduced to help people who have been sick for 20 weeks or more, but can do some work, to remain in their job. This is based on evidence suggesting that those that become disabled whilst working are most likely to find employment with their existing employer and that the longer these people remain out of work the harder it is for them to return to employment.

The effect of the Government's package to make work pay

Tackling the unemployment trap

4.62 These reforms are addressing the unemployment trap, so that work pays. The gap between in and out-of-work incomes has increased while security for those out-of-work has been maintained.

4.63 Evidence suggests that unemployed people may resist taking a job that leaves them less than £40 a week better off in work than remaining on benefits. As a result of this Government's measures to make work pay the amount required to be £40 a week better off in work, for a couple with two children under 11, has fallen from £260 to £160. This amount is very close to the average wage this group would command when moving into work.

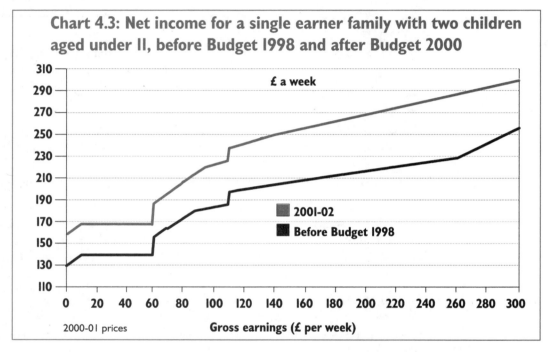

Chart 4.3: Net income for a single earner family with two children aged under 11, before Budget 1998 and after Budget 2000

£ a week

2001-02

Before Budget 1998

2000-01 prices   Gross earnings (£ per week)

4.64 The Government's making work pay package highlights clearly the rewards of work over welfare and by April 2001 guarantees:

- a minimum income of £214 a week for a one earner family with someone in full-time work, over £11,000 a year;

- a family with one part-time worker a minimum income of £155 a week;

- that working families with an income of less than £255 a week will not pay any net income tax; and

- under the Disabled Person's Tax Credit, a minimum income of £246 a week (£12,800 a year) for a family with children and someone in full-time work.

Tackling the poverty trap

4.65 The overall incidence of multiple tapers and very high marginal deduction rates has been greatly reduced by the Government's tax and benefit reforms. Low income families now keep more of each additional pound that they earn.

4.66 Table 4.2 illustrates the estimated number of families facing high withdrawal rates before and after the Government's reforms.

Table 4.2: Combined effect of Government's reforms on high marginal deduction rates

Marginal deduction rate[1]	Before Budget 1998[2]	After Budget 2000[2]
100 per cent or more	5,000	0
90 per cent or more	130,000	30,000
80 per cent or more	300,000	210,000
70 per cent or more	740,000	250,000
60 per cent or more	760,000	950,000

[1] Cumulative figures for working households.
[2] The before and after figures are based on 1997–98 and 1999–00 caseload and take-up estimates respectively.

4.67 In 1997, nearly $3/4$ million families lost over 70 pence of each additional pound of earnings. As a result of previous Budget measures, around half a million fewer families will face effective tax rates of over 70 per cent, significantly reducing the poverty trap for low earning families.

Employment tax credit

4.68 The introduction of the National Minimum Wage and the Working Families' Tax Credit have for the first time guaranteed a minimum income for families in work. As illustrated in Chart 4.3, much has been done to make work pay for families with children.

4.69 The Government has introduced the Disabled Person's Tax Credit and the Employment Credit component of the New Deal for 50 plus, extending the scope of in-work support to people without children. There is a strong case in principle for extending this more widely. The Government is committed to introducing an integrated child credit – a seamless system of child support paid to the main carer from 2003. As set out in Chapter 5 this new system of support, for those in and out of work, will be complemented by an employment tax credit administered by the Inland Revenue and paid through the wage packet. The employment tax credit, which will broadly replicate the adult support in the Working Families' Tax Credit, will be introduced for families with children from 2003. The Government is considering how far to extend the employment tax credit to those without children.

4.70 The National Minimum Wage and tax reforms have increased the gain to work for all workless households. However, the gains to work from low-paid jobs for those without children, are still not large. Currently, the gain to full–time work at the National Minimum Wage for a couple without children is around £15, assuming an average rent. This is much less than the Working Families' Tax Credit delivers for families with children.

4.71 An employment tax credit could increase gains to work for other low paid workers and relieve in-work poverty in working households without children. To maximise the effectiveness of an employment tax credit it may be appropriate to pay a higher rate for couples than single people. For those without caring responsibilities, or a disability, there may be a case for restricting support to households with someone in full-time work.

4.72 Decisions on how far to extend this support to those without children will be taken nearer the time. If an employment tax credit were based around the adult credit in the Working Families' Tax Credit, and were made available to single people and couples with someone over the age of 25, a 30 hour eligibility rule, and with a higher rate for couples, it could reach between 300,000 and 400,000 households without children. Such a credit would:

- deliver a minimum income guarantee of around £165 a week for couples without children and with someone in full–time work;

- double the gain to work for couples in rented accommodation at the minimum wage, and increase it by a third for single people; and

- increase the incomes of the poorest households in work by on average around £20 for couples and £15 for single people.

4.73 An employment tax credit could provide a clearly understood generalised platform for in-work support alongside the National Minimum Wage and the New Deal, demonstrating the benefits of work over welfare and providing additional financial support to people in low paid work. More detail about the employment tax credit is set out in the accompanying Budget paper *Tackling Poverty and Making Work Pay – Tax Credits for the 21st Century*[4]

SECURING PROGRESSION IN WORK

4.74 Moving from welfare into work is the first step in moving out of poverty. But the Government also wants to enable people to progress up the earnings ladder once in employment. The Government has introduced lifelong learning to ensure that everyone in work is equipped with the training and skills necessary to progress in work.

New Deal providing skills   **4.75** Both the New Deal for 18-24 year olds and the New Deal 50 plus offer a £750 in-work training grant. In addition, similar grants are being piloted for lone parents through the New Deal. The New Deal 25 plus offers long-term unemployed people education and training opportunities as well as assistance with associated costs such as childcare, travel and equipment. This access to training through the New Deal programmes helps people develop their skills, thereby providing opportunities for people to climb the earnings ladder.

4.76 Programmes to equip people with the specific skills they need to enter a particular industry, and to progress once in work, are also being run within the New Deal. A customised gateway to train people to enter the construction industry is being trialed in Manchester, and the Government is exploring the possibility of extending this on a national basis. A sector specific strategy for the engineering and manufacturing and hospitality sectors are also being developed. As mentioned in Box 4.2, the Government has been exploring, with sector based intermediaries, how they might help New Deal participants into jobs, with an initial focus on the financial and IT sectors.

Lifelong learning   **4.77** In order to gain the vocational skills businesses require for higher paid work, many people first need to upgrade their basic skills. This can only be done by building a new culture of lifelong learning. The new Learning and Skills Council will work in partnership with employers, Regional Development Agencies and the Small Business Service to deliver the right skills to progress in work.

4.78 The Government has also invested £25 million to make opportunities available for up to 50,000 more people to get the ICT skills they need to increase their employability, and if they need it, to improve their basic literacy and numeracy. This measure complements the ICT learning centres announced in Budget 99. Nineteen pilot projects are testing innovative ways of enabling people to overcome barriers to their acquisition of basic ICT skills. The first tranche of up to 1,000 ICT learning centres will be announced in September 2000.

4.79 Lifelong learning is not just about basic skills. There will also be increased means through individual learning accounts, and increased opportunities through the University for Industry (UfI) for individuals to take responsibility for their own futures, and to continue to increase their knowledge and skills, thereby improving their employability.

---

[4] *Tackling Poverty and Making Work Pay – Tax Credits for the 21st Century*, The Modernisation of Britain's Tax and Benefit System, No. 6, March 2000, available from the Treasury Public Enquiry Unit on 020 7270 4558, or on http://www.hm-treasury.gov.uk

4.80 UfI Limited is currently piloting 24 different on-line courses covering IT and business management through its consumer brand **'learndirect'** in over 70 development centres across the UK in easily accessible locations such as shopping centres, community centres and churches in the run-up to its full launch in the Autumn (see paragraph 3.69).

5 FAIRNESS FOR FAMILIES AND COMMUNITIES

The Government is committed to building a fairer and more inclusive society in which everyone can contribute to and benefit from rising economic prosperity. As set out in the Pre-Budget Report, the Government is pursuing an extensive programme to tackle the causes of poverty, especially child poverty which it is committed to reducing by half within a decade as it moves forward with its commitment to abolishing child poverty within the next 20 years. Budget 2000 builds on the reforms announced in the last two Budgets.

Increasing support for families and tackling child poverty by:

- providing extra financial support by further increasing the Under-16 child credit in the Working Families' Tax Credit by £4.35 and income-related benefits, and by increasing the value of the Children's Tax Credit. This will increase to 1.2 million the number of children taken out of poverty by measures so far this Parliament; and

- setting out future reforms to the tax and benefit system to improve the transparency and administration of financial support for children through a new integrated child credit.

Helping pensioners through:

- increasing the winter fuel payment from £100 to £150 a year for every 60+ household, 8.5 million in total.

Improving public services by:

- an immediate additional £2 billion for the NHS in 2000–01 including extra resources from a rise in tobacco duties;

- 6.1 per cent average annual real terms growth over the next four years – the longest period of sustained high growth in the history of the NHS;

- NHS reforms to tackle variations in efficiency, performance and health outcomes to ensure that a step change in resources can achieve a step change in results; and

- an immediate additional increase of £1 billion for education in the UK, and additional resources of £280 million for transport, and £285 million for the fight against crime.

In addition:

- supporting savings by retaining the current £7,000 contribution limit for Individual Savings Accounts for 2000–01;

- a fairer duty structure for air passenger duty, benefiting passengers on economy and tourist class flights within the UK and Europe; and

- building a fair and efficient tax system by tackling tax abuse and avoidance.

INTRODUCTION

5.1   A strong and efficient economy is one which maximises the potential of every individual regardless of gender, disability, age, family circumstance or where they live. Where work is an option, it provides the best route out of poverty and social exclusion. For those who cannot work, the Government is also providing security through tax and benefit reform and high quality public services for all. The Government recognises that the best solutions do not always come from government, but can originate in the community itself. The best policies bring the private sector, voluntary and community action, and government together.

5.2   This chapter describes how the Government is applying these principles to help deliver a fairer society and a better quality of life for all. It describes the Government's approach to, and support for:

- families and children;
- people with disabilities;
- pensioners;
- savings and pensions;
- high quality public services;
- strengthening community life; and
- fairness in taxation.

SUPPORT FOR FAMILIES AND CHILDREN

5.3   The Government's aim is for every child to have the best possible start in life. Families with children have not had an equal share of income growth over the last 20 years. The tax and benefit system must support all children, recognising the extra costs and responsibilities that parents face, and the importance of children to the country's future.

5.4   The Government has set out a range of indicators to help judge the progress being made towards tackling poverty and social exclusion in *Opportunity for all*.[1] Thirteen of these relate to children. The wide range of indicators reflects the fact that although low incomes are an important part of poverty and social exclusion, poverty is multi-dimensional, and not solely about a lack of money. Other aspects include worklessness, educational failure, and poor health and housing.

5.5   The Treasury paper *Supporting Children Through the Tax and Benefit System*,[2] published alongside the Pre-Budget Report, set out the Government's policy strategy for tackling child poverty. It consists of:

- ensuring a decent family income, with work for those who can, and extra support for all families;

- prevention and support for those with additional needs and at key stages in life, particularly where there are very young children;

- harnessing the power and expertise of the voluntary and community sector, providing support for innovation and good practice, and fostering a strategic partnership between the voluntary and community sector and government through a new Children's Fund; and

- a world-class education system for all, ensuring that children from poor backgrounds have the skills and education they need to break the cycle of disadvantage.

---

[1] *Opportunity for all: Tackling Poverty and Social Exclusion*, The Government's first annual report on poverty and social exclusion (September 1999). Copies can be obtained from 020 7712 2171, or at http://www.dss.gov.uk
[2] *Supporting Children Through the Tax and Benefit System*, No. 5 in the Modernisation of Britain's Tax and Benefit System series (November 1999). Copies can be obtained from the Treasury Public Enquiry Unit on 020 7270 4558, or at http://www.hm-treasury.gov.uk

5.6   The Treasury paper sets out the achievements of Government policies so far and describes the Government's approach to tax and benefit reform for families with children, which is underpinned by two principles:

- providing financial support for <u>all</u> families with children, through the foundation of universal Child Benefit, recognising the additional costs and responsibilities that all parents face when their children are growing up; and

- providing help in the fairest way, and targeting extra financial support on those *who* need it most *when* they need it most, such as mothers with young children, particularly around childbirth, or those on lower or middle incomes through the Children's Tax Credit, the Working Families' Tax Credit, the Disabled Person's Tax Credit and income-related benefits.

5.7   The Government has increased support for all families with children with the largest ever rise in Child Benefit. In addition it has provided greatest help for those most in need. In 2001, financial support for the first child will range from £15.50 to £50 a week. By comparison, it ranged from £11.05 to £27.70 a week in 1997.

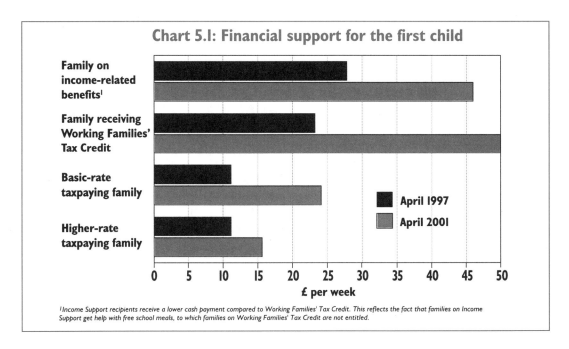

Chart 5.1: Financial support for the first child

Income Support recipients receive a lower cash payment compared to Working Families' Tax Credit. This reflects the fact that families on Income Support get help with free school meals, to which families on Working Families' Tax Credit are not entitled.

Financial support for all families with children

Child Benefit   **5.8**   The Government is committed to the principle of universal Child Benefit, paid to the main carer, as the foundation of its support for children. As announced in Budget 99, Child Benefit will be increased to £15 a week for the first child and £10 a week for subsequent children from April 2000, rising to at least £15.50 and £10.35 from April 2001.

Children's Tax Credit   **5.9**   Budget 99 announced the introduction of the Children's Tax Credit from April 2001, benefiting around five million families with children. It will replace the married couple's allowance and its related allowances which will be abolished from April 2000. Resources are being targeted at lower and middle-income families, with the credit tapered away from families where there is a higher-rate taxpayer.

Box 5.1: Child poverty ambition

Poverty is most damaging when it is persistent and leads to long-term deprivation. Children are now the group most likely to be in poverty, and are more likely to be persistently poor than working-age adults: in August 1999, nearly 800,000 children were living in families that have been on means-tested benefits for at least five years. 2.2 million children live in households where no adult is in work.

In the Pre-Budget Report, the Government announced its long-term economic ambition that, by the end of this decade, child poverty will be reduced by half as the Government moves forward with its commitment to abolish child poverty within 20 years.

The tax and benefit reforms to be introduced over the Parliament have already begun to deliver change, marking the first key steps in reducing child poverty in the UK. Measures in Budgets 98 and 99 will lift 800,000 children out of poverty. Budget 2000 goes further: the measures introduced so far in this Parliament will together lift 1.2 million children out of poverty. Households with children will be on average £850 a year better off.

Number of children lifted out of low incomes

	Below 50% median	Below 60% median	Below 70% median
Children in households lifted out of low income by measures announced this Parliament	1.9 million	1.2 million	500,000

¹ Incomes are measured after housing costs and includes the self-employed.
² Thresholds are the same as those used in 'Opportunity for all'.

A better deal for all families and children

The chart below illustrates the distributional impact of the main children's measures announced by the Government. It shows that all families gain from the increases in Child Benefit. The Working Families' Tax Credit targets working families at the bottom end of the income distribution, and the Children's Tax Credit is better targeted than the married couple's allowance it will replace, being tapered away for families with a higher-rate taxpayer.

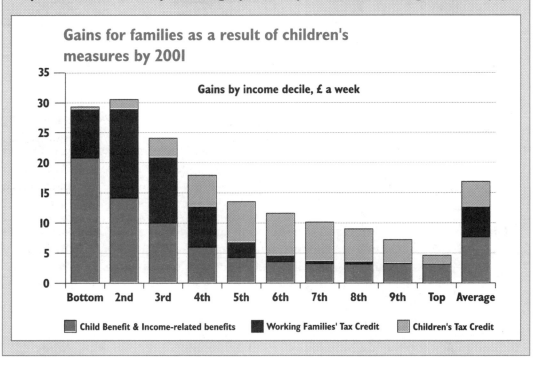

Gains for families as a result of children's measures by 2001

Gains by income decile, £ a week

Child Benefit & Income-related benefits   Working Families' Tax Credit   Children's Tax Credit

5.10   Budget 2000 announces that an additional 50p a week will be added to the Children's Tax Credit when it is introduced in April 2001, making it worth up to £442 a year, or £8.50 a week. This is more than twice the value of the married couple's allowance which it replaces.

5.11   These tax and benefit reforms mean that by April 2001 the tax burden on a typical family on average earnings with 2 children will be at its lowest since 1972.

Working Families' Tax Credit and the Disabled Person's Tax Credit

5.12   The Working Families' Tax Credit and the Disabled Person's Tax Credit were launched in October 1999, integrating the tax and benefit system to make work pay for families with children and for disabled people. Details of the Working Families' Tax Credit and the Disabled Person's Tax Credit are set out in Chapter 4. As announced in Budget 99, the under-11 credit in the Working Families' Tax Credit and the Disabled Person's Tax Credit will be increased by a further £1.10 a week over and above indexation from April 2000, to bring it up to the level of the under-16 credit. These increases will also apply to the under-11 rates for income-related benefits.

5.13   Budget 2000 further increases support for children under 16, with a rise in the child credit in the Working Families' Tax Credit and the Disabled Person's Tax Credit by £4.35 a week from June 2000. These increases will be matched in income-related benefits from October 2000.

5.14   A family with two children earning £12,500 will be £2,600 a year better-off as a result of the measures announced in this and previous Budgets. A family with two children on Income Support will be £1,500 a year better off than they were in 1997.

5.15   The Government has increased the amount spent on children for all family types at all income levels. By the end of the Parliament, the Government will be spending £7 billion extra each year on children. Chart 5.2 shows the composition of this spending.

A new integrated child credit

5.16   Although the reforms so far have made progress in tackling child poverty and delivering new resources fairly, the Government is determined to go further in improving the transparency and administration of income-related payments through the tax and benefit system. The Government will therefore introduce an integrated child credit from 2003.

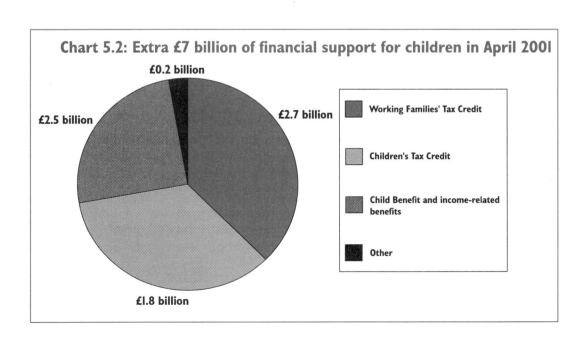

Chart 5.2: Extra £7 billion of financial support for children in April 2001

£0.2 billion

£2.5 billion

£2.7 billion

£1.8 billion

- Working Families' Tax Credit
- Children's Tax Credit
- Child Benefit and income-related benefits
- Other

5.17 The integrated child credit will bring together the different strands of support for children in the Working Families' Tax Credit, the Disabled Person's Tax Credit, Income Support and the Children's Tax Credit, building on the foundation of universal Child Benefit. It will be paid to the main carer in families in and out of work, and as a tax credit it will be administered by the Inland Revenue. The integrated child credit will be complemented by an employment tax credit paid through the wage packet to working households, as described in Chapter 4.

5.18 The integrated child credit will create:

- a more transparent system of support for children to help parents to understand what they can expect to receive, and facilitate public debate about the appropriate level of support;

- a portable and secure income bridge spanning welfare and work to improve work incentives;

- a common framework for assessment and payment to give every family a stake in the system of child payments while allowing extra resources to be directed at those most in need;

- a system where all support for children is paid to the main carer; and

- efficiency gains for Government and reduced hassle for parents.

5.19 Further details of the integrated child credit are set out in the accompanying paper *Tackling Poverty and Making Work Pay – Tax Credits for the 21st Century*[3].

Targeted interventions and additional support

5.20 The Government recognises the challenges and difficulties faced by some families, especially at particular times in their children's lives. The early years of a child's life, in particular, are critical for its future outcome.

Supporting mothers after the birth of a new child   **5.21** Around two fifths of children are born into poverty. Low-income mothers face particularly difficult and restricted choices about how they help their children in the early months. In the past, the tax and benefit system has not provided adequate support. Budget 1999 therefore announced that:

- entitlement to Maternity Allowance would be extended to around 16,000 women earning less than the lower earnings limit (£76 per week) but at least £30 a week, as well as 11,000 low-income self-employed women, from April 2000; and

- to help with the initial costs of having a new child, a new Sure Start Maternity Grant will replace the Maternity Payment from April 2000. The payments will be linked to contact with a healthcare professional to ensure expert advice on child development and services.

Sure Start Maternity Grant   **5.22** Budget 2000 announces a further package of reforms. From this autumn, the Government will increase the Sure Start Maternity Grant to £300, three times the level in 1997. Over 200,000 mothers in low-income families will be able to claim this on the birth of a child.

---

[3] *Tackling Poverty and Making Work Pay – Tax Credits for the 21st Century*, No. 6 in the Modernisation of Britain's Tax and Benefit System series (March 2000). Copies can be obtained from the Treasury Public Enquiry Unit on 020 7270 4558, or at http://www.hm-treasury.gov.uk

Reforms to WFTC and DPTC

5.23   As well as providing this extra lump sum payment, the Government will make the system more responsive to families' financial needs on the birth of a child:

- at present, and previously under Family Credit and Disability Working Allowance, parents have to wait up to six months before they can claim the extra entitlement for their new child. The Government will reform the Working Families' Tax Credit and the Disabled Person's Tax Credit from May 2001 enabling a family to make a new claim as soon as a child is born. Families will therefore be able to get an extra credit for the new baby immediately. Where a working mother has chosen to stay at home with her baby, the family should get extra support reflecting the fall in earnings. This new award will be available right from the start of the child's life, immediately responding to the family's new circumstances. The award will last six months, providing extra help for mothers at home, including those planning to return to work; and

- from May 2001, any mother who works 16 hours or more prior to the birth of a child, and is in receipt of Statutory Maternity Pay or Maternity Allowance, will meet the work criteria for the Working Families' Tax Credit and Disabled Person's Tax Credit. This change means that low-income working families - including where the mother is the sole earner - should be able to get support in these early weeks from the tax credit system, rather than turn to benefits. It also ensures that families who already receive help with their childcare costs will continue to be eligible for these payments.

5.24   These reforms will help low-income families right at the start of their new child's life. Low-income working families could be up to £30 a week better off in these early weeks, on top of the £300 Sure Start Maternity Grant. In making these reforms, the Government is ensuring that help is directed towards the poorest families, to give these mothers more choice about how they support their family around the birth of a child and whether and how to plan a return to work.

5.25   The Government will also review what improvements can be made in maternity pay and parental leave.

Targeted interventions

5.26   The Government is committed to tackling the causes of poverty and social exclusion, not just the symptoms. This principle underlies, for example, the approach taken by the Social Exclusion Unit and several of the cross-cutting reviews that form part of the 2000 Spending Review. There are also new preventative policies that are aimed specifically at children.

Sure Start

5.27   Sure Start is a new policy that works with parents and children to promote the physical, intellectual and social development of pre-school children – particularly those who are disadvantaged – to equip them to thrive when they start school. £450 million has been dedicated to establish 250 Sure Start programmes by 2001–02. By the summer of this year, over half of these programmes will be under way.

5.28   Sure Start programmes are managed by a partnership bringing together voluntary and non-state sector organisations with statutory services in an effective and integrated way to secure the best outcomes for children. When originally planned, it was estimated that the 250 Sure Start programmes would reach around 5 per cent of children in the 0–3 age range.

Improvements in delivery of Sure Start now mean that the programme will reach many more: around 7 per cent of children. Because the programme has been designed especially for disadvantaged areas, this represents nearly 20 per cent of the poorest children.

Additional support   **5.29**   The Government is also providing targeted interventions to children of all ages to provide help when it is needed most:

- *On Track* is a new package of policies targeted specifically at reducing the risk factors that link young children and their family circumstances with future criminal behaviour. Part of the Government's drive to be tough on the causes of crime, *On Track* will provide a range of support including pre-school education, parent support and training, family therapy, home visits, and family/school partnerships. The Government provided an initial £27 million to fund between 20 and 30 pilot projects in 2000–01 and 2001–02; and

- the *Connexions* strategy, which was announced in February 2000, is a package of measures aimed at increasing participation and attainment through the teenage years. The policies will ensure that more young people have access to the services they need, follow appropriate and high-quality learning opportunities, and make a successful transition from adolescence to adulthood and working life.

Working with the voluntary and community sector

5.30   The Pre-Budget Report announced plans for a Children's Fund to invest in the work of the children's voluntary and community sector with children in poverty. The Children's Fund will be a key part of the Government's strategy to eradicate child poverty within a generation.

5.31   Initial consultations with the children's voluntary and community sector identified the need for investment at the most local level in order to make the most impact on children's lives. Consequently, the Government will establish a network of Children's Funds to fund local projects providing local solutions to the problem of child poverty.

5.32   The consultation also considered how to make the most impact on children's lives and arrived at the following four themes:

- **economic disadvantage** - imaginative schemes to enable families to improve their living standards;

- **isolation and access** - prevention and crisis work with hard-to-reach groups;

- **aspirations and experiences** - bridging the gap between the childhood experiences of children in poverty and their contemporaries; and

- **children's voices** - giving children a chance to articulate their own needs.

5.33   A further role for the Children's Fund could be to share good practice that already takes place, building on the diversity and innovation in the sector.

5.34   Over the coming months, the Government will be consulting key groups from the voluntary and community sector to explore how investment in these themes could make a real and measurable difference to the lives of children in poverty and how the local network of children's funds will work in practice.

Box 5.2: Education Ambition

The Pre-Budget Report set out the Government's long-term ambition that by the end of the decade, and for the first time, the majority of the UK's young people can expect to go on from school or college into Higher Education.

Higher Education empowers individuals and can offer a step increase in their life chances. On average, graduates earn 20 per cent more than people with A levels as their highest qualification, and are 40 per cent less likely to be unemployed. Higher Education also equips the UK with the highly skilled workforce it needs to achieve greater productivity and compete with other economies.

While 33 per cent of the UK's young people (aged 18 to 21) already achieve degrees, a higher proportion than in any other EU country, this is not as high as the US.

The Government wants to do more. It wants to ensure that the majority of Britain's young people have the opportunity to benefit from Higher Education, regardless of their background, and that Higher Education courses offer a mix of skills that are relevant to the individual and to society.

The Government's strategy for achieving greater participation in Higher Education includes reforms to the student support system to ensure the help is targeted on those who need it most; coupled with the development of new Foundation Degree courses, which will offer greater vocational content.

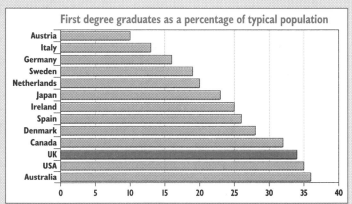

First degree graduates as a percentage of typical population

As part of the current 2000 Spending Review, the Government will determine the next phase of expansion to 2003–04, consistent with its long-term ambition.

Importance of a good start in education

5.35   Education is a vital influence on children's life chances. In recognition of the importance the Government places on giving children the opportunity to fulfil their potential, it is making available an additional £1 billion to education across the UK in 2000–01, raising the growth of spending between 1999–2000 and 2000–01 to 8 per cent in real terms.

5.36   This additional funding will be used to reinforce those policies likely to contribute most to every child fulfilling his or her potential. For example:

- schools will receive extra resources next year. An average primary school will receive an extra payment of £6,000, with grants on top for helping the weakest pupils catch up in literacy and numeracy. In return for meeting new requirements, an average secondary school will receive an extra of £40,000; and

- the pilots for Education Maintenance Allowances (EMAs) are already helping to increase participation of young people in education beyond the age of 16. Accordingly, a further £50 million will be made available to Local Education Authorities where staying on rates are relatively low, extending coverage from 7 per cent of those leaving school to nearly 30 per cent.

5.37   The Secretary of State for Education and Employment will be making further detailed announcements in due course.

FAIRNESS FOR PEOPLE WITH DISABILITIES

5.38   The Government is determined to increase opportunities for people with disabilities to live fulfilling and independent lives:

- the New Deal for Disabled People, described in Chapter 4, assists those who want to work, with advice and support specific to their needs;

- the new Disabled Person's Tax Credit, introduced in October 1999, increases the gains to work and removes the administrative complexity of a separate benefit claim and cheque. Chapter 4 provides more details;

- the disabled child credit in the Disabled Person's Tax Credit will be extended to families in receipt of the Working Families' Tax Credit from October 2000;

- from April 2001, severely disabled people under 60 years of age on income-related benefits will receive a guaranteed income of at least £134 a week for single people, and £176 a week for couples; and

- children aged three to four with severe disabilities will receive an additional £37.40 a week from April 2001 through the extension of the Disability Living Allowance. Reforms to Incapacity Benefit will provide up to £26.70 a week more for people who were disabled before the age of 20.

Anti-discrimination measures   **5.39**   From April 2000 the new independent Disability Rights Commission will promote equalisation of opportunities for disabled people, helping with the enforcement of the Disability Discrimination Act. In December 1999 the Disability Rights Task Force published its report *From Exclusion to Inclusion*. It contained over 150 recommendations for significant extensions and refinements to the Disability Discrimination Act. The Government has endorsed its recommendations ensuring that disabled people have civil rights in schools, and in further, higher and adult education.

FAIRNESS FOR PENSIONERS

5.40   The Government's strategy to ensure fairness for pensioners has three aims:

- lifting the poorest pensioners out of poverty;

- boosting the living standards of pensioners who are on low incomes but who are just above benefit levels; and

- ensuring continuing security for pensioners who are above benefit levels.

Additional help for the poorest pensioners

5.41   Income Support was the mechanism in place in 1997 to support the poorest pensioners. However, it did not provide adequate financial support. Moreover, many of those who were entitled to Income Support did not receive it and the eligibility rules penalised those who, through hard work and thrift, had managed to put away a small amount of savings.

5.42   In response the Government introduced the Minimum Income Guarantee (MIG) for the poorest pensioners. It has announced that it will increase the MIG by earnings this year and throughout the remainder of the Parliament. From April 2000, a single pensioner on the

MIG will have an income of £500 a year more than in 1997. Earnings uprating again in 2001 will bring MIG annual incomes for a younger single pensioner to around £680 more than in 1997, and for a couple to around £1,070 more than in 1997.

Security for all pensioners   **5.43**   In addition, the Government has introduced measures which reach the poorest and those above income-related benefit levels. These measures will ensure that pensioners who have put a little by for their retirement are not penalised:

- winter fuel payments, now paid to every household with someone over 60, 8.5 million in total, each December. Budget 2000 increases the winter fuel payment from £100 to £150 a year from the forthcoming winter; and

- from November 2000, concessionary TV licences for households with someone aged 75 or over. Over 3 million households will benefit – almost half of which are in the bottom three income deciles.

5.44   Taken together these measures mean that from April 2001 a 75 year old on the Minimum Income Guarantee will have an annual income of over £950 more than in April 1997. A couple over the age of 75 will receive over £1,350 a year more.

5.45   These changes will ensure that people who have managed to save something for their retirement benefit from additional support. Budget 2000 sets out the Government's intention to do more:

- the Government wants to reward pensioners who have managed to save something for their retirement. Currently the capital rules attached to the MIG allow £3,000 of saving without any reduction in benefit. Savings over that level reduce benefit entitlement. With over £8,000 of savings, MIG entitlement is removed altogether. The Government has announced that from April 2001 it will double the lower limit to £6,000 and increase the upper limit from £8,000 to £12,000 to reward savers; and

- the Government wants to use the MIG to reward low income pensioners who have made some pension provision for themselves and those who are currently just above MIG levels. With this in mind, the Government will examine for the longer term whether through an income taper or other measures the MIG can provide extra help to people who have provided for themselves. In the light of further work by the Department of Social Security and the Treasury, the Secretary of State for Social Security will publish proposals with a view to implementation during the next Parliament.

Combatting fuel poverty   **5.46**   The Government is also introducing a series of measures, building on the winter fuel payment, to combat fuel poverty among the elderly:

- increased grants under the new Home Energy Efficiency Scheme to reduce the costs of keeping warm for poorer pensioners and other vulnerable groups;

- capital allowances to underpin the Government's Affordable Warmth Programme aimed at combatting fuel poverty to be introduced later this year. The programme will support the installation of efficient central heating systems in up to one million low income homes through a Public Private Partnership with commercial lessors. About two-thirds of those helped are likely to be households aged 60 or above. They will benefit from warmer homes and more efficient heating will also mean lower fuel bills and reduced emissions of greenhouse gases; and

- extending the reduced VAT rate of 5 per cent to grant-funded installation of heating systems and home security goods from April 2000.

Fairness for tax paying pensioners **5.47**   For pensioners who have higher incomes, the Government has made a series of changes to the tax system to ensure that pensioners who have provided for a comfortable retirement continue to enjoy this security:

- an extension of the 10p starting rate of income tax to savings from April 1999, recognising that many pensioners rely on savings as their primary income source. Around 1.5 million pensioners are benefiting;

- increases in the personal tax allowances for people aged 65 or over to: £5,790 for someone aged 65 to 74 and £6,050 for someone aged 75 or more. No one aged 65 or over will pay any income tax until their income reaches at least £111 a week; and

- older people who pay tax can also benefit from the reduction in the basic rate to 22 per cent from April 2000.

5.48   As a result of these measures, six out of ten adults aged 65 and over do not pay any income tax.

SUPPORTING SAVINGS AND PENSIONS

5.49   The Government is committed to creating a stable economy capable of delivering sustained growth with low inflation. Policies including the Working Families' Tax Credit, the National Minimum Wage and cuts in income tax rates increase the financial gains to work. Taken together these measures have increased financial independence. The Government wants to go further and encourage people to make provision for financial security throughout their lives.

5.50   Savings and investments have traditionally been the preserve of the better off. The Government is seeking to create an environment which promotes savings opportunity for all. The Government's savings strategy is therefore based on three principles of:

- fairness;

- flexibility; and

- confidence and transparency.

5.51   In the past, only those who had money to lock away could enjoy the privilege of saving. By ensuring a fair savings strategy, the Government is extending the savings habit to all:

- the Government is working with financial service providers to tackle financial exclusion by, for example, encouraging basic bank accounts which can be easily opened and cannot become overdrawn;

- the new Individual Savings Account (ISA) allows people to save free from tax, while having instant access to their savings. In the first nine months since their launch in April 1999, ISAs attracted over £17 billion in new funds, nearly 40 per cent more than went into Personal Equity Plans (PEPs) and Tax-Exempt Special Savings Accounts (TESSAs) over the same period in 1998. The Government has decided to retain the current £7,000 ISA subscription limit for 2000–01;

- stakeholder pensions, to be introduced in April 2001, recognise the structure of the modern labour market by offering a good value, low cost, tax free means of saving for retirement to groups previously denied it. For example, stakeholder pensions will help those who change jobs regularly and for whom occupational pensions are inappropriate. Similarly stakeholder pensions will, for the first time, allow those on career breaks (such as carers or mature students) to start, or continue to build up, a pension when they are not working; and

- the new all-employee share schemes offers employees the opportunity to invest in their company, tax free. Unlike many past schemes, all employees will have the opportunity to participate.

5.52 Flexibility is the second strand of the Government's savings strategy. The Government recognises that, throughout their lives, people's circumstances and hence their savings needs change. The savings environment must be flexible enough to meet these needs:

- an ISA, allowing easy access to savings, is an ideal way for people to start saving even small amounts. For example, young savers could start with a cash ISA and, as their circumstances become more secure, start to save in an equity ISA;

- ISA savings can be transferred straight into a stakeholder pension. Alternatively they can be used to buy other assets, such as a deposit for a house, or to help start-up a new business; and

- savings built up in a tax-free employee share scheme can be transferred to either an ISA or a stakeholder pension. This allows savers to diversify into other assets, while remaining within a tax-free environment.

5.53 The Government also wants savers to have ready access to transparent products of good quality. Coupled with the Financial Services Authority's new statutory responsibility for educating financial consumers, this should mean that people are able to save with confidence:

- to tackle complexity in savings products, the Government is setting CAT (Charges, Access, Terms) standards for both ISAs and mortgages, and minimum standards for stakeholder pensions. All these products are designed to be straightforward, clear, fair and easy to understand as well as offering decent value to customers;

- pooled pension investments (PPIs) will from 2001 offer pension savers a transparent and straightforward way of building a personalised pension fund which can readily be transferred from one pension scheme to another. They will thus be especially suitable for people who move jobs from time to time; and

- the Financial Services Authority provides a one-stop shop for investor protection, replacing the plethora of different arrangements that existed previously.

HIGH QUALITY PUBLIC SERVICES

5.54 The Government is committed to delivering the high quality public services that people need and expect. As a result of prudent management of the public finances, and through the Comprehensive Spending Review (CSR), the Government has been able to increase investment in public services.

5.55 At the same time the Government is driving up performance through a comprehensive programme of modernisation and reform.

5.56 Public Service Agreements (PSAs) tell Parliament and the public what the Government will achieve with the money it is investing. They set out the real changes that people want to see, and the concrete, measurable improvements to services that the Government will deliver.

5.57 These Agreements are an important part of the Government's programme of public service modernisation. Targets reflect the Government's top priorities in a way that is transparent to the public and accountable to Parliament. They cover policy goals such as small business start-ups, and service changes such as school class sizes. There are tough, stretching targets for the efficiency with which departments manage the resources they are given.

5.58 Targets are being closely monitored to ensure that services become more modern, efficient, and responsive to their users' needs, bringing performance in all areas up to the levels of the best. Progress to date against targets will be set out in Departments' Annual Reports to be published shortly.

The 2000 Spending Review

5.59 The next Spending Review will sustain and increase the additional resources for public mservices announced in the CSR:

- growth in current spending of $2^1/_2$ per cent a year in real terms in the three years to 2003–04, in line with the Government's neutral view of the economy's trend rate of growth of the economy; and

- a more than doubling of net capital investment to 1.8 per cent of GDP by 2003–04, further tackling the legacy of underfunding of Britain's public infrastructure.

5.60 Alongside new spending plans in the 2000 Spending Review, the Government will be publishing revised Public Service Agreements. These will set out the step changes in service delivery which departments must deliver in return for this investment. Box 2.2 provides details of the aims and objectives of the 2000 Spending Review.

A modern National Health Service

5.62 The Government is committed to ensuring that all members of society have access to world class healthcare from the publicly funded NHS, with access based on need.

5.63 Budget 2000 announces the largest ever sustained increase in NHS resources. The Comprehensive Spending Review set out, in July 1998, three year funding for the NHS for 1999–00 to 2001–02. The Government is now able to provide an additional £2 billion for the second year of these plans, 2000–01, including the proceeds of real increases in tobacco duty.

5.63 The Chancellor has also decided to set new three year plans for NHS spending for the following three years covered by the 2000 Spending Review, 2001–02 to 2003–04. The new allocations for the NHS in the UK are set out below.

Table 5.1: NHS spending in the UK, £ billion in current prices

	1998-99	1999-00	2000–01	2001–02	2002-03	2003–04	Average
Previous plans	45.1	49.3	52.2	55.5			
New provision	45.1	49.3	54.2	58.6	63.5	68.7	
Year on year real growth (%)			7.4%	5.6%	5.6%	5.6%	6.1%

Note: these figures include additions to the devolved administrations and the Northern Ireland departments.

5.64   These UK allocations provide for:

- 6.1 per cent average annual real terms growth over the next four years – the longest period of sustained high growth in the history of the NHS.[4] It compares to an average of 3.3 per cent annual real growth since the foundation of the NHS and 2.9 per cent annual real growth between 1978–79 and 1996–97; and

- a 50 per cent cash increase in NHS spending over the five years from the beginning of the first Comprehensive Spending Review – 35 per cent in real terms – equivalent to a rise in NHS cash spending per household from £1,850 in 1998–99 to £2,800 in 2003–4.

5.65   The Government is determined to match new resources with more reform.

5.66   Tomorrow, the Prime Minister will make a statement to Parliament on the work he and the Secretary of State for Health will lead over the next four months to reform and modernise the Health Service.

5.67   The Government's plan, to be published in July alongside the detailed public spending allocations, will address long-standing variations in efficiency, performance and health outcomes, and the right balance between preventative, primary and hospital care – so that a step change in resources can achieve a step change in results.

5.68   Alongside the extra resources must come more reform and modernisation. The Prime Minister, in his statement to Parliament tomorrow, will set out how, with the guarantee of sustained investment, the Government, the professions and the NHS can together rise to the challenge of delivering better healthcare for all.

5.69   The Chancellor is also commissioning a long-term assessment of the technological, demographic and medical trends over the next two decades that will affect the health service to report to him in time for the start of the next spending review in 2002.

Education

5.70   Prudent management of the public finances means that the Government is able to make further targeted additions to key priority programmes.

5.71   Budget 2000 announces an immediate boost for education of £1 billion across the UK. This will include extra payments for all primary and secondary schools and an expansion in Education Maintenance Allowances, that help those aged 16 to stay on in education. The Secretary of State for Education and Employment will be announcing further details in due course. Plans for future years will be announced in the 2000 Spending Review.

Transport

5.72   The Government's goal is a modernised and integrated transport system fit for a new century.

5.73   On top of the investment announced in the CSR, Budget 2000 is making an additional £280 million available across the UK for transport, including new money for both road and public transport schemes. The Deputy Prime Minister will announce further details in due course. Plans for transport spending in future years will be announced in the Spending Review in July.

---

[4] This will be the first period in the history of the NHS with four years of over 5 per cent real terms growth in every year.

Tackling crime

5.74   The Government is already putting significant additional resources into tackling crime and the causes of crime.

5.75   Budget 2000 is making an extra £285 million available for the fight against crime. Capital modernisation projects totalling £185 million have been approved for criminal justice agencies. Another £100 million will be available for modernising policing across the UK. This will help the police to attract and retain good officers over the coming years, initially by accelerating recruitment under the Crime Fighting Fund. Effective policing however is not just about the number of officers. It is also about how to deploy them most effectively. This extra funding will therefore also be available to enhance existing modernisation investments in for example radios and DNA technology. This investment will strengthen the services which the police deliver in cutting crime and catching offenders. The Home Secretary will announce further details in due course.

Public infrastructure

5.76   A key aim of the CSR was to modernise and improve the public infrastructure to improve service delivery. The 2000 Spending Review will continue to redress the under-investment in public capital with significant increases over the period. The Review will provide for a more than doubling of net investment as a share of GDP. Allocations will be made in the Spending Review culminating in July.

5.77   Meanwhile **Budget 2000 is putting an immediate extra £200 million into the** Government's Capital Modernisation Fund to support innovative capital projects which will improve service delivery. Further allocations from the £2.7 billion Capital Modernisation Fund will be announced in the coming weeks.

STRENGTHENING COMMUNITY LIFE

5.78   The best form of economic advance for the country involves communities advancing together. The Government's aim is to build a working and sustainable economy in every community. Strong community networks are an essential foundation for the future success and prosperity of the nation.

5.79   Particular groups and specific geographical areas have their own individual needs. In addition to improving public services for all, Budget 2000 includes a range of measures to strengthen communities by promoting partnerships between government, business and local communities. Chapter 3 sets out the Government's strategy to promote an enterprise culture and encourage private investment flows in deprived areas. This section outlines measures to tackle disadvantage and social exclusion in communities.

The New Deal for   **5.80**   The New Deal for Communities puts local people in charge of their own futures. It
Communities   provides financial resources for communities to work with service providers to develop innovative ways of helping themselves which, if successful, can then be extended to other deprived areas. £800 million has been set aside for the first three years of the programme from April 1999. Ten pathfinder neighbourhoods have now submitted detailed delivery plans. In return, the pathfinder neighbourhoods have made a commitment to deliver quantified improvements against four key outcome goals:

- higher levels of employment;

- better health;

- higher educational attainment; and

- lower crime.

5.81   A further 29 communities have joined the New Deal and are in the process of forming partnerships and drawing up delivery plans.

National   **5.82**   Communities suffering from multiple deprivation need special help. A consultation
Strategy for   document setting out proposals for a *National Strategy for Neighbourhood Renewal* will be
Neighbourhood   launched shortly. It will set out the Government's approach to tackling the problems that
Renewal   social exclusion brings in the most deprived communities. The strategy will draw on the
reports of the 18 inter-departmental Policy Action Teams.

5.83   Building sustainable communities depends in part on ensuring that economic markets can function properly. Drawing on the results of the consultation and the work of a Cross-Cutting Review of Government Intervention in Deprived Areas, set up as part of the 2000 Spending Review, the National Strategy will set out a comprehensive long-term agenda for bridging the gap later this year. The Government is committed to ensuring that the most disadvantaged neighbourhoods are given the support they need to maximise their economic potential.

Housing   **5.84**   The Government will set out its housing vision in a Housing Green Paper which will be published shortly. The Green Paper will underline the Government's commitment to tackling poor housing and improving choice for everyone, particularly those on low incomes. It will set out the Government's strategy for helping home owners, private renters and those in the social housing sector.

5.85   A key element of the Green Paper will be the drive to improve performance in the social housing sector. The Government wants councils and registered social landlords to offer a better service to tenants and, through the Housing Inspectorate, will ensure that councils attain Best Value. The Government will also improve the process of housing transfer to ensure that it delivers a better deal for tenants.

5.86   The Government also wants to see social tenants offered more choice, and believes that social rents should be more coherent. The present chaotic pattern of rents can be confusing both for tenants and landlords. Moving towards a regime that better reflects the value tenants put on different properties will make it easier to give them more choice in the allocation process. The Government's underlying aim is to create a dynamic social housing sector that gives tenants choices and a higher standard of service.

Strengthening   **5.87**   The Government's objective is to sustain and enhance the distinctive environment,
rural   economy and social fabric of the countryside for the benefit of all. Meeting this objective
communities   requires a policy approach which takes account of remoteness and sparsity of population,
structural change in economic activity, and the protection and enhancement of the natural environment.

5.88   As part of the 2000 Spending Review, *the cross-cutting review of rural and countryside programmes* is examining issues specific to rural communities. Its conclusions will inform the Rural White Paper to be published later this year. It will set out the Government's approach to meeting its objective for rural areas. The White Paper will take account of the full range of rural issues: from encouraging sustainable growth in the countryside and a new direction for agriculture, to combatting social exclusion. The White Paper will address the issues raised in the recent Performance and Innovation Unit report on *Rural Economies*, including

- economic instruments;

- innovative approaches to service delivery;

- regulatory changes; and

- organisational arrangements that might be adapted to deliver rural policies more effectively.

The vital role played by the voluntary and community sector

5.89   Volunteering and community activity has a pivotal role to play in the development of a democratic, socially-inclusive society. No-one knows better than local people the needs of their communities. They are ideally placed to be agents of change, pioneering fresh solutions, and delivering personalised services.

Helping communities to help themselves

5.90   The Government is already working with the sector on a series of initiatives aimed at encouraging new volunteers and community-based activities by:

- setting up an internet-based database - *the site* - providing individuals with free and direct on-line access to volunteering opportunities throughout Britain, 24 hours a day, 365 days a year;

- supporting the campaign of the charity one20 and the BBC celebrating volunteering and inspiring people to give time;

- funding the development of the first ever community-based digital TV channel – the media trust's community channel; and

- running five active community demonstration projects testing further ways of strengthening community activity and creating new volunteering opportunities.

Charity Taxation: Getting Britain Giving in the 21st Century

5.91   To further promote social responsibility and voluntary giving, Budget 2000 introduces a radical package of measures to improve incentives for giving to charity and to make the tax system work better for charities themselves. These measures implement and extend the Getting Britain Giving package which was announced in the Pre-Budget Report. They arise out of the comprehensive Review of Charity Taxation which the Government concluded last year. The measures take effect in April 2000.

Gift Aid   5.92   The Gift Aid scheme provides tax relief for one-off donations to charity. There is no maximum limit for donations, but there is currently a minimum limit of £250, which must be paid in a single payment. Following the consultation exercise, which showed strong support for a reduction in the minimum limit, the Government is abolishing entirely the £250 minimum limit on donations. In future, any donation whether large or small, one-off or regular, will qualify for tax relief.

Boosting the Payroll Giving scheme   5.93   Under the Payroll Giving scheme, employees authorise their employer to deduct charitable donations from their pay and receive tax relief on the donation at their top rate of tax. There is relatively low take-up of the scheme by employers and employees. The Government is therefore boosting Payroll Giving with a promotional campaign, starting in the summer, backed by a 10 per cent supplement on donations, to be paid to charities for three years from April 2000. In addition, Budget 2000 abolishes the £1,200 annual maximum limit for Payroll Giving donations.

Measures to encourage corporate giving   5.94   The tax rules for charitable donations by companies are being simplified. The requirement for companies to deduct income tax from their Gift Aid donations, and for the recipient charity to then claim back the tax from the Inland Revenue, is to be abolished. Also, companies will no longer have to give Gift Aid certificates to the charity with their donations. These changes will significantly simplify the tax system for companies and charities.

Other measures to increase giving

5.95 Budget 2000 introduces a new income tax relief for gifts to charity of certain shares and securities. This goes further than the proposed measure announced in the Pre-Budget Report and covers not only listed shares and securities but also other shares dealt on a recognised stock exchange such as AIM shares, units in authorised unit trusts, shares in open-ended investment companies and holdings in similar foreign collective investment schemes. In addition, Budget 2000 removes the charge to tax where income of certain trusts is given to charity.

Making life easier for charities themselves

5.96 Budget 2000 introduces new measures to ease the administration and the tax burden of charities themselves. The Government is introducing a de minimis exemption which will allow charities that engage only in small-scale trading activities to do so directly, without the need to set up a subsidiary company. Broadly the exemption will apply where trading turnover is less than £5,000, or where the trading turnover represents less than 25 per cent of the charity's total income, up to a maximum of £50,000. The existing income tax and VAT exemptions for charity fundraising events will be extended and aligned to exempt a wider range of events. These measures were announced in the Pre-Budget Report.

5.97 Measures will also be introduced to make the VAT system more generous for specific transactions, such as advertising. The VAT zero rate will be broadened for the sale or hire of donated goods, a measure which goes beyond the package announced in the Pre-Budget Report.

FAIRNESS IN TAXATION

Stamp duty

5.98 The Government recognises the importance of good quality housing. Many families on low incomes live in low-rent social housing, which is increasingly provided through Registered Social Landlords (RSLs). Only RSLs which are registered charities enjoy Stamp duty relief at present. Budget 2000 announces the Government's decision to encourage social housing provision and help the voluntary transfer programme by extending that relief. The additional reliefs cover:

- purchases by resident-controlled RSLs;

- transfers of housing stock from local authorities to help the voluntary transfer programme; and

- purchases of property by RSLs which are subsidised by Social Housing Grants.

5.99 In the Pre-Budget Report, the Government signalled the high priority it attaches to encouraging an urban renaissance by tackling the neglect and decline faced by many of Britain's urban areas. Achieving an appropriate balance between greenfield development and making more efficient use of brownfield land is an important element of this. The Government is attracted to the idea of offering relief from stamp duty for new developments on brownfield land. The Government will consult with interested parties on how this measure might be best targeted to help meet its objectives and how the measure could work in practice.

5.100 Budget 2000 also announces new rates for Stamp Duty on property with rates of duty of 3 per cent for transactions over £250,000 and 4 per cent over £500,000. Only 5 per cent of residential transactions in the UK pay at rates above 1 per cent (just over 10 per cent for London and the South East). Over one third of transactions remain exempt because they take place below the £60,000 threshold.

Tobacco

5.101 Tobacco use is detrimental to health with significant wider social costs. The Government's White Papers, *Smoking Kills* and *Saving Lives*, set out ambitious targets for reducing smoking-related diseases such as cancer and heart disease.

5.102 The Government believes that there is a strong health case for year-on-year real terms increases in the price of cigarettes and tobacco. There are two ways of achieving this: through raising taxes and through reducing the supply of cheap smuggled tobacco.

5.103 The Chancellor will continue to form his Budget judgements on the appropriate level and timing of future increases in tobacco taxes, taking into account a wide range of factors, including the Government's health objectives.

5.104 Duties on cigarettes and other forms of tobacco are being increased by 5 per cent in real terms with effect from 21 March. This will release extra resources which will be included in the extra £2 billion for the National Health Service in 2000–01.

Smuggling   **5.105** Tobacco smuggling not only undermines the Government's objective of reducing the levels of smoking in the UK, as cheaper cigarettes become available, but also brings with it widespread and serious criminality. It also cost the Exchequer £2.5 billion in lost revenue in 1999. The Government has demonstrated its determination to tackle this threat. In the Pre-Budget Report, the Government announced a series of measures including the use of scanners and pack marks. This policy will be further underpinned by significant additional resources for Customs and Excise for tackling tobacco smuggling Full details of the Government's strategy are set out in the paper 'Tackling Tobacco Smuggling' to be published on 22 March 2000.[5]

Forestalling   **5.106** The Pre-Budget Report signalled the Government's determination to end tax avoidance through forestalling, whereby manufacturers and importers build up large stocks of cigarettes in the months leading up to a Budget change and pay duty on their accumulated stocks just before the Budget increase takes effect. This has cost the public purse some £300 million a year and leads to greater uncertainty over the timing of revenue flows to the Exchequer.

5.107 In view of the potential compliance costs for wholesalers and retailers of a sell-by-date on the pack mark, the Government has decided instead to impose an anti-forestalling measure involving restricting clearances of tobacco from duty-suspended warehouses in the months immediately preceding a Budget. This will be a less burdensome approach for wholesalers and retailers, and should be more effective in protecting revenue than the proposed sell-by date. The Government will be proceeding with its proposal to introduce a pack mark for anti-smuggling purposes.

Off-shore betting

5.108 The bookmaking and racing industries in the UK need a tax system that allows them to take advantage of the increasing globalisation of the gambling market and the possibilities that e-commerce offers. The tax system also needs to ensure that these industries continue to contribute fairly to government revenues.

5.109 A consultation document issued on 21 March 2000 looks at ways of modernising the basis on which betting is taxed to respond to future threats and opportunities. It focuses on two possibilities:

- changing to a tax based on the place of consumption; and
- a gross profits based tax.

---

[5] *Tackling Tobacco Smuggling* (March 2000). Copies can be obtained from 22 March 2000 from the Treasury Public Enquiry Unit on 020 7270 4558, or at http://www.hm-treasury.gov.uk

5.110   In determining the most appropriate form of taxation for betting, the Government will also wish to take account of proposals for the future funding of the horseracing industry, and looks to the horseracing and betting industries to come forward with sensible and timely proposals. HM Customs and Excise will be conducting a consultation up to 30 June with a view to taking action in Budget 2001[6].

5.111   It is also important that the industry should continue to be protected against unfair competition from offshore bookmakers. The Government therefore welcomes the recent Court of Appeal decision which upholds restrictions on advertising targeted at UK customers. In the light of this decision, the Government currently sees no further need to amend the existing provisions.

VAT on women's sanitary products

5.112   To make the tax system fairer for women, VAT on women's sanitary products will be cut from the standard rate of 17.5 per cent to a reduced rate of 5 per cent. In order to give businesses time to adjust pricing and accounting systems, the reduced rate will be implemented from January 2001.

Air passenger duty

5.113   Budget 2000 announces a new, fairer structure for air passenger duty that will come into effect from 1 April 2001.

5.114   Air passenger duty is currently levied at rates of £10 on departures to destinations within the European Economic Area (EEA), and £20 to other destinations. The Government has recognised that the tax can represent a very significant proportion of the cost of some airfares, and a very small proportion of the cost of others. The duty on economy flights within the EEA will be halved from £10 to £5. The duty on economy flights to other destinations will remain at £20. The rate for club and first class fares for destinations in the EEA will remain at £10, but will rise from £20 to £40 for other destinations. On top of this, all flights from the Scottish Highlands and Islands will be exempt from duty, reflecting the importance of air transport to the daily life of this remote region.

5.115   Part of the cost of these changes will be met by removing the exemption from duty of return flights within the UK, a modification which was necessary to comply with European law. Overall, the changes will produce a fairer duty structure, and will ensure that many millions of passengers on economy or tourist class flights within the UK and Europe will pay less duty than at present.

Anti-avoidance

5.116   Tax-driven schemes, devices and structures, if allowed to flourish unchecked, not only cause ordinary taxpayers to have to make good the resultant loss of revenue but can also give one business an unfair competitive advantage over another. They can also undermine the credibility of the tax system generally. Budget 2000 shows the Government's continuing commitment to protect the revenue base by tackling avoidance across the whole tax system. Among the measures in the Budget are:

- a package of measures to tighten up the controlled foreign company rules, including countering 'designer rate' schemes (as announced in the Pre-Budget Report);

---

[6] The consultation document, *Our Stake in the Future*, is available at http://www.hmce.gov.uk

- a series of measures to combat the avoidance of capital gains tax by the use of trusts, offshore companies and, as announced in the Pre-Budget Report, by exploiting the reliefs for gifts;

- rules to counter the use of a number of devices which seek to reduce the rate of stamp duty payable and a measure to allow new avoidance schemes to be countered as they arise;

- rules to counter rent factoring schemes, equivalent in substance to bank loans, in which borrowers seek excessive relief for repayments;

- action against the avoidance of VAT by foreign lessors on the disposal of assets leased in the UK; and

- legislation to give effect to the proposals already announced to stop avoidance of tax and NICs through the use of personal service companies by workers who would otherwise be treated as employees of their clients.

International exchange of information

The development of the global economy is producing new challenges for business, for international trade and for tax authorities. Taxation is and will remain a national responsibility but globablisation is making international co-operation ever more important.

The UK is playing an active role in helping to modernise international practice within the OECD, the EU and the G7. The Government is seeking to establish exchange of information on as wide an international basis as possible to ensure a level international playing field for individuals and businesses. This approach is reinforced by promoting the principles of fair tax competition and through a commitment to tackling tax evasion and avoidance.

The Government will be legislating to improve the effectiveness of exchange of information agreements under double taxation agreements with other countries, and to allow the UK to enter into new exchange of information agreements to prevent offshore financial centres being used by individuals to evade or avoid UK tax.

Modernising international practice is particularly important in the case of cross-border investment by individuals. The UK Government strongly believes that all individuals should pay the tax due on all their savings income. On cross-border savings this can only be achieved by exchange of information on as wide an international basis as possible.

The Government's recently-published paper, *Exchange of Information and the draft Directive on Taxation of Savings*, explained that the current draft directive would not effectively tackle tax evasion, would not provide a level playing field within the EU and, as an EU alone measure, would not provide a level playing field internationally.

The Government is seeking to establish exchange of information on as wide an international basis as possible to protect the competitiveness of UK and EU financial markets and to ensure a level international playing field for individuals and businesses.

6 PROTECTING THE ENVIRONMENT

The Government's aim is sustainable development - ensuring a better quality of life for everyone, now and for generations to come. To achieve this, economic development needs to take place in a way which protects and, where possible, enhances the environment.

Budget 99 included the largest package of environmental tax reforms ever announced in the UK. Budget 2000 implements and delivers the key reforms – with more of the Finance Bill taken up by environmental tax reform than ever before – as well as announcing a number of new measures. Budget 2000 will put in place policies to tackle climate change, improve air quality, regenerate our cities and protect the countryside.

Tackling climate change:
- extension of reduced Vehicle Exercise Duty (VED) rate to existing cars with engines up to 1,200cc;
- introduction of graduated VED system for new cars based primarily on their carbon dioxide emissions;
- revenue neutral reform of company car tax to encourage use of lower emission vehicles;
- an additional £280 million allocated to tackling congestion hot-spots and modernising public transport;
- further encouragement for emissions trading; and
- implementing the climate change levy to encourage energy efficiency in the business sector, including enhanced capital allowances to encourage energy saving investments and exemptions for electricity generated from "new" renewables and in "good quality" Combined Heat and Power (CHP) plants.

Improving air quality:
- a fiscal incentive to encourage the take up of cleaner Ultra-Low Sulphur Petrol;
- lower rates of tax for vehicles which use less polluting fuels in both company car tax and graduated VED reforms; and
- a freeze in duty on road fuel gases.

Regenerating our cities and protecting our countryside:
- introduction of an aggregates levy to tackle the environmental costs of quarrying and encourage recycling, with all the revenues returned to business through a 0.1 percentage point cut in employers' NICs and a sustainability fund which will deliver local environmental improvements;
- the first year of pre-announced increases in landfill tax to encourage waste minimisation and recycling;
- consultation on possible stamp duty relief for new developments on brownfield land to encourage an urban renaissance; and
- further discussions on a voluntary package to reduce the environmental impacts of pesticides use.

WHY THE ENVIRONMENT MATTERS TO OUR QUALITY OF LIFE

6.1   Too often in the past, economic growth has taken place at the expense of increased pollution and the wasteful use of natural resources. Our quality of life is threatened by climate change, poor air quality and environmental degradation in both urban areas and the countryside.

6.2   Many of the sustainable development indicators published in *'Quality of life counts'* in December 1999 gave clear warnings that action is needed if our quality of life is not to be compromised. Climate change remains a serious global threat. The amount of waste produced is growing while recycling rates remain low. There has been a loss of species, habitats and landscape features, especially in farmland areas.

6.3   Global temperatures have been rising steadily over the last 20 to 30 years. There is increasing scientific agreement that a significant part of this is the result of human activity. Some further climate change is inevitable over the course of the next century. This may mean significant rises in sea levels, leading to an increased risk of flooding in some areas but water shortages in others. In many cases, the world's poorest countries are among those that are most vulnerable to the effects of climate change but the potential economic, social and environmental costs for the UK cannot be ignored.

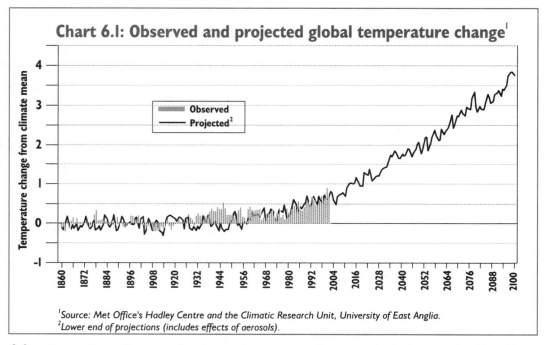

Chart 6.1: Observed and projected global temperature change[1]

[1]*Source: Met Office's Hadley Centre and the Climatic Research Unit, University of East Anglia.*
[2]*Lower end of projections (includes effects of aerosols).*

6.4   Poor air quality degrades the environment and poses risks for human health. The air quality levels at which experts consider there could be harm to human health are, on average, breached on more than 20 days a year. Although everyone suffers on days when air quality is poor, the elderly and those with chronic heart and lung diseases are particularly vulnerable. Poor air quality can bring on asthma attacks among the UK's 3 million sufferers.

6.5   Pressures on land in the UK are growing, with household projections for England indicating that an extra 3.8 million households could form between 1996 and 2021. The rate of new household formation and the geographical distribution of these households will have major environmental impacts. Unrestrained greenfield development can lead to unnecessary loss of countryside, damage biodiversity, detract from quality of life and deplete natural resources.

6.6 The urban and rural environment can be harmed by a number of activities, including aggregates extraction and pesticides use. Household waste is increasing at around 3 per cent a year, and the UK has one of the highest rates of disposing this waste into landfill in the EU. Biodegradable waste emits the powerful greenhouse gas methane as it decomposes, which, unless captured, contributes to climate change. Landfilled waste can also pollute water by leachate, creating a hazard to human health.

THE GOVERNMENT'S APPROACH TO ENVIRONMENTAL TAXATION

6.7 The Pre-Budget Report restated the principles underlying the Government's approach to environmental taxation. Economic instruments, such as taxes, charges and trading can offer scope for delivering environmental improvements in a cost effective way. By making use of the price mechanism, economic instruments allow those involved in environmentally-damaging activities to respond according to their own circumstances. Those facing the lowest costs of abatement have the incentive to make largest reductions. Pricing-in the wider economic costs not only provides a short-term incentive to reduce pollution, but also provides a permanent incentive for innovation and investment in less polluting processes, and encourages the consumption of cleaner products. But, in line with the Government's Statement of Intent on Environmental Taxation, published in July 1997, environmental taxes should meet the tests of good taxation:

- polluters should face the true costs which their actions impose on society;

- the social consequences of environmental taxation must be acceptable;

- economic instruments must deliver real environmental gains cost-effectively;

- environmental policies must be based on sound evidence but uncertainty cannot necessarily justify inaction; and

- environmental policies must not threaten the competitiveness of UK business.

Where environmental taxes meet these tests, the Government will consider introducing them.

Delivering on the Government's commitments

6.8 The Government has developed its environmental tax agenda within this policy framework. This strategy is already delivering real environmental benefits in ways which protect the competitiveness of UK firms and are socially equitable.

Tackling climate change **6.9** At the Earth Summit in Rio in 1992, developed countries agreed a voluntary target to return their emissions of greenhouse gases to 1990 levels by 2000. The UK is one of the few OECD countries which will achieve that target. The Government has already announced a package of measures which will put the UK on track to meet its Kyoto target including:

- the climate change levy and its associated negotiated agreements;

- electricity suppliers will be obliged to provide 10 per cent of electricity from renewable sources from 2010, subject to the cost to consumers being acceptable;

- a new energy efficiency standard of performance, placing an obligation on electricity and gas suppliers to help their domestic consumers save energy and cut fuel bills;

- the Home Energy Efficiency Scheme which improves energy efficiency in the domestic sector, tackling fuel poverty but also reducing energy wastage;

- fuel duties;

- reforms to Vehicle Excise Duty and company car taxation to encourage the use of low emission vehicles;

- European level agreements with car manufacturers to improve the average fuel efficiency of new cars by at least 25 per cent by 2008-09; and

- new targets for improving energy management in public buildings.

These measures mean the Government is now broadly on track to meet its Kyoto target as shown in Chart 6.2.

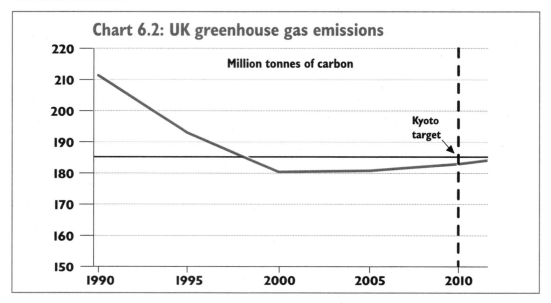

Chart 6.2: UK greenhouse gas emissions

Improving air quality 6.10   Improvements in fuel quality and vehicle emission technology have meant that total road transport emissions of local air pollutants have fallen by around 50 per cent over the last decade. The Government has played an important part in encouraging these changes through setting duty differentials in favour of cleaner fuels:

- favourable tax treatment of unleaded petrol has smoothed the phasing out of leaded fuel from 1 January 2000 in line with EU directives;

- favourable tax treatment of Ultra Low Sulphur Diesel has encouraged almost the whole diesel market to switch over to this less environmentally damaging fuel; and

- favourable tax treatment of road fuel gases has led to a large increase in the purchase and use of vehicles which use these fuels.

Regenerating our cities/protecting our countryside 6.11   The Government is also committed to regenerating our cities and protecting our countryside. As well as measures to improve air quality in both urban and rural areas, the Government has:

- revised planning guidance to help deliver the Government's target that at least 60 per cent of new housing developments should be on brownfield sites; and

- pre-announced a five year programme of increases in landfill tax to give waste producers a clear signal to reduce waste going to landfill and consider recycling.

6.12 Budget 2000 represents the next steps in implementing this strategy and delivering on the Government's commitment to improve the quality of life for all by ensuring that development occurs in a sustainable way, balancing economic, social and environmental considerations.

Box 6.1 Sustainable development

The Government's vision of sustainable development is based on the simple idea of **ensuring a better quality of life for everyone, now and for generations to come.** It means looking at the economic, social and environmental impact of policies, and meeting the four objectives:

- social progress which meets the needs of everyone;

- effective protection of the environment;

- prudent use of natural resources; and

- maintenance of high levels of growth and employment.

To help monitor progress, the Government has developed a set of "headline" indicators of sustainable development, to give a broad overview of trends, backed up by a larger set of almost 150 indicators. Budget 2000 contains a range of measures which will promote sustainable development:

- **maintaining stability and steady growth** is the focus of chapters 2-4, including measures designed to improve productivity, investment and employment;

- Chapter 5 includes many measures which contribute to **social progress**, and are aimed especially at tackling poverty and social exclusion; and

- the measures in Chapter 6 should lead to improvements in headline indicators which monitor **protection of the environment and prudent use of natural resources.** The environmental appraisal in Table 6.2 gives further details.

TACKLING CLIMATE CHANGE

6.13 The UK played a leading role in negotiating the 1997 Kyoto Protocol, in which the developed countries demonstrated their commitment to combat the global problem of climate change by agreeing to reduce greenhouse gas emissions by 5.2 per cent below 1990 levels over the period 2008-12. The EU agreed a joint target of an 8 per cent reduction at Kyoto, with the UK's contribution to this target later set at a $12\frac{1}{2}$ per cent reduction on 1990 levels. The Government has also set itself a more challenging domestic long-term aim to reduce emissions of carbon dioxide by 20 per cent on 1990 levels by 2010.

6.14 The draft UK climate change programme issued for consultation on 9 March 2000 outlined a package of measures designed to ensure that the UK moves towards a sustainable low carbon economy. It shows that the UK is well on course to reduce its greenhouse gas emissions in line with the Kyoto target, and to move beyond that towards the Government's more ambitious domestic goal. A final programme will be published later this year, so that the UK will be ready to ratify the Kyoto Protocol.

Climate change levy

The aim of the levy   **6.15**   The climate change levy will be an important part of the Government's climate change programme. The levy will not only reduce the UK's emissions of carbon dioxide, but will also help to stimulate energy efficiency across the business and public sectors. In addition, recycling all the revenues back to business through a cut in employers' National Insurance Contributions (NICs) and providing additional support for energy efficiency measures will help to promote employment opportunities and stimulate new technologies.

6.16 There will be no net financial gain to the public finances from the introduction of the climate change levy. The levy package is expected to be revenue neutral not only for the private sector, but also broadly neutral between the manufacturing and service sectors.

Developing the levy   **6.17**   The Government has developed the levy proposals in an open and consultative way, first through the work of Lord Marshall's Task Force and then through the extensive consultation exercises that followed the announcement of the levy in Budget 99. The views expressed by business and other interested parties have helped refine the design of the levy.

6.18   The Government's aim in designing the levy has been to maximise its environmental effectiveness while safeguarding the competitiveness of UK business, and the announcements made on the design of the levy in the Pre-Budget Report have been widely welcomed.

Energy efficiency measures   **6.19**   The Government announced in the Pre-Budget Report that it was minded to introduce a system of 100 per cent first year capital allowances for energy saving investments, and that it would be consulting business and others on the possible design of such a scheme. The consultation paper on the support for energy efficiency measures under the climate change levy package was published in December 1999 and around 150 responses were received from a wide range of interested parties.

6.20   The responses to the proposed scheme set out in the consultation paper were broadly supportive. Subject to obtaining EU State Aids clearance, the Government will therefore introduce a system of 100 per cent first year capital allowances from April 2001. In the light of representations received to the consultation paper, the Government plans to extend the list of eligible technologies to include refrigeration equipment, pipe insulation materials and thermal screens in addition to the five technologies (CHP, boilers, motors, variable speed drives and lighting systems) proposed in the consultation document.

6.21   The Government will now begin detailed discussions with the relevant trade sectors and expects that the full list of individual products and systems will be published at around the time of the Pre-Budget Report later this year. In order to avoid distorting the timing of investment decisions, the Government intends to allow investments in approved products and systems made after the publication of the list to qualify for the enhanced allowances, rather than only those made after the start of the next financial year (April 2001) as originally proposed. Formal claims, however, can only be made after April 2001, in line with the legislation for these enhanced capital allowances being included in Finance Bill 2001.

6.22   The Government will update the list of qualifying technologies regularly to take account of and act as a stimulant for new and developing energy saving technologies, subject to cost constraints. In particular, the list could be expanded over time to include investment in developing renewable technologies such as solar and wind power.

6.23   The exact cost to the Exchequer of the enhanced capital allowances scheme will depend on the final list of qualifying technologies and on take-up, but it is estimated to be around £100 million in 2001–02, rising to an estimated £140 million in 2002–03. The cost thereafter will depend on the evolution of the list in terms of which additional technologies could be brought within its scope. The enhanced capital allowances scheme will be an integral component of the climate change levy package and will bring considerable benefits for both the environment and for business, contributing to meeting the UK's Kyoto target while simultaneously rewarding businesses who invest to improve their energy efficiency.

6.24 Views were also sought in the consultation paper on the Government's detailed proposals for using the £50 million "energy efficiency" fund, which is intended to:

- provide energy efficiency advice/audits to small and medium-sized enterprises;

- promote the development of "new" sources of renewable energy; and

- encourage the research, development and take up of low carbon technologies and energy saving measures through a "Carbon Trust".

The responses received are currently being assessed and final decisions on the use of the "energy efficiency" fund will be made in the 2000 Spending Review.

Energy intensive sectors 6.25 The Government recognises the case for giving special treatment to energy intensive sectors because of their high energy costs and their exposure to international competition. Those energy intensive sectors which enter into agreements to implement all cost-effective energy saving measures and achieve carbon or emissions targets which meet the Government's criteria will qualify for an 80 per cent discount from the levy rates.

6.26 The Government proposed in Budget 99 that the basis for defining eligibility to enter a negotiated agreement should be those sites covered by the EU's Integrated Pollution Prevention and Control (IPPC) Directive, defined legally in the UK as sites with processes listed in Parts A1 and A2 of the Pollution Prevention and Control (PPC) Regulations.

6.27 This criterion has a clear rationale. Sites covered by Parts A1 and A2 of the PPC regulations will be subject to a regulatory requirement, in terms of having to operate in an energy-efficient manner, that other non-IPPC sites are not subject to. The Government has said that small sites in sectors covered by Parts A1 and A2 of the PPC regulations, but which fall beneath the size threshold set out in the regulations, will be eligible to be covered by a negotiated agreement. This definition covers the main energy intensive sectors and around 60 per cent of the energy used in manufacturing.

6.28 In the Pre-Budget Report, the Government announced that it remained willing to consider alternative definitions for eligibility which would target relief at energy intensive sectors exposed to international competition. But any alternative definition would have to have a clear rationale, provide legal certainty, administrative simplicity and be consistent with EU State Aids rules.

Box 6.2: Progress on the negotiated agreements

Discussions with the main energy intensive sectors have been underway since spring 1999. Considerable progress has been made. On 20 December 1999, Memoranda of Understanding with the largest ten energy intensive sectors were signed.

The sectors that have already agreed indicative energy efficiency targets are: Cement; Food and Drink (as represented by the Food and Drink Federation); Glass; Non-ferrous metals; Aluminium; Paper; Chemicals; Foundries; Steel; and Ceramics. A number of smaller energy intensive sectors are also involved in negotiations for a sector agreement. Details of the final agreements will be published later this year.

6.29 A number of proposals have been received since the Pre-Budget Report and the Government has assessed them carefully against the criteria listed in it. The Government takes the view that none submitted to date satisfies all of the criteria set out in the Pre-Budget Report. Eligibility for the negotiated agreements will therefore continue to be defined as installations with processes covered by Parts A1 and A2 of the PPC regulations.

6.30 A final consultation paper on the PPC Regulations will be issued shortly by DETR, with the objective of laying the Regulations in Parliament before the summer recess. As part of these wider consultations on the PPC Regulations, and as will be set out in the forthcoming consultation paper, the Government will consider which processes currently covered by Part B of the PPC Regulations should, given their environmental effects, be more appropriately regulated under Part A2.

Horticulture   **6.31** The horticulture sector is a relatively energy intensive sector with a very large number of (often small) businesses and is directly exposed to significant international competition. It is not, however, eligible for a negotiated agreement since it is not covered by the EU's IPPC Directive. Most countries that have introduced energy taxes have afforded special treatment to their horticulture sectors in the form of lower rates or tax exemptions.

6.32 In the light of these considerations – and the scope for energy efficiency improvements in the horticulture sector – the Government intends to introduce a package of measures to help improve energy efficiency in the horticulture sector while protecting its competitiveness. Subject to State Aids clearance from the European Commission, the Government therefore intends to offer:

- **a special package of support for horticulture allocated from the £50 million energy efficiency fund.** This package will aim to improve energy efficiency across the sector and will include activities such as site-specific advice for individual businesses;

- **an extension to the list of investments qualifying for enhanced capital allowances to include thermal screens.** This will provide a further fiscal incentive for horticulture firms to invest in energy saving technologies; and

- **a temporary 50 per cent discount on the levy for a period of up to five years to the horticulture sector** while the energy efficiency measures targeted at the sector take effect.

Liquefied   **6.33** One of the Government's aims in designing the levy has been to avoid providing **Petroleum Gas**   incentives for the take up of more environmentally damaging fuels. The Government believes that, in the light of representations made since the Pre-Budget Report, applying the full rate of the levy to Liquefied Petroleum Gas (LPG) could result in fuel switching to kerosene, which is currently zero rated. In order to avoid such effects, **the Government proposes to halve the rate of levy applying to LPG to the equivalent of 0.07 per kilowatt hour (p/kWh).**

Northern Ireland   **6.34** The energy market in Northern Ireland differs markedly from that in Great Britain. In particular, natural gas is not widely available to firms and households in Northern Ireland. **To help the fledgling gas market to develop, the Government intends to explore with the European Commission the scope for allowing a temporary exemption from the levy for natural gas in Northern Ireland for a period of up to five years.** Such an exemption – which will require EU State Aids clearance – will help reduce carbon emissions by encouraging businesses to switch to natural gas from more polluting fuels.

Design of the levy   6.35   The rates of the levy will be based upon the energy content of the different energy products, and will in 2001-02 be equivalent to:

- 0.07 pence p/kWh for LPG;
- 0.15 p/kWh for gas and coal; and
- 0.43 p/kWh for electricity.

6.36   The Government will continue to monitor and evaluate the contribution that the levy makes to the UK's targets for reducing greenhouse gas emissions. As with excise duties, the Government expects that the rates of the levy will keep pace with inflation over time.

Environmental benefits   6.37   The climate change levy and its negotiated agreements combined are estimated to save at least 5 million tonnes of carbon (MtC) a year by 2010 and therefore form an important part of the UK's draft climate change programme. Full details on the breakdown of these estimated carbon savings are given in Table 6.2, but, in summary, the 5 MtC is comprised of:

- at least $2^1/_2$ MtC arising from the levy package itself, including the additional support for energy efficiency measures and the levy exemptions for electricity generated from renewable sources of energy (excluding large-scale hydro plant with generating capacity more than 10MW) and in "good quality" combined heat and power plant; and
- at least $2^1/_2$ MtC arising from the levy's negotiated agreements.

6.38   The positive responses to the Government's proposals for using the additional support for energy efficiency measures, and the further announcements in Budget 2000 on the intended list of technologies that will qualify for the enhanced capital allowances, mean that the energy efficiency measures are now forecast to save at least $^1/_2$ MtC a year by 2010. When combined with the estimated carbon savings from the price effect of the levy and its associated exemptions (which, following the Pre-Budget Report, were estimated to be around 2 MtC), the estimated carbon savings arising from the levy package itself are estimated to be at least $2^1/_2$ MtC a year by 2010.

6.39   The estimated carbon savings of at least $2^1/_2$ MtC arising from the negotiated agreements are derived from the indicative energy efficiency targets set out in the Memoranda of Understanding signed by the main ten energy intensive sectors on 20 December 1999. These estimated carbon savings are higher than estimated in the Pre-Budget Report, since more complete estimates can be made in the light of the progress on the negotiated agreements. Further carbon savings are expected from the agreements with the smaller energy intensive sectors.

Affordable Warmth   6.40   The Government is committed to ensuring that all sectors play their part in tackling climate change. The Government's "Affordable Warmth" programme tackles fuel poverty, improves the housing stock and reduces wasteful emissions of greenhouse gases by supporting the installation of energy efficient central heating systems in up to one million low income homes. Budget 2000 announces the introduction of capital allowances to underpin this programme. Further details are given in Chapter 5.

> ### Box 6.3: Emissions trading
>
> As indicated in the UK's draft climate change programme, the Government believes that emissions trading has a key role to play in reducing greenhouse gas emissions. The Government is keen to have an operational trading scheme up and running as soon as possible.
>
> The Government welcomes the progress made by the Emissions Trading Group (ETG) in addressing the issues associated with setting up a domestic emissions trading scheme. The work of the group has shown that the early creation of such a scheme could yield significant advantages for the UK, including providing an opportunity for the UK to reduce greenhouse gas emissions in a cost-effective way.
>
> The Government welcomes the proposals put forward by the ETG on ways to encourage participation in a domestic trading scheme. In particular, the Government sees merit in the case put forward by the ETG that some form of financial incentive will be required for companies to take on binding emission targets that generate additional emission reductions. Any incentive would need to be efficient in both economic and environmental terms, have acceptable financial and distributional implications, and be consistent with EU State Aids rules. The Government will continue to work closely with the ETG on the development of a domestic trading scheme and the form such a financial incentive might take.

Transport

6.41   The transport sector has a key role to play in helping to reduce carbon emissions. Over time, rising incomes, demographic shifts and changes in land use have led to rising car ownership and car use. This long-term trend towards increasing car use increases personal mobility, choice and independence but can also lead to increased congestion and pollution.

Providing alternatives to the car

6.42   Reducing emissions depends on tackling congestion and providing people with real alternatives to the car – alternatives which are safe, reliable and accessible to all. This is particularly important for the 28 per cent of households who have no regular use of a car. The Government has already achieved some success in promoting alternatives to car use. For example:

- there has been a 15 per cent increase in rail passenger journeys since May 1997 with an extra 1,100 trains running each day to meet rising demand. Rail investment is now running at £1.7 billion a year, up 34 per cent in the last two years;

- the Rural Transport Fund has already led to the introduction of over 1,800 new or improved rural bus services in England alone, providing longer running times, extended routes, greater frequency and better integration with other bus and rail services;

- bus quality partnerships in 130 towns and cities across the UK have increased bus usage by 10 to 20 per cent. Bus industry investment has doubled to £380 million per year; and

- local authorities have been working with major employers and schools in their areas on developing travel plans which encourage the use of alternatives to the car in getting to work and school.

Transport Strategy

6.43   The publication of the Integrated Transport White Paper *"A new deal for transport-better for everyone"* in July 1998 set out a policy framework for integrated transport. Since then, the Government has introduced the most wide-ranging Transport Bill for a generation to tackle congestion, improve rail and bus services and strengthen air safety. The Government's aim is to publish a ten year transport plan in summer 2000, involving both the public and private sectors and drawing upon the best that technology has to offer.

The ACEA agreement 6.44 Road transport must continue to play its part in helping to achieve the UK's environmental commitments. In October 1998, ACEA, the EU car manufacturers group, agreed to reduce average carbon dioxide emission levels from their new cars from 186g per kilometre to 140g per kilometre by 2008. The agreement has recently been extended to Korean and Japanese car makers.

Green commuting 6.45 Budget 99 introduced a package of tax exemptions to encourage the use of environmentally-friendly modes of transport in travelling to work – notably the removal of the employee benefits charge on employer-provided works buses and on public bus subsidies, and new reliefs for commuter and business cycling. This was widely welcomed as a helpful initiative towards reducing the number of private cars on the road at peak traffic times.

Fuel duties 6.46 Increases in fuel duties in recent years have given motorists and manufacturers clear incentives to design more fuel efficient vehicles, to limit unnecessary journeys and consider alternatives to the car. These increases have played a significant part in putting the UK on track to meet its Kyoto commitments. Real terms increases in fuel duties between 1996 and 1999 are estimated to produce carbon savings of 1 to 2.5 million tonnes of carbon per year by 2010.

6.47 As the Chancellor announced in the Pre-Budget Report, the appropriate level of fuel duties will now be determined on a Budget by Budget basis, taking account of the Government's economic, social and environmental objectives. The price of oil has more than doubled since Budget 99. In the light of this, the Government has decided not to increase fuel duties in real terms in Budget 2000.

Transport spending 6.48 A key part of the Government's transport strategy is to continue to improve Britain's transport infrastructure. To help achieve this, the Chancellor has decided to allocate £280 million to tackle congestion hot-spots and modernise public transport.

Scale charges for employer provided fuel 6.49 Employees who receive free fuel from their employers do not face the full costs of the fuel they use for private motoring, leading to additional congestion and higher emissions. Budget 98 announced a 5 year programme to increase the scale charges for fuel provided for private motoring in company cars by 20 per cent per annum over and above the usual increases in line with pump prices including fuel duty. This reform will discourage employers from providing, and employees from accepting, free fuel so that more company car drivers face the full costs of the fuel they use for private motoring. This should result in fewer private miles being driven, less congestion and lower emissions.

IMPROVING AIR QUALITY

6.50 The Government has set challenging new objectives to improve ambient air quality in order to protect people's health and the environment without imposing unacceptable economic or social costs.

Fuel duty differentials 6.51 The transport sector remains a major cause of poor air quality although improvements in fuel quality and vehicle emission technology have led to a 50 per cent fall in transport related emissions over the last decade. The Government has played an important part in encouraging these changes through setting duty differentials to encourage the manufacture and take up of cleaner fuels.

Unleaded petrol 6.52 A favourable differential for unleaded petrol since 1987 has significantly reduced the use of leaded petrol – which was the major source of lead in the atmosphere – over the last decade. The success of this policy helped facilitate the phasing out of leaded petrol on 1 January 2000, in line with EU directives. As a result of these measures, lead emissions from traffic have been cut to almost zero, with older cars which are unable to use unleaded petrol switching to lead replacement petrol.

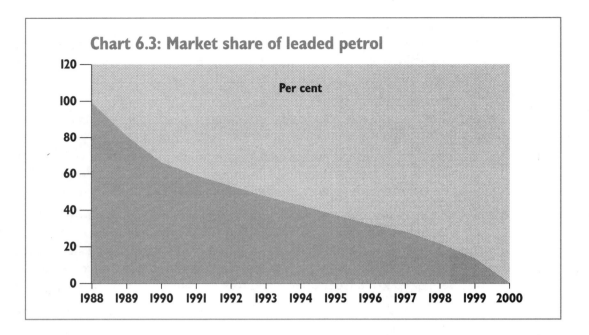

Chart 6.3: Market share of leaded petrol

6.53 The Government has taken steps to encourage the manufacture and use of Ultra-Low Sulphur Diesel (ULSD) which reduces particulate emissions from existing diesel vehicles and allows the introduction of the latest diesel after-treatment devices, such as particulate traps. A 1 pence per litre duty differential in favour of ULSD was introduced in 1997. This was increased to 2 pence per litre in Budget 98 and 3 pence per litre in Budget 99. This policy has led to almost the entire diesel market converting to ULSD, way ahead of most other European countries.

Ultra-Low Sulphur Petrol **6.54** The use of duty incentives to move the diesel and petrol markets to ULSD and unleaded petrol can be counted as major successes in achieving better local air quality. A similar opportunity now exists for Ultra-Low Sulphur Petrol (ULSP). This reduces emissions compared to ordinary petrol and enables the introduction of cleaner vehicle technologies. **The Government therefore intends to introduce a differential of 1 pence per litre in favour of ULSP relative to unleaded petrol from October 2000.**

Road fuel gases **6.55** The Government has recognised that road fuel gases can offer reductions in particulates and nitrogen oxide emissions compared with conventionally fuelled vehicles. The duty rate on road fuel gases had been frozen since 1996, and Budget 99 reduced the duty by 29 per cent.

6.56 The differential in favour of road fuel gases has already led to increased take up of this fuel, with deliveries in the first nine months of 1999-2000 exceeding the total for the preceding year. The number of bi-fuel (petrol and LPG) light vehicles has increased by 10,000 since Budget 99 and the number of refuelling facilities offering road fuel gas has increased from around 150 at the end of 1998 to around 350 today. **To encourage greater use of road fuel gas, Budget 2000 freezes its duty rate, further increasing the differential between road fuel gas and conventional fuels.**

Encouraging cleaner vehicles

6.57 Over time, the Government is committed to targeting the environmental consequences of road use by shifting the burden of vehicle taxation from ownership to use. The Government has also introduced a number of reforms which have sought to provide motorists with a powerful signal to choose more environmentally-friendly vehicles. These measures reinforce the message that the less motorists pollute, the less tax they pay.

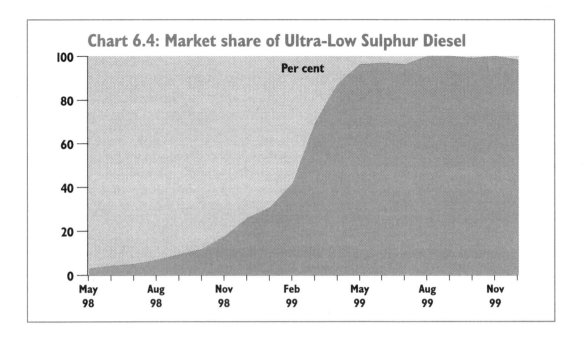

Chart 6.4: Market share of Ultra-Low Sulphur Diesel

VED rates for existing cars

6.58 In Budget 98, the Government announced its intention to reform VED to encourage cleaner cars. A consultation document issued with the 1998 Pre-Budget Report set out options for graduating VED rates by the environmental performance of different cars, looking at factors such as their engine size, carbon dioxide emissions and fuel type.

6.59 Budget 99 cut the VED rate for smaller cars, introducing a reduced annual VED rate of £100 for cars with engines up to 1,100 cc. This delivered a £55 reduction in the VED bill for drivers of 1.8 million smaller cars at a cost of £85 million a year

6.60 From March 2001, this reduced rate will be extended to apply to all existing cars with engines up to 1,200cc – making a further 2.2 million smaller cars eligible for the lower rate. This will provide an incentive for motorists to make their next second-hand car purchase a smaller, more environmentally-friendly model.

Graduated VED for new cars

6.61 Budget 99 announced that, for new cars, a system of graduated VED would be introduced based primarily on their carbon dioxide emissions. Budget 2000 announces details of this new system, which will be introduced from 1 March 2001.

6.62 Newly-registered cars will be placed in one of four VED bands according to their rate of carbon dioxide emissions – the best indicator of their fuel efficiency. Within each band, there will also be a discount for cars using cleaner fuels and technology and a small supplement on diesel cars to reflect their higher emissions of particulates and other local air pollutants. 95 per cent of new cars will pay up to £70 a year less VED under this new system than under the rates for existing cars. The graduated VED system will therefore encourage the purchase of:

- new cars as opposed to older cars;
- cars with lower carbon dioxide emissions and better fuel efficiency; and
- cars using fuels and technology which are better for local air quality.

6.63 The reforms to car VED announced in Budget 99 and Budget 2000 were to have been introduced on a revenue-neutral basis. However, the Government has decided to freeze VED rates for cars until the extension of the reduced rate in March 2001.

Company car taxation

6.64   Budget 99 announced a major revenue neutral reform of the taxation of company cars to help protect the environment. Existing incentives to keep older, more polluting cars and to drive extra business miles will be removed and drivers and their employers will face an incentive to choose cars with lower emissions both of carbon dioxide and local air pollutants.

6.65   From April 2002, the tax charge will be based on a percentage of the car's price graduated according to the level of the car's carbon dioxide emissions measured in grams per kilometre (g/km). The rates have been set to ensure broad revenue neutrality in 2002–03 and will cost the exchequer £100 million over the first three years. The charge will build up from a minimum charge on 15 per cent of the car's price, in 1 per cent steps for every 5g/km CO_2 over a specified level of emissions, up to a maximum charge on 35 per cent of the car's price, the same as the current maximum percentage. The level of CO_2 emissions qualifying for the *minimum* charge will be:

- 165 g/km in 2002/03;
- 155 g/km in 2003/04; and
- 145 g/km in 2004/05.

6.66   Diesel cars will pay a supplement of 3 per cent of the car's price compared to petrol vehicles with similar carbon dioxide emissions to take account of their higher emissions of particulates and pollutants which have adverse impacts on local air quality. Provisions will be put in place so that the supplement can be waived in the future for very low emission diesel cars and discounts can be given to cars using cleaner fuels and technology. This is consistent with the Budget 98 announcement that the extra cost of enabling a company car to run on cleaner road fuel gases would be disregarded when calculating the tax due. In the absence of reliable and complete emissions data, cars registered before 1998 will be charged according to three engine-size bands.

6.67   By encouraging the use of cleaner vehicles, it is estimated that, in the medium to long term, the reform will produce a saving of 0.5 to 1 million tonnes of carbon on a full year basis, making a substantial contribution to meeting the UK's targets for reducing greenhouse gas emissions. The supplement on diesel cars will contribute towards achieving the Government's air quality targets.

The haulage industry

6.68   Budget 2000 demonstrates the Government's commitment to maintaining the competitiveness of the UK haulage industry while recognising the damage which some lorries can do to the environment and the road network.

VED rates for lorries

6.69   The Government has decided to allow 44-tonne lorries meeting Euro II emissions standards onto UK roads from a target date of 1 January 2001, as recommended by the Commission for Integrated Transport. This will be good for the UK haulage industry and the environment. This will increase the fuel-efficiency of haulage operations, reduce congestion and give UK hauliers an advantage over foreign hauliers only permitted to run at 40-tonnes. To encourage their use, a VED rate of £2,950 will apply to this type of lorry.

6.70   The VED rate of £5,750 set for the new, road-damaging 40-tonne lorry on 5 axles in Budget 99 has successfully discouraged its use by domestic hauliers. However, now that domestic hauliers who need the highest weight limits have the option to use the less damaging 44-tonne lorry, the only UK hauliers who still need to use the 40-tonne lorry are international operators using continental roads with 40-tonne weight limits.

6.71   To boost the competitiveness of these international hauliers, the Government will cut the VED rate for the 40-tonne lorry on 5 axles from £5,750 to £3,950. The rate for the less road-damaging 38-tonne lorry on 5 axles will be reduced by £500 to encourage its continued use, and there will also be a reduction of £500 for the lorry typically used to collect freight from UK ports to boost the competitiveness of hauliers in this sector.

6.72 The rates for almost all other lorry types will remain frozen for the third year running, a cut in real terms. In total, the reforms to lorry VED announced in this Budget will cost £45 million.

Enforcement measures to protect legitimate hauliers

6.73 In order to protect the competitiveness of legitimate hauliers, the Government is taking forward a tough package of enforcement measures designed to impose more stringent checks and penalties on hauliers who operate illegally and to reduce the compliance costs of legitimate operators. These include:

- legislation in the Finance Bill to allow impounding of illegally operated lorries;

- reviewing the effectiveness and targeting of current enforcement measures as part of the ongoing work of the Road Haulage Forum; and

- tighter rules on the use of rebated "red diesel" and tougher penalties for its misuse.

6.74 A sub-group of the Road Haulage Forum will continue to review the costs which different lorry types impose on the environment and the roads, with a view to informing future decisions on the VED rates for these vehicles.

REGENERATING OUR CITIES / PROTECTING OUR COUNTRYSIDE

Urban regeneration

6.75 The Government is determined to reverse the physical, social and economic neglect that has scarred some parts of our towns and cities. It will seek a lasting urban renaissance by enhancing the quality of life and competitiveness of all Britain's towns and cities, making them places where people want to live and work. This will, at the same time, relieve pressure on the countryside.

6.76 Last summer the Urban Task Force, chaired by Lord Rogers of Riverside, published its report *Towards an Urban Renaissance*. The Task Force made 105 recommendations aimed at reversing urban decline and attracting people back into cities, towns and urban neighbourhoods. In particular the Task Force considered ways to:

- promote greater efficiency in the use of land by building at higher densities;

- reduce the proportion of new housing built on greenfield land by encouraging more development on brownfield sites;

- improve the balance of urban communities, including achieving a greater mix of housing tenures; and

- physically regenerate deprived urban areas.

Progress in responding to Lord Rogers' report

6.77 The Government has welcomed Lord Rogers' report as making an important contribution to the debate on revitalising our cities. The Government announced new planning policy guidance for housing on 7 March 2000 which responds to a wide range of Lord Rogers' recommendations by:

- promoting greater efficiency in the use of land;

- giving preference to the development of recycled land and buildings before developing greenfield sites – helping to deliver the Government's target that at least 60 per cent of new housing should be built on brownfield sites;

- encouraging higher quality housing development; and

- modernising and streamlining the planning process.

6.78   The Government has also announced that plans to develop the Thames Gateway – the largest tract of brownfield land in the South East – will be given new impetus, and that the area will be extended. This is all part of the Government's commitment to regenerate run-down areas and make our towns and cities more vibrant.

6.79   Since Lord Rogers' report was published the Government has also:

- introduced Urban Regeneration Companies in Liverpool, East Manchester and Sheffield to lead and co-ordinate the regeneration of run-down urban neighbourhoods;

- piloted nine "home zones". These traffic schemes in residential areas will give residents more control over traffic movements in their areas and ensure that the needs of people, rather than traffic, come first;

- invited proposals for a further five millennium villages, building on the experience of the first two at Greenwich and Allerton Bywater in Yorkshire; and

- piloted eight private finance deals for housing pathfinders, helping fulfil the need to attract private investment in local communities.

6.80   The Government is exploring whether fiscal measures – both taxation (national and local) and public spending – including those recommended in Lord Rogers' report, could help meet a number of objectives. For example:

- to encourage the clean up and re-development of brownfield land;

- to help make the private rented sector work better and make investment in rented housing a more attractive proposition;

- to provide an added incentive to local authorities to facilitate development;

- to encourage partnerships with local authorities to promote regeneration;

- to help business to be part of the regeneration of deprived areas; and

- to modernise and streamline the planning system.

Stamp Duty on brownfield   **6.81**   The Government has already recognised the importance of achieving an appropriate balance between greenfield development and improving the use of brownfield land. This is reflected in its national target to place at least 60 per cent of new homes on previously developed land, and its changes to planning guidance. In light of the recommendations made by Lord Rogers, the Government is attracted to the idea of offering relief from stamp duty for new developments on brownfield land. The Government will consult with interested parties on how this measure might be best targeted to help meet the Government's objectives and how it could work in practice.

6.82   The Government also recognises the importance of the provision of good quality housing. Budget 2000 extends the current stamp duty relief for Registered Social Landlords, and announces an extension of the reduced rate of VAT for the installation of energy saving materials to all homes to help tackle fuel poverty and improve energy efficiency in the domestic sector.

6.83   Together these measures contribute to the Government's commitment to generate an urban renaissance by encouraging better use of brownfield land and improvements in the quality of existing housing stock, while at the same time encouraging greater energy efficiency.

6.84   Later this year, the Government will publish an Urban White Paper which will take forward its programme for achieving an urban renaissance. This will tackle the three key elements of the Government's strategy – physical, social and economic development – in a comprehensive and co-ordinated way.

Waste

Limiting the environmental impact of waste   **6.85**   Industry and commerce in England and Wales produce around 70 to 100 million tonnes of waste per year. Local authorities collect a further 30 million tonnes, principally from households, and this is growing by around 3 per cent a year. Disposing of all this waste places further pressure on scarce land, since the UK has one of the highest rates of landfill in the EU. Landfill has other environmental costs, most notably in the emission of methane, a powerful greenhouse gas, from deposits of biodegradable waste.

Landfill tax   **6.86**   Landfill tax rates for active waste were increased from £7 to £10 per tonne from April 1999 and will rise by £1 per tonne each year until at least 2004, when the policy will be reviewed. The lower rate of tax that applies to inert waste (£2 per tonne) has remained unchanged. To ensure a sufficient supply of suitable waste materials to restore landfill sites, Budget 99 introduced an exemption for inert waste used for this purpose.

6.87   By making waste producers take account of the environmental costs they impose on the rest of society, the landfill tax encourages efforts to minimise the amount of waste generated and to develop more sustainable forms of waste management such as recycling, composting and recovery. Raising recycling rates requires a change in our attitude to waste. The Government is giving careful consideration to how it can best promote recycling.

Aggregates

6.88   The extraction and transport of aggregates imposes real costs on local communities in terms of noise and vibration, dust, loss of biodiversity and amenity and visual intrusion. But it is not just local communities which suffer. There is also evidence of wider public concern over the environmental impact of quarrying in protected areas such as national parks.

6.89   In the Pre-Budget Report, the Government welcomed a revised package of voluntary measures brought forward by the Quarry Products Association in July 1999 but said that it continued to fall short of what was necessary to match the overall environmental and economic effects of a tax on primary aggregates. The Government announced it was minded to introduce an aggregates levy in the Budget unless the industry could further improve on the package.

Aggregates levy   **6.90**   Since the Pre-Budget Report, there have been further discussions about the content of the industry's voluntary package. But the industry has made delivery of the voluntary package conditional on undertakings from the Government on procurement policy which were unacceptable. **The Government has therefore decided to introduce an aggregates levy which will come in to effect from April 2002.**

6.91   An aggregates levy will ensure that the environmental impacts of aggregates production not already addressed by regulation are more fully reflected in prices, encouraging a shift in demand away from virgin aggregate towards alternative materials such as recycled aggregate.

6.92   The levy will apply to virgin sand, gravel and crushed rock which is subject to commercial exploitation in the UK – including that dredged from the seabed within UK territorial waters. It will be charged at £1.60 per tonne. The levy will not apply to recycled aggregates, or to certain secondary aggregates such as those derived from reworking old spoil heaps. To protect competitiveness, exports will be relieved and imported aggregates will be subject to the levy when they are first sold or used in the UK.

6.93 There will be a range of exemptions/reliefs for certain rocks (coal, lignite, slate, shale) and industrial minerals (such as metal ores, gypsum, fluorspar); for the production of lime or cement from limestone and for silica sand or limestone used in certain agricultural and industrial processes (such as glass-making and fertiliser production).

6.94 To further the Government's aim of shifting the burden of taxation from "goods" to "bads", the revenues from the levy will be fully recycled to the business community through a 0.1 percentage point reduction in employers' NICS and a new Sustainability Fund. The Government will be consulting shortly on how this fund can best be used to deliver local environmental improvements.

Pesticides

6.95 There is increasing evidence that pesticides use is associated with significant environmental impacts on biodiversity and water quality. The Government is committed to minimising the environmental impact of pesticides, consistent with adequate crop protection.

6.96 The agrochemical and farming industries have made good progress in adopting measures which seek to minimise pesticide usage in recent years but there is scope for further action. A considerable body of research has aimed at identifying additional measures that could be taken to minimise pesticide use[1]. In March 1999, DETR published the most recent research report – *Design of a tax or charge scheme for pesticides*, undertaken by Ecotec Research and Consulting Ltd. This showed that a carefully designed tax or charge scheme could be used to address the environmental impacts of pesticides use.

Voluntary package   **6.97** While the Government believes that a tax could, in conjunction with other measures, be a useful tool in addressing the environmental impacts of pesticides, it has been exploring with the agrochemical industry whether its objectives could be better achieved through a partnership approach. Proposals to minimise the environmental impact of pesticides through voluntary action were brought forward by the British Agrochemicals Association (BAA) in January. The Government recognised that these proposals were a useful basis for discussing with the industry and other interested parties what form a partnership approach might take. The Government also stated that subject to further detailed discussions, it would not proceed with the introduction of a pesticides tax in Budget 2000.

6.98 Following recent discussions with the BAA, the Government has decided not to introduce a tax on the use of pesticides in Budget 2000. Instead, taking the BAA's initial proposals as a starting point, the Government will undertake further discussions with the industry on the form of a possible voluntary package, and the contribution it could make to the Government's objective to minimise the environmental impacts of pesticides use.

6.99 The Government has therefore asked the BAA to further develop their initial voluntary proposals and submit a formal package of measures by mid April. There will then be an opportunity for all interested parties to express their views on the proposed measures and their effectiveness in tackling the environmental impacts of pesticides use. Progress will be considered in Pre-Budget Report 2000.

---

[1] RPA (1997) *Private Costs and Benefits of Pesticides Minimisation;*
ECOTEC (1997) *Economic Instruments for Pesticide Minimisation;*
ECOTEC (1998) *Review and Assessment of Other Countries' Experience with Pesticide Taxes – Lessons for a Possible UK Pesticide/Charge;*
DETR (1999), *Design of a tax or charge scheme for pesticides.*

Water

6.100 As part of the 1998 review of the water abstraction licensing system in England and Wales, the Government outlined the potential for economic instruments to be used alongside regulation to deliver more efficient use of water resources while ensuring adequate protection of the water environment. Subsequently, the Government commissioned research to consider that potential in detail. In the light of that research, the Government will publish a consultation paper later this spring, setting out proposals on how trading in abstraction licences might be facilitated.

ENVIRONMENTAL APPRAISAL OF POLICY MEASURES

6.101 The Government is committed to appraising the environmental impact of all Budget measures and has refined its appraisal techniques in the light of suggestions from the Environmental Audit Committee (EAC) and others. Table 6.1 shows how the Government's environmental tax measures fit in to the overall framework of the Government's environmental policy. An environmental assessment of each of these measures is detailed in Table 6.2.

6.102 It is not always easy to quantify the individual environmental effects of Government policy. Many measures overlap and there are large uncertainties involved in trying to estimate behavioural responses. Wherever possible, an attempt has been made to separate out the effects of individual measures, as in the case of company car tax, or the savings from the climate change levy, but it should be noted that these estimates are subject to large margins of error. Estimates are not included where the precise details of the measure are not yet finalised.

6.103 The Government has made available documentation about the environmental appraisal methodology underlying its estimates including those set out in the draft climate change programme, the associated paper on the derivation of carbon savings, the DTI working paper on emissions projections, the memorandum to the EAC on the environmental appraisal of the fuel duty escalator and an Inland Revenue paper providing an "Integrated Impact Assessment" of the company car tax reform.

Table 6.1: The Government's environmental tax measures and policy objectives

Policy objective	Corresponding environmental tax measures	Other relevant policy initiatives	Sustainability indicator affected
Tackling climate change	• Climate change levy and related measures • Reforms to company car tax • VED reforms • Reduced rate of VAT on energy saving materials	Draft climate change programme[1] New Deal for Transport[2] Breaking the logjam[2]	Emissions of greenhouse gases
Improving the quality of the air we breathe	• Fuel duty differentials • New VED system • Reforms to company car tax	Air Quality Strategy[3]	Days of air pollution
Regenerating our cities and protecting our countryside	• Aggregates levy • Landfill tax increases • Pesticides voluntary package	Quality of Life Counts[4] Less waste more value[5] Limiting Landfill[6] A way with waste[7]	New homes built on previously developed land. Waste arising and management. Rivers of good or fair quality. Population of wild birds.

[1] Draft climate change programme: published on 9 March 2000 by DETR.

[2] A new deal for Transport: Better for everyone, DETR, July 1998; and Breaking the logjam, DETR, December 1998.

[3] Consultation document Report on the Air Quality Strategy, DETR, August 1999.

[4] Quality of Life Counts, DETR, December 1999.

[5] Consultation document, Less waste: More value, DETR, June 1998.

[6] Consultation document, Limiting Landfill, DETR, October 1999.

[7] A draft Waste Strategy for England and Wales, A Way With Waste, DETR June 1999.

Table 6.2: The impact of the Government's environmental tax measures

	Environmental impact[1]	
Climate change levy[2]	Total	at least 5 MtC
	Of which:	
	Negotiated agreements:	at least 2.5 MtC
	Levy Package	at least 2.5 MtC
	Of which:	
	• Price effect of levy[3]:	at least 1 MtC
	• Renewables exemption[3]:	at least 0.5 MtC
	• CHP exemption[4]:	at least 0.5 MtC
	• Energy efficiency measures[4]:	at least 0.5 MtC
Reduced rate of VAT on energy saving materials	Reduction in emissions of CO_2	
Company car tax reform[5]	Estimated to produce savings of around 0.5 to 1 MtC in the medium to long run	
Road fuel duty escalator	The road fuel duty escalator over the period 1996 to 1999 is estimated to produce carbon savings of 1 to 2.5 MtC by 2010 and small reductions in emissions of local air pollutants	
Road fuel duty differentials	The ULSP differential is estimated to reduce NO_x by 1 per cent, reduce CO by 4 per cent and reduce VOCs by 1 per cent in 2004[6]. The ULSD differential is estimated to result in a reduction of 8 per cent of particulates and up to 1 per cent of NO_x. The road fuel gas differential will result in a reduction in emissions of particulates and NO_x	
Reform to car VED	Small reduction in emissions of CO_2, NO_x and particulates	
Changes to VED for lorries	Will increase carrying capacity of lorries and reduce vehicle mileage delivering additional carbon and particulate savings	
Landfill tax	Encourages waste producers and the waste management industry to switch away from landfill towards waste minimisation, re-use and recycling	
Aggregates levy	Reductions in noise, dust, visual intrusion, damage to wildlife habitats and other environmental impacts	
Pesticides tax or voluntary package	Improve water quality, biodiversity and reduce impact on wildlife	

[1] These estimates are subject to significant margins of error.

[2] There are a number of difficulties involved in estimating the emission savings from the individual components of the climate change levy, including the need to avoid double counting. The figures are calculated using cautious assumptions and are shown for illustrative purposes only.

[3] Based on the DTI energy model.

[4] Based on DETR estimates from the draft climate change programme.

[5] This measure is part of a package of measures, including the changes to VED and the ACEA voluntary agreements. There are a number of difficulties involved in estimating the emission savings from the individual components of this package, including the need to avoid double counting.

[6] Using the NETCEN emissions model – further detail on the methodology used in the model is provided in "NETCEN's January 2000 report *UK Road Transport Emissions Projections*.

ILLUSTRATIVE LONG-TERM FISCAL PROJECTIONS

It is important that short-term Budget decisions are consistent with long-term sustainability. The illustrative 30 year projections presented in this annex assist in assessing sustainability and generational equity. The key points are:

- the impact of ageing on the UK's public finances is projected to be less than for most European countries;

- given the projected profile for transfers and the assumption of a constant tax share, public current consumption can increase as a share of GDP in the long term and still remain consistent with the fiscal rules;

- net debt is projected to stabilise slightly below 40 per cent of GDP in the long term; and

- increases in labour market participation will improve the sustainability of the public finances, creating the potential for long-term improvements in the quality and quantity of public services or reductions in taxation.

INTRODUCTION

A1 In setting fiscal policy it is important for the Government to enure that its short-term decisions are consistent with a sustainable long-term framework. Failure to do so would see the costs of current policy being pushed on to future generations with detrimental effects to long-term economic growth. This outcome would also be inconsistent with the principles of fiscal management set out in the *Code for Fiscal Stability* and, in particular, with achieving fairness between generations.

Code requires illustrative long-term projections
A2 For this reason, the Code requires the Government to publish illustrative long-term projections for a period of at least 10 years. The first set of these projections was published in Budget 99. They showed that the UK was in a relatively strong long-term fiscal position and that current consumption could grow at a slightly faster rate than economic growth and remain consistent with meeting the fiscal rules.

A3 The projections in this annex build on those published last year to provide an update on the sustainability of UK fiscal policy. As the factors affecting long-term sustainability are not likely to change significantly from year to year, the overall position has not changed markedly. However, this set of projections incorporates updated demographic projections and some minor refinements to the assumptions and methodology to provide additional insight.

A4 The analysis of long-term sustainability is still being developed, not only in the UK but also in a number of other countries. The Government will continue to analyse long-term spending trends to ensure the public finances remain sustainable and provide fair outcomes to present and future generations.

DEMOGRAPHIC TRENDS

A5   The demographic challenges the UK faces, along with other EU and OECD countries, emphasise the importance of a sound long-term fiscal strategy. As shown in Chart A1, around one in four people in the UK will be aged 65 or over by 2036, compared to around one in six in 2000.

The UK is ageing ...

Chart A1: UK population by age and sex

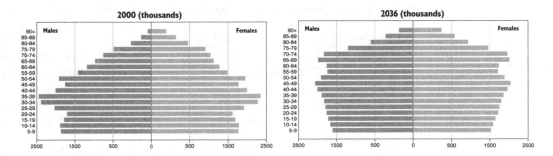

A6   This future ageing of the UK population, however, is broadly comparable with past trends. Over the period 1981 to 2000, the average age in the UK across the entire population has risen from just over 37 to nearly 39 years. The increase projected for the next 20 years is only a little faster with the average age rising to around 41½ years.

A7   The ageing of the population in the UK is expected to be less pronounced than in most European countries. This is reflected in the low projected increase in the age dependency rate shown in Table A1.

... but not as much as the rest of Europe

Table A1: Dependency rates for selected countries

	Age[1] per cent			Total[2] per cent		
	2000	2020	Increase	2000	2020	Increase
United Kingdom	26.3	32.3	6.0	68.9	70.4	1.5
France	27.1	35.4	8.3	70.0	75.8	5.8
Germany	26.2	35.5	9.3	60.0	64.5	4.5
Italy	29.1	40.2	11.1	60.1	67.1	7.0
United States	21.2	28.2	7.0	69.4	69.8	0.4
Japan	27.4	48.0	20.6	60.7	83.0	22.3

[1] *Age dependency is population aged 65 and over as a percentage of those aged between 20 and 64.*

[2] *Total dependency is population aged 19 and under and aged 65 and over as a percentage of those aged between 20 and 64.*

Sources: Government Actuary's Department for UK, United Nations for all other countries.

A8   These factors mean the impact on the UK of an ageing population is expected to be manageable. Nonetheless, the issue cannot be ignored. The reduced proportion of the population of traditionally working age and the greater demand for services for the aged will both have implications for government spending and revenue.

ASSUMPTIONS AND METHODOLOGY

A9   The Treasury's model for long-term fiscal projections examines the sustainability of the public finances by determining at what rate current consumption (current spending on health, education,) can grow while still allowing the Government to meet its fiscal rules. This is done by projecting forward taxation and transfer payments and capital consumption (depreciation), with the difference indicating the resources available for current consumption. This methodology is set out in more detail in Box A1.

Box A1: Long-term projections methodology

The methodology used for calculating long-term projections starts from assuming that the Government's golden rule will be met over the long term. As the model uses a steady state without any economic cycle, this is equivalent to meeting the golden rule in every year, or in other words, that:

$$CS_t = CR_t \qquad (1)$$

Where CS_t = current spending in year t; and
                   CR_t = current revenue in year t.

Current spending consists of current consumption, capital consumption (depreciation) and transfer payments (namely social security and debt interest payments). This can be written as:

$$CS_t = CC_t + KC_t + Tr_t \qquad (2)$$

Where CC_t = current consumption in year t;
                   KC_t = capital consumption in year t; and
                   Tr_t = transfers in year t.

Inserting equation (2) into equation (1) then gives:

$$CC_t = CR_t - KC_t - Tr_t \qquad (3)$$

The model then solves for current consumption by using projections of current revenue, transfers and capital consumption as discussed in this chapter.

A10   The projections of taxation, transfers and capital consumption are intended to show the impact of extending current policy settings forward. In many cases, however, it is difficult to define what represents current policy from a modelling perspective. As such a number of assumptions are made to approximate the current settings. These assumptions are set out below.

Economic assumptions

A11   Table A2 sets out the key economic assumptions underlying the projections[1]. Over 30 years the range of plausible assumptions is large. However, consistent with the approach to projecting the public finances in the short term, the assumptions used here take a cautious view. In particular, the expected effects of the Government's reforms to increase labour market activity and productivity are not taken into account in the baseline scenario. The importance of labour market participation is examined as an alternative scenario later in this annex.

---

[1] For the period to 2004–05, the projections presented in Chapter B of the FSBR are used.

Table A2: Long-term economic assumptions

| | Average annual real growth, per cent | |
	2005–06 to 2009–10	2010–11 to 2029–30
Productivity	2	$1^3/_4$
Labour force	$^1/_4$	0
GDP	$2^1/_4$	$1^3/_4$
Inflation	$2^1/_2$	$2^1/_2$

Cautious economic assumptions for the long term A12 The overall long-term rate of economic growth used in the projections is lower than the Government's neutral projection of trend economic growth[2]. This reflects the use of cautious assumptions for both labour force and productivity growth. The reason for introducing this additional caution is twofold. First, the greater uncertainty involved over the long term suggests taking a more cautious approach. Second, a number of the effects driving higher short-term economic growth may not continue in perpetuity. For example, higher productivity growth may reflect "catch-up" effects for a while and female participation rates cannot be expected to continue to grow forever.

Taxation assumptions

A13 Tax revenues are subject to a number of influences in both the short and long term. For example, changing patterns of income and spending give rise to considerable uncertainty about tax bases.

Constant overall tax revenue as a share of GDP A14 The long-term implications of these effects, however, are difficult to project in a meaningful way. For this reason, the approach used is to project total current receipts as a constant share of GDP without making assumptions about the source of that revenue. This approach is equivalent to saying that the Government will continue to raise the same relative amount of revenue as is currently the case. Although pressure may arise on certain tax bases in the long term and it is quite likely that some sources of taxation will decline or grow in relative importance, it is assumed that the Government will offset these effects in a revenue neutral way.

Spending assumptions

A15 As current consumption is calculated as the difference between receipts and other spending, the main spending assumptions relate to transfers and capital consumption.

Social security projections use the current framework A16 Transfers are made up of three separate components: social security transfers, interest payments and other transfers. The projections of social security transfers are calculated in conjunction with the Department of Social Security and take into account the current social security framework.

Interest payment projections use market interest rates A17 The calculation of interest payments requires assumptions both about interest rates and the level of investment. As for the short-term forecasts, interest rates are modelled using market expectations and the existing spread of financial assets to which those rates apply. The amount of investment is determined by assuming a constant investment profile at the same proportion of GDP from 2004–05 to 2019–20. From 2020–21 the rate of investment is reduced slightly to stabilise net debt at 40 per cent of GDP. This approach is consistent both with meeting the sustainable investment rule and, in the absence of an explicit investment target beyond 2004–05, current policy settings. The net debt trend is discussed in more detail in the following section.

---

[2] See *Trend Growth: Prospects and Implications for Policy*, HM Treasury, November 1999.

Capital consumption projections use historical data

A18   Capital consumption is based on the forward profile for investment which provides information on additions to the capital stock. The consumption of both the existing stock of assets and these new additions is then calculated on the assumption that future public sector asset lives are broadly similar to those evident in the past.

A19   As with all projections, the outcomes reflect the inputs and assumptions. The assumptions set out above reflect current policy settings but cannot, and do not, attempt to preempt future policy decisions. For this reason, they should be interpreted as illustrating a potential long-term position rather than presenting an expectation about the future.

THE BASELINE PROJECTIONS

A20   The baseline projections are set out in Chart A2. These illustrative projections show that, given the assumptions for transfer payments and taxation, public sector current consumption can grow at an average real rate of around 2½ per cent a year and still remain consistent with meeting the fiscal rules.

A broadly sound long-term fiscal position

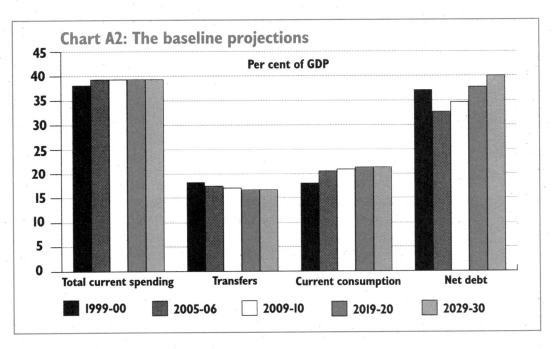

Chart A2: The baseline projections

A21   The main reason that current consumption can grow faster than GDP is the declining trend for transfers as a share of GDP. This in turn is primarily driven by the projected path for social security benefits. As the majority of benefits are indexed by prices, they remain constant in terms of purchasing power and fall as a share of GDP over time. Falling debt interest payments as a share of GDP in the medium term also contribute to the reduction in transfers.

A22   These illustrative projections produce a broadly similar picture to that presented last year. There have, however, been some small changes. Most notably, the long-term rate of growth of transfers has increased slightly primarily as a result of updated demographic projections. In addition, the projected rate of investment is higher than that used last year producing higher net debt and debt interest payments in the long term. As a result, the sustainable rate of current consumption growth has fallen slightly and current consumption broadly stabilises as a share of GDP between 2019–20 and 2029–30. This situation is offset by short-term improvements in the public finances so that the overall picture is largely unchanged.

Net debt is projected to stabilise below 40 per cent of GDP in the long term

A23   The projected changes in net debt emphasise the importance of ensuring sound public finances in the short term to prepare for future developments. On current projections net debt falls to 32.6 per cent of GDP in 2004–05. This downward trend, however, is not projected to continue indefinitely. Rather, net debt is projected to rise, and stabilise slightly below 40 per cent of GDP.

A24   The main reason for this longer-term increase in the net debt ratio is the combination of continuing strong public sector investment and the cautious projection of trend growth over this period. Should real economic growth be closer to 2 per cent a year then the debt to GDP ratio would stabilise at around 38 per cent of GDP. However, it is important to take a cautious approach in the baseline projections and not to anticipate the long-term effects of the Government's policies to raise productivity and labour market participation.

A25   The general conclusion of the baseline projections has been supported by work undertaken by the National Institute of Economic and Social Research (NIESR). NIESR's generational accounts[3] for the UK suggest only a modest generational imbalance and a broadly sustainable position. Further information on generational accounts is set out in Box A2.

No scope for complacency

A26   It is important, however, that the Government does not become complacent in the light of these positive projections. These data need to be interpreted with caution as they are subject to a number of uncertainties over a long period. Changing mortality, fertility or migration trends may produce a different population profile from that currently expected with consequential effects on the demand for social security, health and education services. In addition, the demographic trends provide no information on 'expected healthy life', which adds uncertainty to projections of health and social security spending.

A27   Aside from demographic uncertainty, there are a number of expenditures which the Government will face in the future about which the cost is uncertain – such as nuclear decommissioning. In addition, there are uncertainties about the demand for, and cost of providing public services over time. For example, changes in the structural level of unemployment and deviations in public sector pay, particularly relative to productivity, may affect spending pressures. Similarly, efficiency gains in all spending areas should reduce the cost of providing services.

---

[3] See *Generational Accounting in the UK* by Roberto Cardarelli, James Sefton and Laurence Kotlikoff, November 1998.

Box A2: Generational Accounting

An alternative method of analysing long-term fiscal sustainability and generational equity is through the use of generational accounts. These accounts calculate the net tax burden (the difference between taxation and government benefits) that an individual will pay over their remaining lifetime. By comparing the net tax burden faced by newborns (a proxy for the current generation) with that of future generations it is possible to examine the extent to which current policies imply a transfer between generations.

The National Institute of Economic and Social Research (NIESR), partly funded by the Treasury, has produced a set of generational accounts for the UK[1]. These accounts suggested that the UK was in a broadly sustainable long-term position and that any generational imbalance was relatively modest.

Generational accounts are also available for a number of other countries. A recent publication by the National Bureau of Economic Research (NBER)[2], compares generational accounts for 17 countries. As is evident in the chart below, this study shows widely differing long-term situations across the various countries as measured by the increase in taxes required to restore generational balance.

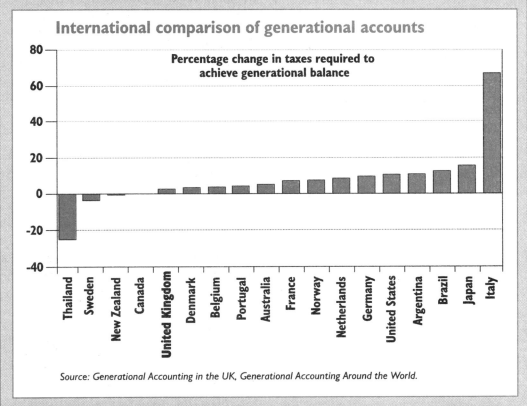

International comparison of generational accounts

Source: Generational Accounting in the UK, Generational Accounting Around the World.

This comparison also clearly shows the UK's sound long-term position. However, given the uncertainty associated with these, and other long-term, projections this position must be interpreted cautiously.

---

[1] *Generational Accounting in the UK* by Roberto Cardarelli, James Sefton and Laurence Kotlikoff, November 1998.

[2] *Generational Accounting Around the World*, edited by Alan Auerbach, Laurence Kotlikoff and Willi Leibfritz, 1999.

A28   These future uncertainties require the Government to develop policies that take the ageing of the population into account and minimise the risk of the public finances becoming unsustainable. The future increase in the retirement age for women from 60 to 65 will play an important role in reducing long-term spending pressures. In addition, the Government has announced:

- programmes to raise productivity and labour market participation, and hence increase trend economic growth;

- policies to deliver welfare reform and service modernisation;

- assistance for people to provide for retirement incomes for themselves through stakeholder pensions; and

- reforms, such as Public Service Agreements and the Public Service Productivity Panel, aimed at raising productivity throughout the public services and ensuring resources are used to their best effect.

A29   These developments will all play an important role in ensuring sustainable public finances in the long term.

ALTERNATIVE SCENARIO

A30   It is important to examine the effect that changes in the key assumptions may have on fiscal sustainability. Last year's Economic and Fiscal Strategy Report illustrated the effects of stronger economic growth and higher investment. This year an alternative scenario examines the importance of the Government's labour market programmes.

Higher labour market participation

A31   One of the main concerns about the ageing of the population is the effects that it could have on the labour market and in turn economic growth. This concern is based on the existing trend of people – males in particular – reducing their involvement in the labour market before reaching the statutory retirement age. There is, however, no reason why this trend should continue. Improvements in health and the demand for the skills developed by older members of society mean that employment opportunities will continue to exist for all. In addition, policies such as the New Deal are helping to get people back into the labour market right across the age spectrum.

A32   The effects of increasing labour market activity are shown in Chart A3. This chart presents a scenario in which the participation rate across all ages increases by 4 percentage points between 2010 and 2020 (with the increase weighted towards older age groups).

A33   This scenario clearly emphasises the importance of labour market participation. The increase modelled here allows real growth in current consumption to rise by $1/4$ per cent to average $2^3/4$ per cent a year over the projection period. This would allow the Government either to increase spending and/or reduce taxes by an average additional amount of almost £1 billion each year in 1999–2000 terms.

A34   The main driver of this outcome is the fact that economic growth has increased along with the increase in the labour force. In addition, spending on transfers falls slightly as benefit recipients move into the workforce. The resulting combination of higher tax revenues and lower social security transfers leaves the Government in a stronger fiscal position.

Higher labour
market
participation
will improve
long-term
sustainability

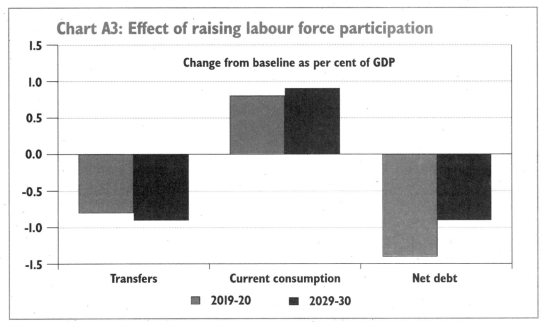

Chart A3: Effect of raising labour force participation

Change from baseline as per cent of GDP

Transfers   Current consumption   Net debt

■ 2019-20   ■ 2029-30

A35 This outcome emphasises the importance of the Government's programmes to improve labour market participation. Even small increases in participation rates can support relatively large increases in current consumption. However, it should be noted that the scenario does not model the expected effect of the Government's policies to reform the labour market although it does show the importance of these policies.

CONCLUSIONS

A36 As indicated in previous long-term projections by the Treasury, as well as by NIESR, the UK's public finances are broadly sustainable in the long term. The strength of this position is in contrast with that expected in many European countries.

A37 The Government will, nonetheless, continue to examine the potential impact of both the ageing of the population and other long-term effects. This reflects the high degree of uncertainty surrounding long-term analysis of fiscal trends and the fact that small changes in economic and policy variables can have significant effects over the long term.

A38 It is for this reason that the Government already has in place a number of measures designed to offset the effect of ageing on public spending and revenue. The importance of some of these measures is demonstrated in the alternative scenario modelled above. This emphasises the reasons for the Government's efforts to improve labour market participation. These measures, and the publication of illustrative long-term projections, will help to ensure that short-term policy decisions are set firmly within a sustainable long-term framework.

FINANCIAL STATEMENT AND BUDGET REPORT

BUDGET MEASURES

INTRODUCTION

This chapter sets out the measures in Budget 2000 and includes those announced since Budget 99. The effects[1] of the Budget measures on Government revenues are set out in Tables A.13 and A.14 and explained in Appendix A1. Tax changes announced in Budget 99 or earlier which take effect after this Budget are set out in Appendix A2. Appendix A3 provides estimates of the revenue costs of some of the main tax allowances and reliefs.

PERSONAL TAXES AND SPENDING MEASURES

Income tax 2000–2001

Bands, rates and personal allowances
The personal allowance will increase to £4,385 as already announced. The age-related personal allowances and income limit, the starting and basic rate limits, blind person's allowance and, where applicable, the married couple's allowance and widow's bereavement allowance will all rise in line with statutory indexation.(14)

Working Families' Tax Credit and Disabled Person's Tax Credit
The tax credit for children under 16 in the Working Families' Tax Credit (WFTC) and Disabled Person's Tax Credit (DPTC) will be increased by £4.35 from June 2000.(22) Other weekly rates and thresholds will rise in line with the Rossi index from April.(c) In addition, the credit for children under 11 rises by £1.10 above indexation in April 2000 to align it with the credit for children aged 11-16.(22)

The DPTC additional child credit for each disabled child will be extended to WFTC from October 2000.(d)

Two administrative reforms to the WFTC and DPTC from May 2001 will allow a new claim to be made immediately on the birth of a child to reflect the family's change of circumstances and will enable any mother who works 16 hours or more prior to the birth of a child and who is in receipt of Statutory Maternity Pay or Maternity Allowance to meet the work criteria for WFTC and DPTC.(23)

10p rate extended to savings
As announced in the Pre-Budget Report, the 10p starting rate of income tax will be extended to savings income with effect from 6 April 1999. Whether an individual has income from earnings, a pension or savings they will now benefit from the 10p rate on the first £1,500 of their taxable income in 1999–2000.(b)

Stakeholder pensions
A simplified and integrated tax regime for defined contribution pensions will be introduced in April 2001. This will facilitate the introduction of stakeholder pensions as announced by the Secretary of State for Social Security on 22 February 2000.(e)

ISA subscription limits
The higher ISA overall subscription limit of £7,000 and the £3,000 cash sublimit available for 1999–00 will be extended for a further year.(43)

Other measures
The rate of relief on the first £30,000 of certain life annuity loans (often called Home Income Plans) taken out before 9 March 1999 will be fixed at 23 per cent. (*)

---

[1] The contents of the brackets after each measure in this chapter refer to the line(s) in Tables A.13 and A.14 where its yield or cost is shown. The symbol "–" means that the proposal has no Exchequer effect. "*" means that the effect is negligible, amounting to less than £3 million a year.

The maximum earnings for which pension provision may be made with income tax relief (the "earnings cap") will be increased in line with statutory indexation to £91,800.(*) As announced on 7 March 2000, the tax charge on the repayment by occupational pension schemes of surplus employee additional voluntary contribution funds will be reduced from 33 per cent to 32 per cent from 6 April 2000.(*)

Individuals who file their Self Assessment tax returns over the internet in 2000–01 and pay any tax due electronically will receive a discount of £10.(10)

As announced on 25 February 2000, from 6 April 2000 the rate of deduction applying to payments made to subcontractors who have not been granted a certificate under the Construction Industry Scheme will fall from 23 per cent to 18 per cent.(47)

Payments to participants under the Employment Zones initiative will be exempt from tax and NICs from April 2000.(*)

Table A.1: Bands of taxable income 2000–2001

1999–00	£ a year	2000–01	£ a year
Starting rate 10 per cent	0 – 1,500	Starting rate 10 per cent	0 – 1,520
Basic[1,2] rate 23 per cent	1,501 – 28,000	Basic[1,2] rate 22 per cent	1,521 – 28,400
Higher[2] rate 40 per cent	over 28,000	Higher[2] rate 40 per cent	over 28,400

[1] The rate of tax applicable to savings income in Section 1A ICTA 1988 remains at 20 per cent for income between the starting and basic rate limits.
[2] The rates applicable to dividends are 10 per cent for income up to the basic rate limit and 32.5 per cent above that.

Table A.2: Income tax allowances 2000–2001

	£ a year		
	1999–00	2000–01	Increase
Personal allowance			
age under 65	4,335	4,385	50
age 65–74	5,720	5,790	70
age 75 and over	5,980	6,050	70
Married couple's allowance[1]			
age 65 before 6 April 2000	5,125	5,185	60
age 75 and over	5,195	5,255	60
minimum amount[2]	1,970	2,000	30
Income limit for age-related allowances	16,800	17,000	200
Widow's bereavement allowance[3]	1,970	2,000	30
Blind person's allowance	1,380	1,400	20

[1] Tax relief for these allowances is restricted to 10 per cent.
[2] This is also the maximum relief for maintenance payments where at least one of the parties is aged 65 before 6 April 2000.
[3] This will not be available in respect of deaths occurring after 5 April 2000.

Table A.3: Working Families' Tax Credit and Disabled Person's Tax Credit

	£ a week		
	1999–00	2000–01	Increase
Working Families' Tax Credit (WFTC) – basic credit	52·30	53·15	0·85
Disabled Person's Tax Credit (DPTC) – single person	54·30	55·15	0·85
Disabled Person's Tax Credit (DPTC) – lone parent/couple	83·55	84·90	1·35
30 hours tax credit (for both WFTC and DPTC)	11·05	11·25	0·20
Child tax credits (for both WFTC and DPTC)			
under 11	19·85	25·60[3]	5·75
11 – 16[1]	20·90	25·60[3]	4·70
16 – 18	25·95	26·35	0·40
Disabled child tax credit – WFTC[2]	–	22·25	22·25
Disabled child tax credit – DPTC	21·90	22·25	0·35
WFTC threshold	90·00	91·45	1·45
DPTC threshold – single person	70·00	71·10	1·10
DPTC threshold – lone parent/couple	90·00	91·45	1·45

[1] The 11–16 and 16–18 child tax credits apply from the September following the 11th and 16th birthday respectively.
[2] The disabled child tax credit in the Working Families' Tax Credit is to be introduced from October 2000.
[3] The rate applies from June 2000. The rate for April and May is £21.25 a week.

Income tax 2001–2002

Children's Tax Credit The Children's Tax Credit will be worth up to £442 a year. This is an increase of £26 on the amount announced in Budget 99.(21)

Effects on the Scottish Parliament's tax varying powers – statement regarding Section 6 of the Scotland Act 1998

A one penny change in the Scottish variable rate in 2000–2001 could be worth approximately plus or minus £240 million, broadly unaffected by these changes. In the Treasury's view, an amendment of the Scottish Parliament's tax-varying powers is not required as a result of these changes.

Inheritance tax

Threshold The threshold will be increased by statutory indexation to £234,000.(42)

Taxes on capital gains

Capital gains tax rates and annual exempt amount As announced in the Pre-Budget Report, from 6 April 2000 capital gains falling within the starting rate band will benefit from the 10p rate.(*) The annual exempt amount will be increased by statutory indexation to £7,200.(–)

Capital gains tax business assets taper The business asset taper will be reduced to four years for business assets disposed of on or after 6 April 2000, with the gain tapered as shown below. From 6 April 2000, employee shareholdings in all trading companies and all shareholdings in unquoted trading companies will qualify for the business asset taper. In addition, the business asset taper will apply to shareholdings of 5 per cent or greater in quoted trading companies.(4)

Table A.4 Capital gains tax business assets taper

No. of years	Percentage of gain chargeable	Effective tax rate, per cent	
		Higher rate taxpayer	Basic rate taxpayer
0	100	40	20
1	87½	35	17½
2	75	30	15
3	50	20	10
4+	25	10	5

Stamp duty

Rates and thresholds
From 28 March 2000, stamp duty rates will be increased on transfers of land and property (excluding shares) over £250,000 and less than £500,000 from 2.5 per cent to 3.0 per cent and from 3.5 per cent to 4.0 per cent for land and property over £500,000.(37)

The threshold for the zero rate of stamp duty applying to rents for leases for up to 7 years is increased from £500 to £5,000.(*)

Intellectual property
The stamp duty charge on transactions in intellectual property, including patents, trademarks and copyrights, will be abolished with effect from 28 March 2000.(2)

Registered Social Landlords
From Royal Assent, additional reliefs will be introduced for property transfers to Registered Social Landlords (RSLs). These include a general relief for resident-controlled RSLs and a relief for transfers from local authorities to RSLs to help the Large Scale Voluntary Transfer Programme.(38)

National insurance 2000–2001

Table A.5: National insurance contribution rates 2000–2001

Total weekly earnings[1]	Employee (primary) NICs rate[2]	Employer (secondary) NICs rate[3]
Below £67 (LEL)	0	0
£67 to £76 (PT)	0[4]	0
£76 to £84 (ST)	10	0
£84 to £535 (UEL)	10	12·2
Above £535	0	12·2

[1] The limits are defined as LEL – lower earnings limit; PT – primary threshold; ST – secondary threshold; and UEL – upper earnings limit.

[2] The contracted-out rebate for primary contributions in 2000–01 is 1.6 per cent of earnings between the LEL and UEL for all forms of contracting out – contracted-out salary-related schemes (COSRS), contracted-out money purchase schemes (COMPS) and appropriate personal pensions (APPs).

[3] The contracted-out rebate for secondary contributions is 3 per cent of earnings between the LEL and UEL for contracted-out salary-related schemes. For contracted-out money purchase schemes, the employer's contracted-out rebate varies according to the age of the employee. For appropriate personal pensions, the total rebate (primary and secondary combined) applicable to earnings is, like the rebate for COMPS, related to the age of the employee.

[4] No NICs are actually payable but a notional primary Class 1 NIC will be deemed to have been paid in respect of earnings between LEL and PT to protect benefit entitlement.

Table A.6: Self-employed national insurance contribution rates 2000–2001

Total annual profits	Self employed NICs
Below £3,825 (SEE)	0[1]
£3,825 to £4,385	£2 (Class 2) a week
£4,385 to £27,820	£2 (Class 2) a week
	plus 7% of profit above £4,385
Above £27,820	£2 (Class 2) a week
	plus 7% of profit between £4,385 and £27,820

[1] The self-employed may apply for exception from paying Class 2 contributions if their earnings are less than, or expected to be less than, the level of the Small Earnings Exception (SEE).

National insurance 2001–2002

As announced in the Pre-Budget Report, the rate of employer national insurance contributions will be reduced by 0.3 percentage points from April 2001. This will help ensure that all the revenues from the climate change levy are recycled to business.

Table A.7: National insurance contribution rates 2001–2002

Total weekly earnings[1]	Employee (primary) NICs rate[2]	Employer (secondary) NICs rate[3]
Below £69 (LEL)	0	0
£69 to £87 (PT/ST)	0[4]	0
£87 to £575 (UEL)	10	11·9
Above £575	0	11·9

For footnotes see Table A.5.

National insurance contributions 2002–2003

The revenues from the aggregates levy will be recycled through a further reduction in the rate of employer national insurance contributions of 0.1 percentage points from April 2002.(15)

Table A.8: National insurance contribution rates 2002–2003

Total weekly earnings[1]	Employee (primary) NICs rate[2]	Employer (secondary) NICs rate[3]
Below £71 (LEL)	0	0
£71 to £90 (PT/ST)	0[4]	0
£90 to £590 (UEL)	10	11·8
Above £590	0	11·8

For footnotes see Table A.5.

Benefits 2000–2001

Sure Start Maternity Grant From autumn 2000, the Sure Start Maternity Grant will be increased by a further £100 to £300.(24)

Income-related benefits Income-related benefits for children under 16 will be increased by £4.35 from October 2000 in line with the increases in the Working Families' Tax Credit.(22)

New Deal 50 plus payments Payments made under the New Deal 50 plus programme are exempted from tax from 25 October 1999, when the scheme commenced.(*)

Pensioners From December 2000, the Winter Allowance to every household with a person aged 60 or over will be increased to £150 from the current level of £100.(26)

Benefits 2001–2002

Transition to work From spring 2001, the Government will introduce a package of measures to ease the transition into work.(16, 17, 18, 19, 20)

Pensioners As announced in the Pre-Budget Report, the minimum income guarantee for pensioners will be uprated by earnings rather than prices. The lower capital limit will be doubled from £3,000 to £6,000 and the upper limit increased from £8,000 to £12,000.(25)

BUSINESS TAXES AND SPENDING MEASURES

Tax on business profits

Capital allowances Permanent first year capital allowances for small and medium sized enterprises will be introduced at a rate of 40 per cent.(8)

100 per cent first year allowances will be introduced for investments by small enterprises on information and communications technology in the three years starting 1 April 2000.(9)

From Royal Assent, capital allowances will be made available to lessors under the Government's Affordable Warmth Programme.(54)

A package of measures will be introduced to simplify, clarify and deregulate the capital allowances system. In addition, lessors will be able to claim capital allowances on the original cost to the lessee where new machinery and plant is sold and leased back provided certain conditions are met.(*)

Capital allowances will be available for oil companies using machinery and plant under an oil production sharing contract. This will apply to expenditure on or after 21 March 2000.(*)

As announced in the Pre-Budget Report, 100 per cent first year capital allowances for energy saving investments (see climate change levy below) will be introduced from April 2001.

Quarterly payments of corporation tax The rate of interest charged on underpayments of corporation tax under the quarterly instalment arrangements will be reduced by 1 percentage point from 2 per cent to 1 per cent over base rate. The change will be made by regulation as soon as possible after 21 March 2000. In addition, the de minimis exemption for quarterly instalment arrangements will be increased from £5,000 to £10,000 for accounting periods ending on or after 1 July 2000.(13)

Loans with interest rates linked to profits From 21 March 2000, companies will be able to claim relief for interest paid on certain commercial loans ('ratchet loans') with interest rates linked to profits. Transfers of ratchet loans will also be exempt from Stamp Duty.(*)

Notional transfers of assets within groups From 1 April 2000, simplification to capital gains rules will allow companies in groups to match gains and losses without the current need to move assets around the group prior to disposal(*).

Modernisation of rules for groups of companies From 1 April 2000, the rules for group relief and company gains will be modernised to include groups established through companies resident anywhere in the world and will be extended to include UK branches of overseas companies.(11)

Rollover relief for substantial shareholdings Subject to consultation in the summer, the Government is minded to introduce in Budget 2001 rollover relief for gains on the disposal by companies of shareholdings in other companies that amount to a substantial percentage of the shares in issue. This measure would broadly align the treatment of gains from the disposal of such shareholdings with the treatment of gains from the direct disposal of qualifying business assets other than shares.

Changes to double taxation relief Double taxation rules will be changed from April 2000 to help branches of international companies avoid being taxed twice. From 1 July 2000, the double taxation relief rules will be changed to limit the use of so called mixer companies to shelter low taxed foreign profits from UK tax.(12)

Overseas life assurance business The definition of this business will be relaxed to enable life assurers to write more business with overseas policyholders. (–)

Abolition of withholding tax on international bonds Withholding tax rules for Paying and Collecting Agents of international bonds and foreign dividends will be abolished from April 2001 and instead the Inland Revenue will collect routine information about the savings income of all individuals. Provisions for new Tax Information Exchange Agreements and extended powers to meet requests for information from other tax authorities will take effect from Royal Assent.(5)

Other measures As announced on 14 January 2000, the arrangements for traders to compute their profits in a non-sterling currency used in their accounts will be extended to all companies for accounting periods beginning on or after 1 January 2000 and ending on or after 21 March 2000.(*)

For accounting periods beginning on or after 1 January 2001, the benefits gained by insurance companies and Lloyds members through setting excessive provisions for future liabilities will be removed.(30)

Capital gains roll-over relief was extended to UK oil licences with effect from 1 July 1999. (*)

As announced on 12 August 1999, subject to state aid clearance, an optional tonnage-based tax regime for shipping will be introduced for accounting periods starting on or after 1 January 2000.(a)

The Inland Revenue will publish in the summer a further technical note on reform of the taxation of intellectual property. This will consider whether tax relief should be given to companies for the cost of purchasing goodwill and other intangible assets.

The Inland Revenue will consult in the summer on changes proposals to modernise the rules for deduction at source from payments for the use of intellectual property.

As announced on 25 November 1999, a new transitional relief scheme will phase in changes in rate bills arising from the revaluation of non-domestic rates in England on 1 April 2000, with greater protection offered to smaller properties.(j)

Relief will be given for the cost of acquiring capacity (Indefeasible Rights of Use) on submarine telecommunications cables.(*)

The rules governing tax relief for films are being clarified, defining film rights eligible for tax relief and the income and expenditure covered by current legislation.(–)

Value added tax

Registration thresholds The VAT registration threshold will be increased broadly in line with inflation to £52,000 from 1 April 2000. The deregistration threshold will increase from £49,000 to £50,000.(46) The level at which businesses deregistering from VAT can ignore tax due on goods on hand at deregistration will be increased from £250 to £1,000.(*)

Modernising VAT A power to impose a penalty for businesses in the gold trade who fail to comply with key requirements of the investment gold scheme will be introduced from Royal Assent.(*) Two other minor changes to VAT exemptions are included in the Budget.(48, 49)

Extending the reduced VAT rate for energy saving materials

A new reduced VAT rate for installation of energy saving materials in all homes will be introduced. In addition, the existing reduced VAT rate for grant funded installations of energy saving materials will be extended to include publicly funded installations of central heating and security measures in the homes of poorer pensioners and energy efficient heating measures in the homes of the less well-off. The changes apply from 1 April 2000.(53)

Reduced rate of VAT for women's sanitary products

From 1 January 2001, the rate of VAT on women's sanitary products will be reduced from 17½ per cent to 5 per cent.(41)

Securing the tax base

Direct taxes

A number of measures will be introduced, with effect from 21 March 2000, to prevent avoidance of CGT by individuals using trusts and offshore companies.(27)

As announced in the Pre-Budget Report, legislation will be introduced to withdraw from 9 November 1999 business assets gifts relief on the transfer of shares or securities to companies.(g)

Budget 2000 includes measures to strengthen the Controlled Foreign Company provisions, in addition to the designer rate measure announced on 6 October 1999.(32, k)

New rules for apportioning interest payable and income of life assurance companies will be introduced for accounting periods beginning after 31 December 1999 and ending on or after 21 March 2000.(29)

Schemes which allow stamp duty to be avoided when property is transferred to a company will be closed from 28 March, four other loopholes will be closed from Royal Assent and a mechanism will be introduced to allow new avoidance schemes to be countered as they arise.(28)

New rules will prevent oil companies reducing Petroleum Revenue Tax liabilities by deferring expenditure claims to periods when safeguard relief no longer applies. This will apply to expenditure on or after 21 March 2000.(33)

Measures were introduced with effect from 1 July 1999 to close a loophole that could allow oil companies to avoid paying PRT on tariff income by re-structuring their company interests in North Sea oil and gas fields.(–)

Legislation will be introduced to counter rent factoring schemes to take effect from 21 March 2000.(31)

Value Added Tax

From 21 March 2000, overseas businesses will no longer be able to dispose of their assets VAT-free where they have previously been allowed to recover VAT on the purchase of those assets.(34)

Incentives for investors and entrepreneurs

Corporate venturing

Budget 99 set out the Government's intention to introduce measures to promote corporate venturing. New tax reliefs will be introduced from 1 April 2000 to encourage companies to invest in small higher risk trading companies and form wider corporate venturing relationships.(3)

Improvements to EIS and VCT

The minimum holding period for investments under the Enterprise Investment Scheme (EIS) and Venture Capital Trusts (VCTs) will be reduced from 5 years to 3 years for new shares issued on or after 6 April 2000. Other technical improvements will be made to both schemes.(7)

Contributions to Enterprise Agencies

Tax reliefs on contributions by traders to Local Enterprise Agencies, Training and Enterprise Councils, Local Enterprise Companies and Business Link organisations, due to expire on 1 April 2000, will be extended indefinitely.(*)

Incentives for employees and managers

New all-employee share plan

The Finance Bill will legislate for the new all-employee share plan announced in Budget 99. From April, companies will be able to send in draft plans to the Inland Revenue for approval.(1)

Enterprise Management Incentives

From Royal Assent, smaller high risk companies will be able to issue tax-advantaged share options to key staff. The number of employees per company will be 15, 9 more than the maximum 6 proposed in Budget 99.(6)

Administrative help for small businesses

More support for small employers

From April 2000, the Inland Revenue will expand the range of help available on payroll issues. This will include: doubling the size of the Inland Revenue Business Support Teams; increasing both the size and the scope of the work carried out by the New Enterprise Support Initiatives (NESI) helpline for new employers; and offering new employers a visit by a Business Support Team to help them with various payroll issues. New businesses will also be offered a detailed "health check" of their payroll systems. Business support teams will look to establish clear links with the Small Business Service.

The threshold for quarterly payments of employer deductions (including Pay As You Earn (PAYE)) will be increased to £1,500, allowing more small employers to pay quarterly rather than monthly.(–)

The Inland Revenue will publish a payroll software standard on 21 March 2000 providing accreditation for software that can accurately meet payroll commitments.

As announced on 16 February 2000, small businesses that file their 2001–02 VAT or PAYE end of year returns via the internet and pay the tax due electronically will receive a one off discount of £50 (or £100 for both). Unincorporated businesses can also qualify for the £10 discount on self-assessment income tax returns (see Income Tax 2000–2001 above). There will be an extra discount of £50 for small employers who pay tax credits to employees and qualify for the £50 PAYE discount. The PAYE and tax credits discounts will also be available to small employers using an internet payroll service.(10)

Other measures

Concessionary TV Licences

From November 2000, pensioners aged 75 and over will be entitled to have their household's TV licence paid for by Department of Social Security. The costings include the cost of giving refunds to eligible pensioners who will, by November, still have unexpired months left to run on their current licences.(i)

Charities tax package

As announced in the Pre-Budget Report, a package of measures will be introduced in April 2000 to boost giving to charity. Extra measures are included in Budget 2000. (39, h)

Capital gains tax

Legislation was introduced in Section 75 Finance Act 1999, to take effect from the date of the announcement on 16 June 1999, to counter avoidance of CGT through the purchase of trust losses.(f)

ENVIRONMENTAL TAXES AND SPENDING MEASURES

Climate change levy

The Pre-Budget Report announced changes to the design of the climate change levy. Further refinements are included in Budget 2000.(l)

Transport and the environment

Company car taxation

Budget 2000 confirms that from April 2002, the tax charge for company cars will be linked to exhaust emissions. A 3 per cent supplement to this charge will apply to diesel cars. The Government will consult on waiving the supplement for very low emission diesels and on giving discounts to cars using fuels and technologies that are particularly environmentally friendly.(*)

Car fuel scale charge

The scales used to charge VAT on fuel used for private motoring in business cars will be increased from 6 April 2000 to reflect changes in fuel prices. (52)

Fuel duties

Road fuel, gas oil and fuel oil duties will rise from 21 March 2000 in line with inflation as shown in Table A.9 (See Appendix A1).(50)   The rate of duty for road fuel gases will be frozen.(52)

Table A.9: Changes to duties on road fuels and other hydrocarbon oils

	Changes in duty (per cent)	Effect of tax[1] on typical item (increase in pence)	Unit
Leaded petrol	3·40	2·12	litre
Unleaded petrol	3·41	1·89	litre
Higher octane unleaded petrol	3·41	1·97	litre
Diesel	3·21	1·89	litre
Ultra-low sulphur diesel	3·41	1·89	litre
Ultra-low sulphur petrol	1·29	0·72	litre
Gas oil	3·41	0·10	litre
Fuel oil	3·41	0·09	litre
AVGAS	3·40	1·06	litre
Road fuel gas	–	–	kg

[1] Tax refers to duty plus VAT, except for gas oil and fuel oil, which are shown exclusive of VAT.

The Government intends to introduce a differential of 1 pence per litre for ultra-low sulphur petrol relative to unleaded petrol from 1 October 2001. (51)

Penalties will be introduced to prevent misuse of rebated oils and the definitions of vehicles able to use rebated oil will be tightened from 1 May 2000.

The water content of water/diesel emulsions will be exempt from road fuel duties from Royal Assent.(–)

Vehicle Excise Duties

The 12 month standard and rate of Vehicle Excise Duty (VED) for cars, taxis and vans will rise in line with inflation by £5 to £160 (and the reduced rate for smaller cars will rise by £5 to £105) for licences taken out after 1 March 2001.(59)

From 1 March 2001, the reduced VED rate for smaller-engined cars will be extended from 1,100cc to 1,200cc. Owners of qualifying cars who take out licences at the standard rate up to 28 February 2001 will automatically receive a rebate of up to £55 in March 2001.(58)

From 1 March 2001, all cars registered for the first time will be placed into one of four VED bands based on their rates of carbon dioxide emissions. Within each band, there will also be a discount rate for cars using cleaner fuels and technology and a small supplement for diesel cars.(57)

Table A.10: Bands and rates for the graduated VED system for new cars

VED band	CO₂ emission level (grammes per kilometre)	Cars using cleaner fuels	Petrol car	Diesel car
A	Up to 150g	90	100	110
B	151g/km to 165g/km	110	120	130
C	166g/km to 185g/km	130	140	150
D	186g/km and above	150	155	160

The rate for new vans and other new vehicles for which CO_2 emissions data are not currently available will be £160.

A VED rate of £2,950 will apply to 44-tonne lorries on 6 axles meeting Euro II emissions standards, permitted for general use on UK roads from a target date of 1 January 2001. As a result, the VED rate for 40-tonne lorries on 5 axles will be cut by £1,800 to £3,950 for licences taken out after 21 March 2000.(56)

VED rates will also be cut by £500 for licences taken out after 21 March 2000 for the UK-standard 38-tonne lorry on 5 axles, for the 36-tonne lorry on 5 axles and for the lorry typically used for collecting 'unaccompanied' freight from UK ports.

VED rates for lorries currently paying £155 or £160 rise by £5 in line with the standard rate for cars. VED rates for all other lorries will be frozen for the third year running.(56)

A package of enforcement measures is being taken forward to tackle hauliers operating illegally, including legislation to allow the impounding of their lorries and measures to tighten regulations and penalties governing the use and misuse of rebated red diesel.

Land use

Landfill Tax From Royal Assent, landfill tax will be payable by either the holder of the waste management licence or the operator of a landfill site. This measure ensures that the person carrying out the landfilling activity is responsible for the tax.

The temporary disposal rules will be extended to allow the storage or sorting of material suitable for landfill site restoration to take place without incurring tax.(*)

Aggregates levy An aggregates levy will be introduced from 1 April 2002. This will apply to virgin sand, gravel and crushed rock which is subject to commercial exploitation in the UK – including that dredged from the seabed within UK territorial waters. It will be charged at £1.60 per tonne.(55)

Revenues from the levy will be returned to the business community through a 0.1 percentage point cut in employer national insurance contributions and a new sustainability fund to deliver local environment improvements.

The levy will not apply to recycled aggregate, or to certain secondary aggregates such as those derived from reworking old spoil heaps. To protect competitiveness, exports will be relieved and imported aggregates will be subject to the levy when they are first sold or used in the UK.

Tax relief for waste disposal sites

From 21 March 2000, a waste disposal firm that takes over sites previously run by another waste disposal operator will be entitled to tax relief for their predecessor's site preparation expenditure. This changes the current rules which only allow the person incurring the expenditure to claim relief. (*)

Other indirect taxes

Excise duties

Tobacco duties

The duties on all tobacco products will be increased by 5 per cent in real terms, typically 24.8 pence on a packet of 20 cigarettes, on 21 March 2000 (see Appendix A1).(44)

From Royal Assent, the basis of ad valorem duty on cigarettes will be based on the higher of the marked price or the listed recommended price.

Table A.11: Changes to tobacco duties

	Changes in duty (per cent)	Effect of tax[1] on typical item (increase in pence)	Unit
Cigarettes	8·41	24·8	packet of 20
Cigars	8·41	8·1	packet of 5
Hand-rolling tobacco	8·41	21·7	25g
Pipe tobacco	8·41	13·3	25g

[1] Tax refers to duty plus VAT.

Alcohol duties

From 1 April 2000, the duty on beer, wine and cider will increase in line with inflation. There will be no change in the duty on spirits (see Appendix A1).(40)

Table A.12: Changes to alcohol duties

	Changes in duty (per cent)	Effect of tax[1] on typical item (increase in pence)	Unit
Beer	3·41	1·1	pint of lager
Wine	3·41	4·5	75cl bottle
Fortified wine	3·41	6·0	75cl bottle
Lower strength sparkling wine	3·41	4·8	75cl bottle
Higher strength sparkling wine	3·41	6·4	75cl bottle
Spirits	0·00	0·0	70cl bottle
Still cider	3·41	1·0	litre
Strong cider	3·41	1·5	litre
Sparkling cider	3·41	4·8	75cl bottle

[1] Tax refers to duty plus VAT.

Betting and gaming duties

From 5 August 2000, the duty bands for amusement machine licence duty will be restructured to align them more closely to prize levels and price per play. The effect will be to create five duty bands instead of three and introduce concessions for seaside arcades and non-profit making clubs.(45)

Duty restructuring will be accompanied by some minor administrative changes.(*)

The gaming duty bands will be adjusted on 1 April 2000 in line with inflation.(-)

There will be a period of consultation up to 30 June on the Government's plans to modernise the structure of general betting duty.

Air passenger duty

From 1 April 2001, the duty on economy flights within the European Economic Area (EEA) will be reduced from £10 to £5. In addition, all flights from the Scottish Highlands and Islands will be exempt from duty. The duty on economy flights to other destinations will remain at £20. The rate for club and first class fares for destinations in the EEA will remain at £10, but will rise from £20 to £40 for other destinations.(35, 36)

The current return leg exemption for flights within the UK will be abolished from 1 April 2001, in line with EU Treaty obligations.

Modernising indirect taxes

From Royal Assent, Customs will be given a new power to search articles accompanied by a person where there are reasonable grounds to believe that the person has with them goods on which payment of excise duty is outstanding and has not been deferred. This will align the power to search accompanied articles for excise goods with the power to search vehicles.(–)

Powers of Customs officials to search premises under a Writ of Assistance will be modified to ensure that they are compatible with the provisions of the Human Rights Act 1998 (HRA) which comes into force on 2 October 2000. The changes take effect from Royal assent.

A financial security requirement will be introduced from Royal Assent to cover any potential excise duty liability for goods in transit between EU member states.(-)

Table A.13: Budget 2000 Measures

		(+ve is an Exchequer yield)		£ million
	2000–01 indexed	**2001–02 indexed**	**2002–03 indexed**	**2000–01 non-indexed**
MEETING THE PRODUCTIVITY CHALLENGE				
1 New all-employee share plan	-120	-280	-370	-120
2 Abolition of stamp duty on intellectual property	-5	-5	-5	-5
3 Corporate venturing scheme	-5	-25	-50	-5
4 Capital gains tax reform	0	-225	-275	0
5 Abolition of withholding tax on international bonds and foreign dividends	0	-300	*	0
Small business				
6 Enterprise Management Incentives	-30	-50	-60	-30
7 EIS/VCTs: reduction in minimum holding period and technical changes	-5	-15	-25	-5
8 Permanent first year capital allowances for small and medium sized enterprises at 40%	*	-190	-330	*
9 First year capital allowances for small enterprises for information and communication technology at 100% for three years	0	-90	-90	0
10 Discount for filing of tax returns over the internet and electronic payment	-5	-30	0	-5
Large business				
11 Extending group rules for corporation tax losses and company gains	-60	-100	-65	-60
12 Changes to double taxation relief	+40	+140	+120	+40
13 Reduction in interest rates on overdue quarterly instalments and de-minimis limit for CT instalments raised to £10,000	-5	*	*	-5
INCREASING EMPLOYMENT OPPORTUNITY FOR ALL				
14 Income tax: indexation of allowances and limits	0	0	0	-470
15 Reduction in employer national insurance contribution rate by 0.1 percentage points from April 2002	0	0	-350	0
Transition to work package				
16 £100 Job Grant	0	-20	-20	0
17 Income Support Mortgage Interest run-on for 4 weeks on taking work	0	-10	-10	0
18 Income Support Mortgage Interest 52 week linking rule	0	-5	-5	0
19 Simplification of Housing Benefit Extended Payments Scheme	0	-15	-15	0
20 Increasing £15 earnings disregard in income-related benefits to £20	0	-20	-20	0
FAIRNESS FOR FAMILIES AND COMMUNITIES				
Measures for families with children				
Tackling child poverty				
21 Increase Children's Tax Credit by £0.50 from April 2001	0	-100	-130	0
22 Increase Working Families' Tax Credit under 16 child credit and income related benefits by £4.35 from June 2000 and October 2000 respectively	-665	-1,260	-1,295	-665
Maternity package				
23 Extension of Working Families' Tax Credit to those receiving maternity pay	0	-40	-80	0
24 Increase Sure Start Maternity Grant by £100	-5	-20	-20	-5
Fairness to pensioners				
25 Increase minimum income guarantee capital limits for pensioners from April 2001	0	-145	-145	0
26 £150 Winter Allowance from December 2000	-430	-430	-430	-430
Securing the tax base				
27 Capital gains tax: use of trusts and offshore companies	0	+120	+125	0
28 Stamp duty: transfer of property and company reorganisations	+50	+100	+100	+50
29 Life assurance company taxation: modification of apportionment rules	+50	+115	+120	+50

Table A.13: Budget 2000 Measures

	(+ve is an Exchequer yield)			£ million
	2000–01 **indexed**	**2001–02** **indexed**	**2002–03** **indexed**	**2000–01** **non-indexed**
30 Insurance companies and Lloyds: reserves	0	+30	+120	0
31 Rent factoring	+20	+50	+80	+20
32 Controlled Foreign Companies	+40	+120	+150	+40
33 Petroleum Revenue Tax: preventing misuse of safeguard relief	0	+10	+30	0
34 VAT: capital asset disposals	+5	+5	+5	+5
Duties and other tax changes				
35 Relaxation for flights from Scottish Highlands and Islands from April 2001	0	-5	-5	0
36 Other reforms to Air Passenger Duty	-5	-75	-85	0
37 Stamp duty: 3 per cent rate for transfer of land and property above £250,000 and 4 per cent above £500,000	+290	+295	+365	+290
38 Stamp duty: Registered Social Landlords	-10	-20	-20	-10
39 Enhancement to charities tax package	0	-5	-15	0
40 Alcohol: freeze duty on spirits and revalorise all other alcohol duties	-25	-25	-20	+140
41 VAT: reduced rates on sanitary protection	-10	-35	-35	-10
42 Inheritance tax: index threshold	0	0	0	-15
43 Extending current Individual Savings Account subscription limits for 1 year to April 2001	-40	-70	-75	-40
44 5% real increase to tobacco duty	+235	+405	+415	+375
45 Reform of amusement machine licence duty	-5	*	*	-5
46 VAT: indexation of registration and deregistration thresholds	0	0	0	-5
47 Construction industry scheme: reducing the deduction rate	-150	-50	-50	-150
48 VAT: exemption	+15	+15	+15	+15
49 VAT: credit supplies	-20	-20	-20	-20
PROTECTING THE ENVIRONMENT				
50 Revalorisation of hydrocarbon oil duties	0	0	0	+715
51 Ultra low sulphur petrol – introducing a 1p differential with unleaded petrol	*	-15	-35	*
52 VAT: revalorisation of fuel scale charges for business cars	0	0	0	+60
53 Extending reduced VAT rate for energy saving materials	-35	-35	-35	-35
54 Affordable warmth scheme: capital allowances	*	-10	-20	*
55 Aggregates levy	0	0	+385	0
Vehicle Excise Duty:				
56 Reduce VED rates for goods vehicles	-45	-45	-45	-45
57 Introduction of graduated VED system for new cars from March 2001	0	-80	-140	0
58 Increase threshold for reduced VED rates for private and light goods vehicles tax class to 1,200cc (from 1,100cc) from March 2001	-120	-120	-120	-120
59 Revalorisation of VED rates for existing Private and Light Goods Vehicles deferred until March 2001	-110	0	0	-110
TOTAL	**-1,165**	**-2,580**	**-2,480**	**-570**

*negligible.

Table A.14: Measures included in Pre-Budget Report

	(+ve is an Exchequer yield)			£ million
	2000–01 indexed	**2001–02** indexed	**2002–03** indexed	**2000–01** non-indexed
MEETING THE PRODUCTIVITY CHALLENGE				
a Tonnage tax: an optional alternative regime for shipping companies	-10	-25	-40	-10
INCREASING EMPLOYMENT OPPORTUNITY FOR ALL				
b Extension of the starting rate of income tax to savings income	-140	-160	-180	-140
c Indexation of Working Families' Tax Credit (WFTC) and Disabled Person's Tax Credit	0	0	0	-125
d Extending of Disabled Child Tax Credit to WFTC	-10	-25	-25	-10
e Stakeholder pensions	0	-150	-620	0
FAIRNESS FOR FAMILIES AND COMMUNITIES				
f Capital gains tax: countering abuse of gifts relief	+30	+75	+75	+30
g Capital gains tax: countering abuse of trust losses	+120	+150	+150	+120
h Charities tax package	-100	-200	-275	-100
i Concessionary TV licences for pensioners aged 75 and over	-345	-355	-360	-345
j Transitional relief scheme for non-domestic rates revaluation	-580	-120	+320	-580
k Controlled Foreign Companies	0	+20	+50	0
PROTECTING THE ENVIRONMENT				
l Changes to climate change levy package since Budget 99	0	-150	-240	0
TOTAL	**-1,035**	**-940**	**-1,145**	**-1,160**

In the Pre-Budget Report the Chancellor announced that future decisions about changes in fuel and tobacco duties would be taken on a Budget by Budget basis. Accordingly, the current revenue forecast revalorises these duties in line with expected inflation for future years. The Budget 99 assumed that these duties would rise in line with previous commitments to increase fuel duties by 6 per cent in real terms and tobacco duties by 5 per cent in real terms each year. Compared to continuing the escalators, revalorising road fuels has a revenue cost of £1.2 billion in 2000–01, £2.6 billion in 2001–02 and £4.0 billion in 2002–03; for tobacco the comparable revenue costs are £0.2 billion, £0.8 billion and £1.3 billion.

APPENDICES

APPENDIX AI: EXPLAINING THE COSTINGS

This appendix explains how the Exchequer effects of the Budget measures are calculated. In the context of these calculations, the net Exchequer effects for measures may include amounts for taxes, national insurance contributions, social security benefits and other charges to the Exchequer and, for Customs and Excise, penalties.

The general approach

The net Exchequer effect of a Budget measure is generally calculated as the difference between that from applying the Pre-Budget and post-Budget tax regimes to the levels of total income and spending at factor cost expected after the Budget. The estimates do not therefore include any effect the changes themselves have on overall levels of income and spending. They do, however, take account of other effects on behaviour where they are likely to have a significant and quantifiable effect on the yield and any consequential changes in revenue from related sources. These include estimated changes in the composition or timing of income, spending or other tax determinants. For example, the estimated yield from increasing the excise duty on petrol includes the change in the yield of VAT on that duty and the change in the yield of VAT and other excise duties resulting from the new pattern of spending. Where the effect of one tax change is affected by implementation of others, the measures are generally costed in the order in which they appear in Tables A.13 and A.14.

The non-indexed base column in Table A.13 shows the revenue effect of changes in allowances, thresholds and rates of duty (including the effect of any measures, such as the increases in the standard rate of landfill tax, previously announced but not yet implemented) from their pre-Budget levels. The indexed base columns strip out the effects of inflation by increasing the allowances, thresholds and rates of duty in line with prices in this and future Budgets.

Where the Government has a pre-announced policy, such as the increases in the standard rate of landfill tax previously announced but not yet implemented, this is also stripped out of the indexed numbers. Measures announced in this Budget are assumed to be indexed in the same way in future Budgets.

The indexed base has been calculated on the assumption that each year fuel, tobacco, and alcohol duties and allowances and thresholds, other than VAT, gaming duties and tax credits, rise in line with the projected increase in the RPI over 12 months to the September following the Budget, assuming implementation dates of March for fuel and tobacco and April for alcohol. Tax credits are assumed to rise in line with the Rossi index. The VAT thresholds and all other duties are assumed to rise in line with the RPI increase over the year to the previous December (1.76 per cent in the year to December 1999). Increases in VAT, gaming duty bands and landfill tax are assumed to be implemented in April, amusement machine licence duty in August and air passenger duty in November.

These costings are shown on a National Accounts basis. The National Accounts basis aims to recognise tax when the tax liability accrues irrespective of when the tax is received by the Exchequer. However, some taxes are scored on a receipt basis, principally due to the difficulty in assessing the period to which the tax liability relates. Examples of such taxes are corporation tax, self assessment income tax, inheritance tax and capital gains tax. This approach is consistent with other Government publications.

Notes on Individual Budget Measures

Anti-avoidance measures

The yields represent the estimated direct effect of the measures with the existing level of activity. Without these measures, there could be a significant future loss of revenue currently included in the baseline.

New all-employee share plan

The cost includes relief from income tax and national insurance contributions and is net of liabilities arising from the taxation of shares withdrawn from the plan prior to the typical five year holding period.

The cost is expected to increase to around £450 million by 2002-03 before falling to around £400 million by about 2006-07 due to charges on early withdrawal of shares from the plan.

Corporate venturing

The cost is expected to reach £100 million after five years.

Capital gains tax reform

The long term cost is expected to be about £400 million, after first rising to £600 million.

Abolition of withholding tax on international bonds and foreign dividends

In 2001-02 the cost arises from part of the tax liability deducted at source under current rules being met through self assessment for companies with payment in the following year. By 2003–04 there will be a yield of about £25 million.

Enterprise Management Incentives (EMIs)

The cost includes income tax and national insurance contributions and is net of capital gains tax liabilities arising from disposal of shares acquired under EMIs. The expected long term cost is £45 million due to future revenues from capital gains and the normal charges applying to discounts.

EIS/VCTs: reduction in minimum holding period and technical changes

The full effect of reducing the minimum holding period will not arise until 2003-04 when the cost will be £30 million. The technical improvements made to both schemes have negligible cost.

Permanent first year allowances for SMEs

The revenue effect covers both companies and unincorporated businesses. The cost declines slowly after 2002-03.

100 per cent first year allowances for information and communication technology equipment for small enterprises

The revenue effect covers both companies and unincorporated businesses. From 2004-05, there will be some increase in tax liability as the balance of unrelieved capital expenditure carried forward is reduced by higher allowances.

Extending group rules for corporation tax losses and company gains

The cost is expected to fall to a small full year figure from 2004–05.

Changes to double taxation relief

The annual yield is expected to be £100 million from 2004-05.

Life company apportionment rules

The annual yield is expected to increase steadily to reach £150 million after 5 years.

Insurance companies and Lloyds: reserves

The annual yield from this measure will increase gradually and is expected to reach £250 million after 10 years.

Rent factoring

The full effect will not arise until 2004-05 when the yield will be £150 million

Petroleum revenue tax: preventing misuse of safeguard relief

The long term yield is expected to be under £10 million a year, after first rising to £50 million.

Charities tax package

The full combined effect of the packages in the Pre-Budget Report and Budget 2000 will be a cost of some £400 million after 5 years.

Affordable Warmth Scheme – capital allowances

The cost will rise to £45 million in 2004-05 and 2005-06, declining gradually thereafter.

Tonnage tax

The cost will depend on the number of companies that opt into the new arrangements.

Stakeholder pensions

The cost includes: income tax relief on contributions to stakeholder pensions, extra costs from a combined tax regime for personal pensions and stakeholder pensions, national insurance contribution rebates to stakeholder pensions and tax relief associated with the employee's part of national insurance contribution rebates to stakeholder pensions. The annual cost is expected to reach £5 billion by about 2050. This full year cost includes higher NIC rebates to appropriate personal pensions (beginning in 2003-4 following the year of accrual) and the effect of higher rebates to stakeholder pensions and appropriate personal pensions following the change from SERPS to State Second Pension.

Quarterly deductions for small employers

The cost of this measure is shown as 'nil' under the National Accounts basis. The cost in receipts terms as employers defer paying tax by up to two months is estimated as £40 million in 2000-01 and £10 million in 2001–02.

Excise duties

The cost of changes in excise duty rates depends partly on the extent to which manufacturers and wholesalers anticipate expected increases by releasing their goods early so as to pay duty at pre-Budget rates. Costings for excise duties normally take into account the anticipated level of such forestalling on the timing of accrued liability. This effect can be significant, particularly for tobacco products.

The calculation of the expected effect of changes in duty rates on consumer demand for excise goods assumes that any change in duty is passed on in full to consumers. Details of the main own and cross price elasticities used to calculate the cost of Budget measures were published in Government Economic Service Working Paper no. 138 "Consumers' Demand and Excise Duty Receipts Equations for Alcohol, Tobacco, Petrol and Derv" in November 1999.

Air Passenger Duty

The costs of changes in air passenger duty do not allow for any change in the yield from other indirect taxes resulting from the new pattern of spending. This is due to uncertainty about whether spending abroad or in the UK would be affected.

The indexed base has been calculated on the assumption that each year air passenger duty increases in November in line with the increase in RPI. The £20 million full year cost of not revalorising the duty rates is included in the indexed costings.

The cost of exempting Scottish Highlands and Islands flights allows for the abolition of the domestic return leg exemption but not the other elements of the APD package.

APPENDIX A2: TAX CHANGES ANNOUNCED IN BUDGET 99 OR EARLIER

This Appendix sets out a number changes to tax, national insurance contributions, social security benefits and other charges to the Exchequer which were announced in Budget 99 or earlier, the effects of which are taken into account in the forecast.

Table A2.1: Measures announced in Budget 99 or earlier which take effect after this Budget

	(+ve is an Exchequer yield)			£ million
	2000–01 **indexed**	**2001–02** **indexed**	**2002–03** **indexed**	**2000–01** **non-indexed**
INLAND REVENUE TAXES				
1 Corporation tax: new 10 per cent rate for the smallest companies from April 2000	0	–100	–140	0
2 Research and development tax credit	*	–100	–150	*
3 Individual Learning Accounts: making employer contributions to employee tax and NICs free	–5	–10	–10	–5
4 Abolition of Vocational Training Relief	+30	+55	+55	+30
5 Basic rate of income tax reduced to 22 per cent from April 2000	–2,350	–2,900	–3,000	–2,350
6 Alignment of NICs threshold with income tax personal allowance, in two stages, beginning April 2000	–925	–1,840	–1,950	–1,035
7 Increase to the NICs upper earnings limits for employee contributions in April 2000 and April 2001	+390	+630	+660	+460
8 Reform of self-employment NICs rates and profit limits from April 2000	+210	+230	+250	+220
9 Abolition of married couples allowance from April 2000 for those born after 5 April 1935	+1,400	+1,850	+2,000	+1,400
10 Introduction of Children's Tax Credit from April 2001	0	–1,600	–2,050	0
11 Abolition of mortgage interest relief from April 2000	+2,050	+2,150	+2,200	+2,050
12 Countering avoidance in the provision of personal services	+900	+400	+300	+900
13 Extension from April 2000 of employer NICs to all benefit in kinds subject to income tax from April 2000	+225	+225	+250	+225
14 Child Benefit: uprating from April 2000 to £15 per week for first child and £10 per week for subsequent children	–255	–255	–255	–255
15 Maternity pay reforms	0	–15	–15	0
16 Sure Start Maternity Grant	–20	–20	–20	–20
17 Increase minimum income guarantee for pensioners	–220	–220	–220	–220
18 Equalisation of child credits in WFTC and DPTC	–75	–110	–110	–75
19 Car fuel scale charge	+150	+250	+375	+150
Customs and Excise taxes				
20 £1 per tonne increase in landfill tax each year	+25	+45	+60	+30
TOTAL	**+1,530**	**–1,335**	**–1,770**	**+1,505**

* Negligible

Inland Revenue taxes

The new starting rate of corporation tax takes effect from 1 April 2000 for profits up to £10,000, also benefiting companies with profits up to £50,000. (1)

Tax credits will be available for spending by small and medium sized enterprises on research and development from April 2000. Following consultation, the measure has been expanded to include more companies and payable credits per company limited to the total of PAYE and national insurance liabilities. These changes leave the net cost unaltered. (2)

A new tax relief will ensure that employees pay no tax or national insurance contributions on their employer's contributions to their Individual Learning Accounts provided the employers make available such help to their entire workforce on similar terms.(3)

Basic rate relief on vocational training will be abolished in September 2000. (4)

From 6 April 2000, the basic rate of income tax will be reduced from 23p to 22p.(5)

From April 2000, the level of earnings above which people will pay national insurance contributions will increase as a consequence of the introduction of the new primary threshold. The level of earnings above which employees will pay no national insurance contributions (the upper earnings limit) will also increase to maintain the earnings base upon which national insurance contributions are paid. (6, 7)

From April 2000, the class 2 NICs charge will be reduced from £6.55 to £2 per week. At the same time the starting point for paying class 4 NIC will be aligned with the income tax personal allowance and the contribution rate increased to 7 percent. The upper profits limit rises with the upper earnings limit described above.(8)

The married couple's allowance for a husband and wife both born after 5 April 1935 (and related allowances) will be removed from 6 April 2000. Couples in which at least one of the spouses was born before 6 April 1935 will remain entitled to claim the allowance. Widow's bereavement allowance will be removed in respect of deaths after 5 April 2000. Tax relief for maintenance payments will cease for payments made and falling due on or after 6 April 2000. Tax relief for maintenance payments will be retained where one or more of the parties was born before 6 April 1935.(9)

A new Children's Tax Credit will be introduced from 6 April 2001 for families with children. The credit will be up to £8.50 per week, tapered away from families where one or both partners is a higher rate taxpayer.(10)

Relief on mortgage interest payments for home loans will be removed from 6 April 2000. (11)

Budget 99 announced that legislation would be introduced in April 2000 to tackle avoidance of tax and national insurance contributions through the use of personal services companies. The full year yield of this measure is £350 million with cash receipts of £400 million in both 2000-01 and 2001-02 and £300 million in 2002-03. The larger apparent first year yield arises because the National Accounts basis uses an accruals method for receipts of PAYE and national insurance contributions but only recognises corporation tax as received. (12)

From April 2000, employers' Class 1A NICs will be extended to all benefits in kind that are currently chargeable to income tax, where a national insurance contributions charge is not already payable. (13)

The credit for children under 11 in the Working Families' Tax Credit and the Disabled Person's Tax Credit will be increased by £1.10 above indexation to make it equal to the credit for children aged 11-16 from 6 April 2000.(18)

The Chancellor announced in Budget 98 that scale charges for fuel provided for private motoring in company cars would increase by 20% above revalorisation from 6 April 1998 and in each of the following four years. (19)

Relief will be available directly for the cost of buying 3rd generation mobile phone licenses. (*)

A new 'fast-track' to the Disabled Person's Tax Credit will be introduced from October 2000 to help with the retention of employees who become sick or disabled while working and are able to work for reduced hours or rates of pay.(*)

Customs and Excise taxes

Landfill tax was introduced on 1 October 1996. In Budget 99, the Chancellor announced the introduction of a landfill tax escalator of an additional £1 per tonne on active waste each year to encourage waste managers to look for more environmentally friendly alternatives to landfill.

APPENDIX A3: TAX ALLOWANCES AND RELIEFS

This appendix provides estimates of the revenue cost of some of the main tax allowances and reliefs.

Tax reliefs can serve a number of purposes. In some cases they may be used to assist or encourage particular individuals, activities or products. They may thus be an alternative to public expenditure. In this case they are often termed "tax expenditures". There may, for instance, be a choice between giving tax relief as an allowance or deduction against tax, or by an offsetting cash payment.

Many allowances and reliefs can reasonably be regarded (or partly regarded) as an integral part of the tax structure - called "structural reliefs". Some do no more than recognise the expense incurred in obtaining income. Others reflect a more general concept of "taxable capacity": the personal allowances are a good example. To the extent that income tax is based on ability to pay, it does not seek to collect tax from those with the smallest incomes. But even with structural reliefs of the latter kind, the Government has some discretion about the level at which they are set.

Many other reliefs combine both structural and discretionary components. Capital allowances, for example, provide relief for depreciation at a commercial rate as well as an element of accelerated relief. It is the latter element which represents additional help provided to business by the Government and is a "tax expenditure".

The loss of revenue associated with tax reliefs and allowances cannot be directly observed, and estimates have to be made. This involves calculating the amount of tax that individuals or firms would have had to pay if there were no exemptions or deduction for certain categories of income or expenditure, and comparing it with the actual amount of tax due. The Government regularly publishes estimates of tax expenditures and reliefs for both Customs and Excise and Inland Revenue taxes. Largely because of the difficulties of estimation, the published tables are not comprehensive but do cover the major reliefs and allowances.

The estimates in Table A3.1 below show the total cost of each relief. The classification of reliefs as tax expenditures, structural reliefs and those elements combining both is broad brush and the distinction between the expenditures and structural reliefs is not always straightforward. In many cases the estimated costs are extremely tentative and based on simplifying assumptions. The figures make no allowance for the fact that changes in tax reliefs may cause people to change their behaviour or larger claims for social security benefits. This means that figures in Table A3.1 are not directly comparable with those of the main Budget measures.

Estimation of behavioural effects is notoriously difficult. The sizes of behavioural change will obviously depend on the measure examined and possible alternative behaviours. For example, removing the tax privileges of one form of saving may just lead people to switch to another tax privileged form of saving.

Table A3.1 also gives details of reliefs relating to VAT, which is collected by Customs and Excise. It shows the estimated yield forgone by not applying the standard rate of VAT ($17^1/_2$ per cent) to goods and services which are currently zero-rated, reduced-rated, exempt or outside the scope of VAT. Estimates of the scale of structural reliefs for local authorities and equivalent bodies are also shown. Again, the figures are estimates and must be treated with caution. In line with the treatment of Inland Revenue taxes, they make no allowance for changes in behaviour.

The estimated costs of reliefs and allowances given in Table A3.1 cannot be added up to give a meaningful total. The combined yield of withdrawing two related allowances would therefore be higher than the sum of individual costs. Similarly the sum of the costs of component parts of reliefs may differ from the total shown.

More details on individual allowances and reliefs can be found in the HM Treasury publication "Tax Ready Reckoner and Tax Reliefs", November 1999.

Table A3.1: Estimated costs of main tax expenditure and structural reliefs

	£ million Estimated cost for	
	1998–1999	1999–2000
TAX EXPENDITURES		
Income Tax		
Relief for:		
Approved pension schemes	11,400	12,900
Approved profit sharing schemes	170	200
Approved discretionary share option schemes	110	90
Approved savings-related share option schemes	490	420
Personal Equity Plans	1,000	1,000
Individual Savings Accounts	0	100
Venture Capital Trusts	70	80
Enterprise Investment Scheme	80	100
Profit related pay	1,500	900
Vocational training	45	55
Exemption of:		
First £30,000 of payments on terminatin of employment	1,100	1,200
Interest on National Savings Certificates including index-linked certificates	230	190
Tax Exempt Special Savings Account interest	400	350
Premium Bond prizes	110	90
SAYE	110	90
Income of charities	925	950
Foreign service allowance paid to Crown servants abroad	100	100
First £8,000 of reimbursed relocation packages provided by employers	300	300
Tax Credits:		
Life assurance premiums (for contact made prior to 14 March 1984)	115	115
Mortgage interest	1,900	1,600
Working Families' Tax Credit	-	900
Capital gains tax		
Exemption of gains arising on disposal of only or main residence	1,400	2,200
Retirement relief	210	240
Inheritance tax		
Relief for:		
Agricultural property	90	100
Business property	110	130
Heritage property	50	50
Exemption of transfers to charities on death	310	350
Value Added Tax		
Zero-rating of:		
Food	7,750	7,750
Construction of new dwellings (includes refunds to DIY builders)	2,450	2,750
Domestic passenger transport	1,700	1,750
International passenger transport	1,800	1,850
Books, newspapers and magazines	1,200	1,300
Children's clothing	1,050	1,100
Water and sewerage services	900	950
Drugs and supplies on prescription	600	600
Supplies to charities	150	150
Ships and aircraft above a certain size	300	350
Vehicles and other supplies to disabled people	200	200
Lower rate on domestic fuel and power	1,800	1,800

Table A3.1: Estimated costs of main tax expenditure and structural reliefs

	£ million Estimated cost for	
	1998–1999	1999–2000
STRUCTURAL RELIEFS		
Income tax		
Personal allowance	31,200	31,900
Income tax and corporation tax		
Double taxation relief	5,500	5,500
Corporation tax		
Reduced rate of corporation tax on policy holders' fraction of profit	300	300
National insurance contributions		
Contracted-out rebates		
of which:		
Occupational schemes deducted from national insurance		
contributions received	5,700	5,990
Occupational schemes (COMPS) paid by the Contributions Agency		
direct to scheme	110	110
Personal pensions	2,340	2,660
Value Added Tax		
Refunds to:		
Local authorities and Northern Ireland government of VAT incurred		
on non-business purchases	3,350	3,450
The BBC and ITN of VAT incurred on non-business purchases	200	200
Central Government, Health Authorities and NHS Trusts on contracted-out		
services and projects under private finance initiative	1,750	1,800
RELIEFS WITH TAX EXPENDITURE AND STRUCTURAL COMPONENTS		
Income Tax		
Married couple's allowance	2,800	2,000
Age-related allowances	1,100	1,250
Additional personal allowance	220	150
Relief for maintenance payments	90	90
Exemption of:		
British government securities where owner not ordinarily resident in		
the United Kingdom	1,000	1,000
Child benefit (including one parent benefit)	800	850
Long-term incapacity benefit	450	400
Industrial disablement benefits	80	80
Attendance allowance	275	210
Disability living allowance	350	350
War disablement benefits	110	90
War widow's pension	70	60
Income tax and corporation tax		
Capital allowances	19,300	19,900
of which:		
Temporary first year allowances for SMEs	*	230
Corporation tax		
Small companies' reduced corporation tax rate	1,500	1,600

Table A3.1: Estimated costs of main tax expenditure and structural reliefs

	£ million Estimated cost for	
	1998–1999	1999–2000
Capital gains tax		
Indexation allowance and rebasing to March 1982	1,400	1,500
Taper relief	60	160
Exemption of:		
Annual exemption amount (half of the individual's exemption for trustees)	1,500	2,000
Gains accrued but unrealised at death	750	900
Petroleum revenue tax		
Uplift on qualifying expenditure	240	240
Oil allowance	240	350
Safeguard: a protection for return on capital cost	310	320
Tariff receipts allowance	70	70
Exemption for gas sold to British Gas under pre-July 1975 contracts	160	140
Inheritance tax		
Nil rate band for chargeable transfers not exceeding the threshold	5,500	5,900
Exemption of transfers on death to surviving spouses	1,000	1,000
Stamp Duties		
Exemption of transfers of land and property where the considerations do not exceed the threshold	230	240
National insurance contributions		
Reduced contributions for self-employed not attributable to reduced benefit eligibility (constant cost basis)	2,800	2,700
Value Added Tax		
Exemption of:		
Rent on domestic dwellings	2,550	2,650
Rent on commercial properties	1,600	1,700
Private education	850	900
Health Services	550	550
Postal Services	400	400
Burial and cremation	100	100
Finance and insurance	100	100
Betting and gaming and lottery	900	900
Small traders	100	100

B THE ECONOMY

> **The Government has taken long-term action to lock in economic stability, opening the way for sustained increases in output, employment and living standards:**
>
> - a sound and credible platform of economic stability has been delivered. The pause in economic growth last year was short-lived and damaging falls in output and employment were avoided;
>
> - robust growth of $2\frac{3}{4}$–$3\frac{1}{4}$ per cent is forecast in 2000, materially stronger than expected a year ago. GDP is set to expand at its sustainable rate of $2\frac{1}{4}$–$2\frac{3}{4}$ per cent in later years;
>
> - the balance of growth has improved over the past year, with stronger activity spreading to most sectors and regions of the UK economy;
>
> - inflation is historically low and is expected to remain close to target in the period ahead. The outlook is protected by a credible forward-looking policy commitment to low inflation;
>
> - employment has risen by 800,000 since spring 1997. Against a backdrop of increased employment opportunity in all regions of the UK economy, the Government is implementing a comprehensive strategy to get more people into work; and
>
> - some clear risks to the outlook remain, both at home and abroad, despite pre-emptive monetary policy action already having been taken and the much tighter than expected fiscal stance over the past year. Policymakers must remain vigilant, acting decisively where necessary.

INTRODUCTION[1,2]

BI This chapter sets out the economic background to Budget 2000, providing updated forecasts for the UK and world economies over the next three years. The overview section discusses recent developments in the UK economy and gives a summary of the outlook for growth and inflation. The second half of this chapter focuses on domestic forecast issues and risks, and sets out the world economy background.

Table B1: Summary of forecast

	1999	Forecast 2000	2001	2002
GDP growth (per cent)	2	$2\frac{3}{4}$ to $3\frac{1}{4}$	$2\frac{1}{4}$ to $2\frac{3}{4}$	$2\frac{1}{4}$ to $2\frac{3}{4}$
RPIX inflation (per cent, Q4)	$2\frac{1}{4}$	$2\frac{1}{4}$	$2\frac{1}{2}$	$2\frac{1}{2}$

---

[1] The forecast is consistent with output, income and expenditure data to the fourth quarter of 1999 released by the Office for National Statistics (ONS) on 28 February 2000. This release also contained revisions to earlier quarters of 1999 which the Treasury has carried through to other national accounts series that the ONS did not revise, such as household saving and sectoral net borrowing. A fully consistent national accounts dataset for 1999 will not be published by the ONS until 27 March. A detailed set of charts and tables relating to the economic forecast is available on the Treasury's internet site (http://www.hm-treasury.gov.uk), and copies can be obtained on request from the Treasury's Public Enquiry Unit (020 7270 4558).

[2] The forecast is based on the assumption that the exchange rate moves in line with an uncovered interest parity condition, consistent with the interest rates underlying the economic forecast.

UK ECONOMY OVERVIEW

The UK economy in 1999

B2   In early 1999, many commentators were predicting weak short-term prospects for the UK economy. The February average of independent forecasts showed GDP rising by just 0.6 per cent in 1999, with growth expected to remain well below trend in 2000 (Budget 99 Table A2). Within total GDP, the average expectation was for growth in domestic demand of around 1 per cent in 1999, partly offset by falling net exports and hence a significant decline in manufacturing output. Claimant unemployment was projected to rise by around 230 thousand on average in the year to the fourth quarter of 1999.

B3   The Budget 99 forecast, by contrast, projected greater resilience in economic activity. Interest rates had already been reduced by 2 percentage points from a relatively low peak of $7^1/_2$ per cent in mid-1998, subsequently reaching a low of 5 per cent in summer 1999. This timely response to the deterioration in global and UK prospects came against a background of considerable strength in private sector balance sheets, partly reflected in still high levels of consumer confidence. The good prospect of a continued expansion in domestic demand underpinned the relatively buoyant Budget 99 GDP growth forecast of 1 to $1^1/_2$ per cent, despite a larger expected negative contribution from net trade compared to outside forecasts.

B4   The preliminary estimates of output and expenditure now available to the fourth quarter of 1999 broadly confirm the Budget 99 forecast judgements. GDP rose by 2 per cent in 1999, exceeding the upper end of the Budget 99 forecast range. Rapid growth in domestic demand, up 3.4 per cent in aggregate and spread fairly evenly among the components of final demand, more than accounted for buoyant activity overall. This was partly offset by somewhat weaker than expected net trade, which reduced growth by 1.7 percentage points. Moreover, claimant unemployment also confounded outside expectations, falling by 140 thousand during the course of the year.

B5   Activity strengthened rapidly during 1999, with quarterly growth rising from 0.4 per cent at the beginning of the year to an average of 0.9 per cent in the third and fourth quarters. The balance of growth between sectors and the components of demand also improved. Manufacturing output grew by 1.7 per cent between the first and second halves of 1999, surpassing all expectations and so more than recouping the losses of the previous 12 months. The service sector recorded growth of 1.6 per cent over the same period, up from 1.0 per cent in the first half of 1999. This strengthening in activity through the year was shared across all regions of the UK (see Box B1).

B6   Both the level and growth of GDP at market prices in the second half of 1999 were slightly stronger than forecast in the Pre-Budget Report. Export volumes of goods and services strengthened considerably, rising 6.2 per cent compared to the first half of the year. Around mid-year this helped eliminate the previously strong negative contribution to growth from net trade, though export volumes fell back in the fourth quarter. Growth in import volumes was stronger than expected during the second half of 1999, contributing to a slightly weaker than anticipated net trade performance overall. Growth in final domestic demand has eased somewhat, largely reflecting the unsurprising dip in business investment growth which followed the earlier deterioration in survey investment intentions. Household consumption, by contrast, rose by 0.8 per cent in the fourth quarter of 1999, and was up 4.4 per cent on a year earlier. With total domestic demand growing by 1.9 per cent in the fourth quarter of 1999, albeit boosted by exceptional inventory accumulation, some further rebalancing in demand was clearly required.

Box B1: Regional economic activity in 1999

The dramatic improvement in business survey indicators over the past year has, in part, reflected a correction from excessively pessimistic readings recorded during the second half of 1998 (see Box A1 of the Pre-Budget Report). It also reflects the underlying strengthening in manufacturing and service sector growth illustrated, for example, by the improvement in the British Chambers of Commerce (BCC) deliveries balances[1] between the first and fourth quarters of 1999. This survey is useful in providing a snapshot of activity across the UK regions on a much more timely basis than official indicators allow.

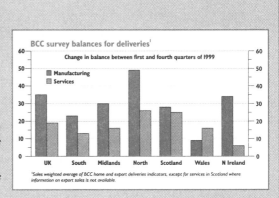

BCC survey balances for deliveries[1]

Change in balance between first and fourth quarters of 1999

[1]Sales weighted average of BCC home and export deliveries indicators, except for services in Scotland where information on export sales is not available.

The BCC survey recorded strong gains in the pace of manufacturing activity in nearly all areas during 1999, with a particularly sharp improvement registered in the northern regions. Unsurprisingly, given a starting position of growth much closer to trend, the strengthening in activity recorded in the service sector was less dramatic overall. Again, the survey evidence shows all regions sharing in stronger growth last year, though with gains tilted towards the north. These improvements lifted the BCC activity indicators to healthy levels in virtually all regions by the fourth quarter of 1999. This points to a buoyant expansion in activity across the board, though with Scotland and manufacturing in Wales still lagging behind the national survey results in terms of the current pace of growth.

[1]Positive survey balances signal an expansion in sales, and so an increase in the balance indicates a strengthening in output growth.

B7 Measured from the output side, 1.8 per cent growth in non-oil gross value added in 1999 was exactly as forecast in the Pre-Budget Report, with stronger than expected manufacturing output growth offset by a slightly weaker expansion in the service sector. Non-oil output therefore is still estimated to have risen just above trend in the third quarter of 1999, with the positive output gap rising to $^1/_4$ per cent of GDP by the end of the year. At current rates of expansion, this signals upward pressures on domestic costs, though such judgements are subject to wide margins of uncertainty.

B8 RPI excluding mortgage interest payments (RPIX) inflation of 2.2 per cent in the fourth quarter of 1999 was marginally higher than forecast in November. It has remained just below target since spring 1999, and is in line with the majority of forecasts made a year ago despite the rapid strengthening in UK growth. Currently subdued retail price pressures are also reflected in UK Harmonised Index of Consumer Prices (HICP) inflation of 1.2 per cent in the fourth quarter, lower than the Eurozone average for only the second time in over five years. Since then UK HICP inflation has come down further, and is now the lowest rate in the EU. This current conjuncture of strong growth combined with low retail price pressures is examined in detail later in this chapter.

The labour market

B9   Labour market performance was strong throughout 1999, with growth in employment remaining relatively firm even during the temporary slowing in GDP growth. The Labour Force Survey (LFS) measure of employment rose by 290,000 over the year to the fourth quarter to new record highs, driven by service sector jobs, and both the claimant count and ILO measures of unemployment now stand at 20-year lows. Sustained employment growth appears to have prompted a modest increase in labour market participation, lowering working age inactivity by around 200,000 over the past 18 months. Higher participation should also partly reflect the effects of Government policies to increase labour supply.

B10   Over the past year there has been a switch towards the creation of full-time rather than part-time jobs as the economy has strengthened. Full-timers have accounted for more than three quarters of the 1 per cent increase in employment; and involuntary temporary employment – those on short-term contracts who would prefer more permanent work – has fallen over the same period.

B11   Approaching three quarters of the working age population are now employed, just below the previous peak in spring 1990. Moreover, a range of indicators, including record numbers of vacancies and positive survey evidence, suggest that labour demand is likely to remain robust. Further sustained advances in the employment rate will increasingly need to be accompanied by rising labour market participation.

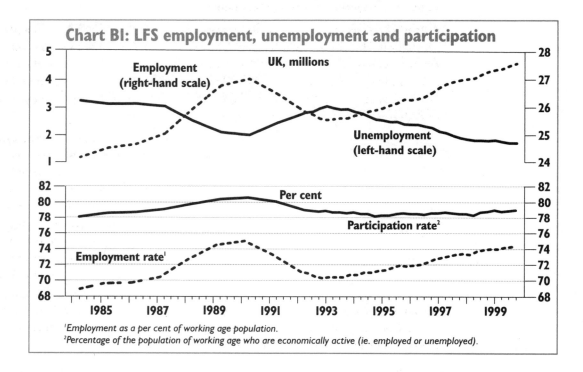

Chart B1: LFS employment, unemployment and participation

¹Employment as a per cent of working age population.
²Percentage of the population of working age who are economically active (ie. employed or unemployed).

B12   LFS employment growth towards the end of 1999 continued in line with the ¹/₄ per cent average quarterly rate of expansion seen throughout the year. The strengthening in output growth has therefore led to a marked cyclical improvement in productivity growth back towards its assumed trend rate. Much as anticipated in the Pre-Budget Report, non-oil productivity growth is now estimated to have risen to over 1¹/₂ per cent in the fourth quarter of 1999. The slowing in productivity growth was particularly marked in this cycle, with low levels of unemployment probably encouraging firms to retain labour through a relatively shallow slowing in activity. Stronger pressures in the manufacturing sector have contributed to an increase in productivity growth to more than 5 per cent recently, helping offset sterling's impact on export competitiveness.

Box B2: Regional labour markets

Unemployment has fallen across all regions during the 1990s, and the working age employment rate is now only a little below its previous peak of 75 per cent in 1990. Moreover, the divergence in unemployment rates between regions has fallen by roughly a third over this period, with regions of above average unemployment having seen the largest falls. Given evidence that the sustainable aggregate level of unemployment rises with regional dispersion in unemployment, this reduction in regional mismatch should contribute to a sustained improvement in national labour market performance.

Unemployment, as a measure of unused labour supply, can be considered alongside vacancies as a measure of unfilled demand. Longer-term comparisons suggest that regional labour markets have become much more evenly balanced, with supply better matched to demand right across the country. While regional divergences tend to narrow in recoveries and widen in downturns, the lower dispersion in unemployment-vacancy ratios in recent years goes beyond a purely cyclical effect[1].

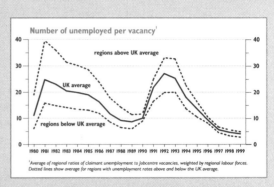

Number of unemployed per vacancy[1]

regions above UK average

UK average

regions below UK average

[1]Average of regional ratios of claimant unemployment to Jobcentre vacancies, weighted by regional labour forces. Dotted lines show average for regions with unemployment rates above and below the UK average.

Indeed there have been continued improvements in the matching of supply and demand throughout the UK over recent years, a period when the economy has remained relatively close to trend. This may reflect structural improvements such as reduced mismatch or more active job search by the unemployed. With each region now relatively well supplied with vacancies in relation to its workforce, the key to reducing unemployment further lies in addressing labour market inequalities within regions.

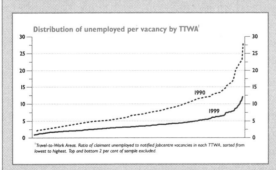

Distribution of unemployed per vacancy by TTWA[1]

1990

1999

[1]Travel-to-Work Areas. Ratio of claimant unemployed to notified Jobcentre vacancies in each TTWA, sorted from lowest to highest. Top and bottom 2 per cent of sample excluded.

At the sub-regional level, the distribution of unemployment per vacancy across Travel To Work Areas – defined as a local labour market in which at least 75 per cent of the population both live and work – also shows a clear improvement since 1990. However, further analysis reveals that areas of high unemployment still coexist within all regions alongside others where labour is in short supply[2]. Indeed, throughout the 1990s differences in unemployment rates within regions were greater than those between them. Budget 2000 includes a package of measures to tackle low employment in Britain's most deprived areas.

---

[1]Although the chart uses claimant unemployment, ILO unemployment data shows very similar results. However, the ILO data are available only from 1984, and prior to 1992 are only available seasonally unadjusted for spring quarters.

[2]A detailed analysis is given in *The Goal of Full Employment: Employment Opportunity for all Throughout Britain,* HM Treasury, February 2000.

BI3   Unemployment has continued to decline modestly on both the ILO and claimant measures, though falls in working age inactivity tended to flatten its downward trend during the second half of 1999. The ILO unemployment rate is now 5.9 per cent, $1\frac{1}{2}$ percentage points below the rate in spring 1997, and numbers unemployed for more than one year have fallen by around two thirds over the same period. As the ILO measure includes only those who are both actively seeking and available to work, it is a better indicator of the downward pressure on wages than wider measures of worklessness. Although the sustainable level of unemployment is impossible to estimate with any precision, it seems likely to have fallen broadly in line with actual unemployment over the two years to summer 1999, judging by the absence of any clear trend in earnings growth over this period. However, the most recent upturn in wage growth, albeit partly influenced by millennium-related bonus payments, is a cautionary signal. Prospects for sustainable growth depend on responsible wage behaviour in both the private and public sectors.

BI4   The key to further sustained improvements in labour market performance lies in expanding the effective supply of labour, allowing the economy to grow more rapidly while avoiding skills shortages and inflationary pressures. This will be helped by the improved balance between regional labour markets (see Box B2). However, in addition to the current 1.7 million ILO unemployed there are a further 2.3 million people who want a job but are economically inactive. The Government's policies are designed to help re-attach these individuals to the labour market and make them more effective at competing for jobs. Its comprehensive welfare to work strategy and policies to make work pay are described in Chapter 4 of the EFSR.

Demand and output

BI5   Forward-looking indicators have yet to provide clear evidence of the anticipated slowing in domestic demand in early 2000. Although the millennium is a possible complicating factor, it appears to have had fairly limited real economy impacts. The vast majority of business surveys, for example, have signalled only a very partial easing in the pace of activity during the first quarter of 2000.

BI6   Household spending in particular continues to be driven by rising real incomes, falling unemployment and continued strong gains in wealth, the latter underpinned by the recent acceleration in house prices. Retail sales volumes grew rapidly in the three months to February, and headline consumer confidence has remained close to record levels early this year, despite higher interest rates. Household consumption is forecast to grow at an annualised rate of 4 per cent during the first half of 2000. For a period, this is likely to be partially offset by more moderate business investment growth, with company spending strengthening only gradually from its temporary dip in autumn 1999. Growth in export volumes during the first half of 2000 is also likely to be much less rapid than in mid-1999, when trade performance rebounded exceptionally from a weak base.

BI7   Domestic demand growth is expected to rise to $3^{3}/_{4}$ to 4 per cent during 2000 as a whole, 1 percentage point higher than forecast in the Pre-Budget Report. This largely reflects much stronger than anticipated underlying strength in consumer demand. Household consumption is now forecast to grow by $3^{1}/_{2}$ to $3^{3}/_{4}$ per cent in 2000, only partly reflecting higher real income growth, and the saving ratio is now projected to fall to $5^{1}/_{2}$ per cent, $^{3}/_{4}$ percentage point lower than forecast in the Pre-Budget Report. Stronger household spending is accompanied by similar upward revisions to forecast growth in fixed investment and government consumption.

B18   More buoyant domestic demand is offset by a weaker forecast for net trade, partly due to correspondingly faster growth in import volumes. However, the recent unexpected strength in sterling is also likely to impact on underlying trade performance, and net exports are now forecast to reduce growth by 1 percentage point in 2000. Overall, GDP is expected to grow by $2^3/_4$ to $3^1/_4$ per cent in 2000 as a whole, an upward revision of $^1/_4$ percentage point from the Pre-Budget Report forecast.

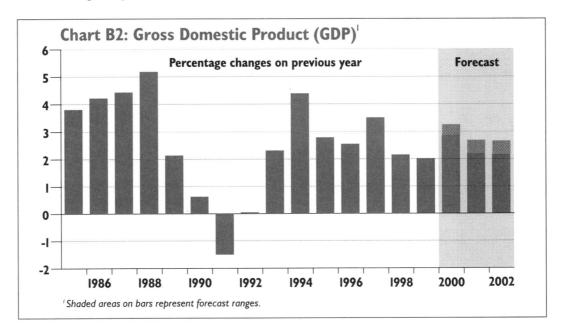

Chart B2: Gross Domestic Product (GDP)[1]

Percentage changes on previous year   Forecast

[1] Shaded areas on bars represent forecast ranges.

B19   The starting point of RPIX inflation below the Government's target creates headroom for above trend economic growth in 2000. The economy is expected gradually to rise further above trend in the first half of 2000, with a positive non-oil output gap of around $^1/_2$ per cent projected at the end of the year. Although downward retail price pressures can be expected to persist for a period, the positive output gap means that the economy cannot afford to out-run its trend growth rate in later years. This underlines the importance of a return to more sustainable rates of expansion in domestic demand, and household consumption in particular.

B20   The Monetary Policy Committee of the Bank of England has again moved pre-emptively, raising base rates by 1 percentage point since September last year. Within a credible policy framework, such moves are likely to have a significant impact, and a marked slowing in household spending growth is expected from the second half of 2000. Household consumption growth is forecast to fall to 2 to $2^1/_2$ per cent in 2001. This is expected to drive a deceleration in domestic demand next year, much in line with the latest independent consensus. With the negative net export contribution to activity projected broadly to unwind, this implies a more modest easing in overall GDP growth back to its trend rate of $2^1/_4$ to $2^3/_4$ per cent in 2001, and remaining within this range in 2002.

B21   As always, the economic outlook is subject to considerable uncertainties – average absolute errors in forecasts over the past ten years are reported in Table B6. In particular, there is a strong risk of more rapid growth in domestic demand, at least in the near term. Upside risks to the outlook for consumption and investment spending are discussed in the second half of this chapter. They are balanced, to some extent, by the possibility of a correction in global equity prices and sharper slowing in US and world growth. This would have direct implications for UK stock prices, export demand and sterling. Moreover, it would pose the risk of a sudden deterioration in private sector balance sheets, prompting a much sharper deceleration in domestic spending.

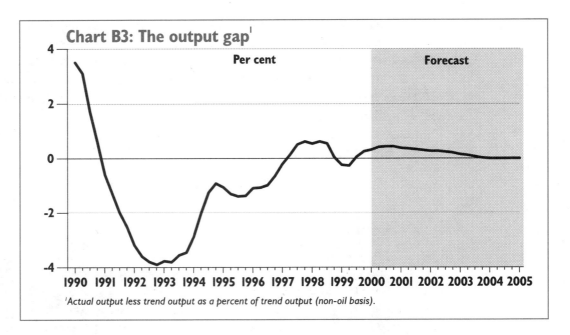

Chart B3: The output gap[1]

Per cent

Forecast

[1]Actual output less trend output as a percent of trend output (non-oil basis).

Trend output growth

B22   The mid-points of the GDP forecast ranges are anchored on an assumption of $2^1/_2$ per cent a year trend output growth in the medium term. This neutral assessment of non-inflationary growth prospects was set out in detail in the Pre-Budget Report. Projections for the public finances (Chapter C) are still based on the low end of the forecast ranges, consistent with a deliberately cautious assumption of $2^1/_4$ per cent trend growth.

B23   The neutral $2^1/_2$ per cent assumption is broadly in line with most independent analyses, though a wider range of views exists in terms of the prospective contributions from trend productivity growth and changes in the employment rate. Within the neutral assumption, productivity is projected to grow by 2 per cent a year which, in underlying terms, is in line with trend performance during the 1990s. As forecast in November, latest data now signal a cyclical recovery in productivity growth back towards this neutral rate. The neutral view also includes a modest 0.1 percentage points a year contribution to trend growth from an increasing employment rate, comprising small falls in both inactivity and unemployment rate components. The trend decline in inactivity reflects some assumed continuation of longer-term trends, particularly towards higher female labour market activity, outweighing the expected upward shift in the population distribution towards age cohorts with lower activity rates.

B24   In all areas, the Government is aiming for a better outcome. Its comprehensive range of policies to raise productivity growth and get more people into work is described fully in EFSR Chapters 3 and 4. Building upon the platform of economic stability on which sustained increases in output and employment depend, they offer the clear potential for stronger non-inflationary growth in the medium term. This is illustrated by the upper ends of the forecast ranges, based on $2^3/_4$ per cent a year trend growth in the medium term.

B25   However, there are still further possibilities for upside potential. The share of business investment in real GDP has risen to record levels over recent years and, within that, spending on Information and Communications Technology (ICT) appears to have been particularly strong. It is too early to assume that the rapid adoption of 'new economy' technologies has raised potential output growth, though the highly favourable growth and inflation performance of the US economy in recent years suggests this is possible.

B26   In particular, the growth of e-commerce has the potential to increase competition and efficiency, through a combination of lower market entry costs, enhanced price transparency, rationalisation of supply chains and reduced inventory holdings. However, whereas the overall effect could be higher sustainable growth and lower prices, the process of transition could see greater dispersion in economic performance. Businesses failing to keep up with the pace of diffusion of e-commerce may risk falling casualty to on-going margin squeeze. Significant impacts will probably take time to emerge, even though the current low weight of e-transactions in overall UK activity probably understates its influence. Behaviour of firms, even in sectors where internet usage is low, is likely to be increasingly affected by the spur of competition associated with e-commerce.

Inflation

B27   RPIX inflation has been just below its target level since April 1999, averaging $2^1/_4$ per cent for the year as a whole. This modest undershoot has persisted rather longer than expected a year ago, despite stronger than expected growth in output and unit labour costs, and the oil price more than doubling during 1999. These factors were outweighed by a sharp squeeze in business margins and continued weakness in non-oil import prices.

B28   The deflationary trend in retail goods prices more than accounts for recent inflation outturns. Retail goods inflation has fallen to around zero, down from well over 1 per cent early last year. However, abstracting from the impact of higher petrol prices, goods prices have fallen quite sharply. Underlying output price inflation (excluding food, beverages, tobacco and petroleum) has also remained subdued. Falling import prices have intensified competitive pressures on both domestic producers and retailers, prompting a very sharp compression in aggregate business margins during 1999. There is much evidence of keener price competition and discounting among retail outlets, with recent inflation rates for both food and clothing and footwear standing at 40-year lows. A similar story is found even in some areas of strongest demand last year, such as household goods.

B29   Such factors have had much less impact in the services sector, which is less directly exposed to the level of sterling. Excluding rent and utilities, services inflation rose from $4^1/_4$ per cent to $5^1/_2$ per cent during the course of 1999, providing a clear reflection of rapid growth in domestic demand and a tight labour market. While stronger productivity growth led to some moderation in unit wage cost pressures during 1999, nominal earnings have accelerated sharply recently and are now growing in excess of the $4^1/_2$ per cent rate that the Bank of England has said is consistent with the inflation target in the medium term. Growth in total costs is also being buoyed by the flatter trend in non-oil import prices.

B30   RPIX inflation is expected to remain below target throughout 2000, gradually returning to $2^1/_2$ per cent in early 2001. This partly reflects a moderating contribution to inflation from indirect taxes compared with 1999 and also utility price cuts in water, electricity and gas from April 2000 onwards. Sterling's recent strength is likely to extend the deflationary trend in goods prices in the near term, slightly prolonging RPIX inflation's undershoot of target compared to the Pre-Budget Report forecast. However, even at constant UK interest rates, for example, an uncovered interest parity exchange rate condition would imply a growing contribution from rising import price inflation thereafter. Together with a declining negative contribution from falling business margins during the course of 2000 and into 2001, this is expected to offset some further easing in unit wage cost growth, returning RPIX inflation to its target level early in 2001.

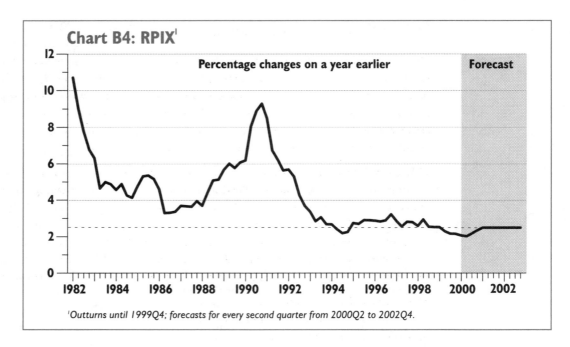

Chart B4: RPIX[1]

Percentage changes on a year earlier

Forecast

[1]*Outturns until 1999Q4; forecasts for every second quarter from 2000Q2 to 2002Q4.*

B31   On the HICP measure, which was developed to facilitate comparisons between EU countries, the UK now has the lowest inflation rate in the EU. In February UK HICP inflation was just 1 per cent, following a record low of 0.8 per cent in January. This provides a further reflection of weak price pressures in the UK goods sector. In the Eurozone, by contrast, goods inflation has been pushed up by the euro's depreciation and related stronger impact from rising oil prices. As in the Pre-Budget Report forecast, the current 1.2 percentage point divergence between UK HICP and RPIX inflation is expected to narrow over the next few years.

B32   The main upside risk to the inflation outlook is that domestic cost pressures could turn out to be stronger than expected. An examination of previous cycles shows that current inflation outturns are a poor guide to prospects (Box B3). With the economy estimated to be above its trend level and, as yet, few signs that the pace of domestic demand has slowed to more sustainable rates, there is a risk that domestically-generated inflationary pressures could pick up rather than ease. Combined with rising import price inflation, this could lead to stronger than forecast RPIX inflation later this year and into 2001.

B33   The December national accounts release included major upward revisions to GDP deflator inflation over the past two years, with implied inflation rates for both private and government consumption now higher. However, GDP deflator inflation is still forecast to fall from 3.3 per cent in 1998–99 to around $2^{1}/_{2}$ per cent in 1999–2000 overall. This reflects a smaller contribution from the terms of trade and lower consumers' expenditure deflator (CED) inflation, subsequently pushing GDP deflator inflation down further to $2^{1}/_{4}$ per cent in 2000–01. GDP deflator inflation is forecast to return to $2^{1}/_{2}$ per cent in 2001–02.

Box B3: Inflation and the economic cycle

Output gap analysis suggests that inflation tends to rise when output is above its trend level and fall when output is below potential. This relationship is far from precise: it depends on changes in inflation being unanticipated, and also on external price pressures and hence exchange rate movements. Moreover, the output gap is difficult to measure. Nevertheless, the deviation of output from its trend level typically appears to offer a fairly reliable gauge of domestically-generated inflationary pressures.

This model conforms with the familiar view that upward or downward pressures on inflation take time to build following either an upturn or slowing in output growth. However, its conclusions are in fact much stronger than this, particularly if cycles are fairly symmetric. GDP growth is likely to be at its strongest around the point at which the economy approaches trend from below, and yet downward inflationary pressures will persist until the output gap is fully closed. Conversely, inflation is likely to peak just around the point where growth hits a low point as the economy returns to trend from above.

These stylised predictions seem to fit the facts of recent cycles. Following the recession of the early 1980s, stronger growth gradually returned the economy to its trend level by the middle of the decade. Inflation fell sharply over this period, and did not bottom out until mid-1986 (albeit helped by the oil price). Broadly as the output gap model predicts, this coincided with the onset of the strongest output growth, with GDP growth averaging more than $4^1/_2$ per cent from 1986 to 1988.

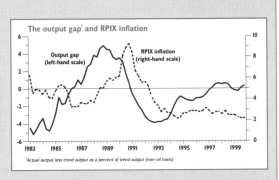

The output gap[1] and RPIX inflation

Output gap (left-hand scale)

RPIX inflation (right-hand scale)

[1] Actual output less trend output as a percent of trend output (non-oil basis).

As the economy moved above trend after 1986, inflation began to turn upwards. But, at around 4 per cent in the first half of 1988, it appeared still subdued even three years into the boom in domestic demand and despite the preceding sharp depreciation in sterling. Partly in response to these subdued inflation outturns, monetary policy failed to act early enough to prevent the substantial boom of the late 1980s, notwithstanding clear warning signals from rising capacity utilisation, house prices and the current account deficit. From mid-1988 prices accelerated sharply, with inflation approaching double-digits during 1990. This led to a sharp policy tightening, and by October 1989 interest rates had doubled to 15 per cent, eventually tipping the economy into recession. Inflation meanwhile peaked in autumn 1990, just as the sharpest output losses took output back to trend, thus marking the end of a turbulent 11-year cycle.

Direct parallels with previous cycles must be treated with great caution. Consistent with the Government's commitment to delivering economic stability, the economy has remained much closer to its sustainable position over the past three years. This limits the usefulness of the output gap approach, given the substantial margins of error. However, one of the key lessons of the 1980s was that surprisingly benign inflation outturns can persist alongside a peak in output growth. Under the output gap framework, they should be expected to. This underlines the importance of setting monetary policy in a forward-looking context.

Independent forecasts

B34   Independent forecasts for the UK economy have strengthened further since the publication of the Pre-Budget Report. The independent consensus for GDP growth is 3.1 per cent for 2000, an increase of $^1/_2$ percentage point since the autumn. For 2001, the average independent forecast is for GDP to grow by 2.6 per cent, a modest easing to a more sustainable rate of growth. The Budget 2000 growth forecasts, following the small upward revision in 2000, are almost exactly in line with the independent consensus both this year and next.

Table B2: Budget and independent[1] forecasts

	Percentage changes on a year earlier unless otherwise stated					
	2000			2001		
		Independent			Independent	
	March Budget	Average	Range	March Budget	Average	Range
Gross domestic product	2³/₄ to 3¹/₄	3.1	2.0 to 3.7	2¹/₄ to 2³/₄	2·6	1·6 to 3·8
RPIX (Q4)	2¹/₄	2·1	1·3 to 2·8	2¹/₂	2·4	1·5 to 2·8
Current account (£ billion)	–20¹/₂	–15.6	–28.0 to –9.3	–21	–16.4	–39.0 to –5·0

[1] 'Forecasts for the UK Economy: A Comparison of Independent Forecasts', March 2000.

B35   Like the Budget 2000 forecast, independent forecasters expect the current combination of strong growth and subdued retail price pressures to persist for a period. The average independent forecast for RPIX inflation in the fourth quarter of 2000 is now 2.1 per cent, down around $^1/_4$ percentage point since November. It is expected to return gradually to the Government's $2^1/_2$ per cent target by the end of next year.

B36   Independent forecasts for the balance of payments current account have changed little over recent months, and deficits equivalent to between $1^1/_2$ and $1^3/_4$ per cent of GDP are expected in both 2000 and 2001. However, there exists a considerable range of views around these average forecasts. Larger than expected current account deficits would provide a warning signal of stronger than expected demand, borrowing and inflationary pressures.

FORECAST ISSUES AND RISKS

The household sector

B37   Household consumption rose by 4 per cent in 1999, in line with the Pre-Budget Report forecast, and readily explicable in terms of the fundamental drivers of consumer demand. Growth in real household disposable incomes was somewhat weaker than forecast, despite a sharp rise to $3^1/_4$ per cent, which reflected a continued robust expansion in employment incomes and a significant decline in growth in taxes on income as the impact of self-assessment worked through. Stronger underlying growth in spending therefore led to an unexpected fall in the saving ratio, with rapid gains in household wealth perhaps boosting spending by more than 1 percentage point relative to incomes last year. In particular, house prices accelerated unexpectedly sharply from mid-1999. Falling interest rates in the year to June 1999 also supported above trend consumption growth during the first half of the year.

B38   While growth in total spending is reported to have eased during the course of 1999, latest indicators are very strong. Slower recorded growth in vehicles spending is uncertain due to the change in the system of vehicle registrations, and reported easing in purchases of non-durable goods and services contrasts with the sharp acceleration in retail sales volumes and still strong services output growth. Household consumption is now forecast to grow by $3^1/_2$ to $3^3/_4$ per cent in 2000 as a whole, 1 percentage point higher than in the Pre-Budget Report, reflecting both stronger growth in employment incomes and lower than previously expected saving. Precautionary motives for saving have fallen sharply with enhanced macroeconomic and job prospects: the proportion of households expecting higher unemployment has fallen sharply over the past year and consumers' confidence in their future financial situation has stabilised around record levels.

Table B3: Household sector[1] expenditure and income

	Percentage changes on previous year			
		Forecast		
	1999	2000	2001	2002
Household consumption[2]	4	$3^1/_2$ to $3^3/_4$	2 to $2^1/_2$	$1^3/_4$ to $2^1/_4$
Real household disposable income	$3^1/_4$	$3^3/_4$ to 4	$2^3/_4$ to $3^1/_4$	$2^1/_2$ to 3
Saving ratio (level, per cent)	$5^3/_4$	$5^1/_2$	6	$6^3/_4$

[1] Including non-profit institutions serving households.
[2] At constant prices.

B39   Consumption growth is, however, expected to ease later in 2000, subsequently falling just below trend rates during 2001 with the saving ratio rising to 6 per cent. This slowing will partly reflect the direct impact of recent increases in interest rates. Rising mortgage interest payments, together with the abolition of MIRAS and increased stamp duty, are likely to dampen growth in housing demand and prices. This should indirectly restrain growth in consumer spending into 2001 via the effects on household wealth and borrowing. Household consumption growth is forecast to fall to 2 to $2^1/_2$ per cent in 2001, broadly in line with independent forecasts, and to ease a little further in 2002.

B40   There are clear upside risks to the outlook. The tight labour market poses a direct upside risk to growth in earnings and hence consumer spending, at least in the short term. Moreover, there remains a strong possibility that households may choose to react more positively to rapid gains in wealth over recent years. As a proportion of household income, total household wealth is estimated to have risen to a record level in the fourth quarter of 1999. One way of releasing such gains to boost spending is through secured borrowing above that needed for house purchase or improvements, known as mortgage equity withdrawal. Although still substantially lower than in the 1980s, the Bank of England estimates that equity withdrawal rose quite sharply in the second half of 1999, bolstering already strong growth in consumer credit. Box B4 discusses the housing market outlook and risks in more detail.

Box B4: Housing and the wider economy – outlook and risks

House price inflation rose sharply from mid-1999, recently reaching around 15 per cent. Housing transactions also stepped up markedly, rising 9 per cent during the year as a whole, while secured borrowing grew by over 8 per cent in the year to January 2000 compared to under 6 per cent a year earlier.

Box A4 of the Pre-Budget Report discussed the potential links between the housing market and wider economic performance. Direct impacts, such as the boost to spending associated with higher levels of housing transactions, are uncontroversial, and non-vehicle durables spending has been very strong. But indirect effects on spending are not straightforward. While recent growth in housing values, lending and equity withdrawal has been rapid, this may be more a symptom of the underlying strength in consumer demand rather than an explanation or cause. The strong past association between changes in household wealth and consumer confidence does, however, raise the risk of much stronger growth in household consumption in 2000. This depends on whether current housing market signals add to existing knowledge of the underlying momentum in consumer demand.

Annual growth in real household disposable incomes is estimated to have recently risen to around 5 per cent. Given a fairly fixed supply of housing in the short run, this is probably sufficient to explain house price inflation close to double digit rates in the context of conventional models of housing demand. Current house price gains have moved beyond this reflecting, among other things, the still relatively low mortgage interest payments burden, although the level of prices does not appear out of line with fundamentals.

House price-earnings ratio[1]

1995=100

Long-run average

[1]Ratio of house prices to wages and salaries per employee. House prices are measured by the DETR index up to 1995 to obtain a long time-series. Thereafter they are measured by the average of DETR, Halifax and Nationwide indices in view of short-term divergences.

The regional dimension of recent housing market performance is also a concern. While less marked than in previous economic cycles, house price gains have been most rapid in London and the South East. This is likely to reflect the relatively fixed supply of land and housing, and perhaps greater cyclicality in local incomes and demand. Unchecked, it would raise the possibility of stronger house price inflation elsewhere.

The risk that housing market developments could encourage wider macroeconomic instability highlights the importance of the Government's monetary framework. The new arrangements are designed to promote forward-looking policy setting taking full account of all available economic indicators. Despite currently subdued retail price pressures, interest rates have risen by 1 percentage point since their low of 5 per cent in June last year. The removal of MIRAS from April 2000 and increased stamp duty will also contribute to greater sustainability in housing and consumer demand.

House price inflation and transactions are expected to remain high for a while, given strong near-term economic growth and the significant stock of approved mortgage lending. However, pressures are likely to ease later in 2000 and into 2001 as higher house prices, increased post-tax interest rates and some slowing in income growth dampen housing demand. Nevertheless, past housing cycles have been characterised by stronger and more persistent overshooting in activity and prices relative to longer-term sustainable levels. While the new macroeconomic framework provides a more credible guard against speculative behaviour, policy will need to remain alert to the risks.

Companies and investment

B41   Business investment growth eased further in the second half of 1999, as slower private service sector spending combined with continuing weakness in manufacturing. A temporary retrenchment was anticipated in the Pre-Budget Report and earlier forecasts, in lagged response to the earlier deterioration in business optimism, profit and output expectations. These factors were subsequently reflected in an estimated $3/4$ percentage point reduction in private non-financial companies (NFCs) profits as a per cent of GDP in 1999. Fears of potential millennium bug related problems may also have contributed to the slowdown, with major ICT projects increasingly held off as the date change drew near.

B42   Most indicators suggest that the climate for investment has improved significantly over the past year. With stronger economic growth, NFC profits have begun to recover, rising an estimated 4 per cent by the fourth quarter of 1999 from their trough in the first quarter, though partly reflecting buoyant North-Sea incomes. Rising capacity utilisation and buoyant output expectations have prompted continued improvements in investment intentions overall. BCC survey evidence shows that plant and machinery investment intentions have risen back to their strong 1995–97 average in the service sector. In manufacturing they are also above the longer-run average, though CBI survey evidence paints a weaker picture. These cyclical improvements have reinforced existing incentives to invest. Company rates of return are high relative to the cost of capital, the buoyant stock market has tended to lower the cost of equity finance, and corporate income gearing (the ratio of debt service costs to corporate income) remains low.

B43   However, NFC's net borrowing is estimated at around 2 per cent of GDP in 1999 and is forecast to rise to around 3 per cent of GDP in 2000. While larger deficits were recorded in the late 1980s, the forecast cautiously assumes that companies will aim to curtail borrowing gradually in the period ahead, implying more modest rates of expansion in capital spending compared to recent years. Overall business investment is forecast to grow by $2^{1}/4$ to $2^{3}/4$ per cent in 2000, strengthening fairly gradually from its dip last autumn in lagged response to stronger output growth. It is forecast to rise by 2 to $2^{1}/2$ per cent in 2001, reflecting the general easing in economic growth, remaining within this range in 2002.

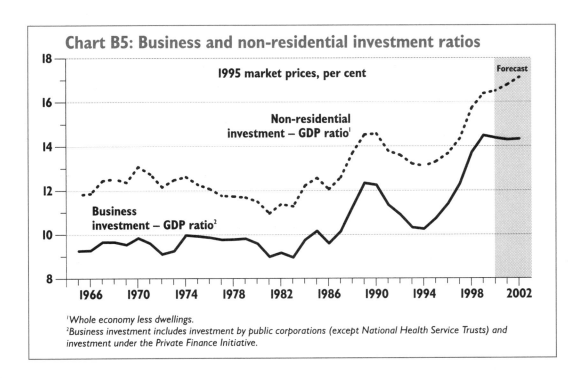

Chart B5: Business and non-residential investment ratios

Whole economy less dwellings.
Business investment includes investment by public corporations (except National Health Service Trusts) and investment under the Private Finance Initiative.

Box B5: Business investment in the UK and G7 countries

The capital stock per worker in the UK business sector is estimated to be around 20 per cent lower than in the US and 40 per cent below that in Germany[1]. This is a reflection of past low levels of business investment and is a major factor in the UK's relatively low level of labour productivity. In recent years, however, business investment has increased rapidly in the UK, with growth averaging more than 11 per cent a year since 1997.

As a result, the share of business investment in GDP rose to 14.5 per cent in 1999, easily surpassing the previous peak of 12.3 per cent recorded in 1989. Indeed, for the first time since at least 1965, the UK business investment ratio may have exceeded the average of the other G7 countries. This also rose strongly from the mid-1990s, though mainly reflecting strong growth in the US. Business investment ratios in other G7 economies were little changed.

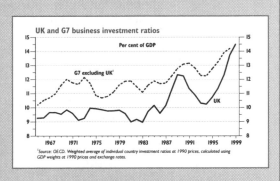

The possible causes of the improved UK investment performance were discussed in the Pre-Budget Report. With the economy remaining relatively close to trend in recent years, the increase in the investment ratio goes well beyond cyclical factors. As in the US, an increasing share of ICT investment has been important. Enhanced macroeconomic stability in output, inflation and interest rates is also likely to have played a key part.

[1] *See Britain's productivity performance 1950-1995, O'Mahoney M. (1999).*

B44   As a per cent of GDP, this would maintain the business investment ratio very close to its recent record level, locking in the strong gains of recent years (see Box B5). However, the forecast is subject to upside risks, and a return to much more rapid rates of investment growth is quite possible. Strong capital spending has partly reflected faster depreciation as a result of the increasing share of ICT and other specialist equipment with shorter asset lives, and such investment might be expected to move progressively into higher gear as new technology opens up ever more opportunities. Moreover, company balance sheets on standard aggregate measures remain strong, suggesting larger financial deficits to support stronger investment spending might be readily financeable. Against that, the comfortable levels of capital gearing and the ratio of company financial assets to loans outstanding are vulnerable to equity valuations; and company liquidity, as measured by the ratio of deposits and currency to loans outstanding, declined through 1999.

B45   Total fixed capital formation is likely to be boosted this year by a stronger expansion in private dwellings investment, as house builders react to strong price gains and enhanced profitability. It is also buoyed by strong growth in general government investment over the forecast period reflecting the Government's commitment to the renewal and modernisation of the public sector capital stock, delivering the desired level of improvement within the fiscal rules (see EFSR Chapters 2 and 5).

Table B4: Gross fixed capital formation

| | Percentage changes on previous year | | | |
| | | Forecast | | |
	1999	2000	2001	2002
Whole economy[1]	$5^1/_4$	$3^1/_4$ to $3^3/_4$	$3^3/_4$ to $4^1/_4$	$3^3/_4$ to $4^1/_4$
of which:				
Business[2,3]	$7^3/_4$	$2^1/_4$ to $2^3/_4$	2 to $2^1/_2$	2 to $2^1/_2$
Private dwellings[3]	$-^3/_4$	3 to $3^1/_2$	$1^3/_4$ to $2^1/_4$	2 to $2^1/_2$
General government[3,4]	$^1/_2$	$18^1/_4$	20	$17^1/_2$

[1] Includes costs associated with the transfer of ownership of land and existing buildings.

[2] Private sector and public corporations' (except National Health Service Trusts) non-residential investment. Includes investment under the Private Finance Initiative.

[3] Excludes purchases less sales of land and existing buildings.

[4] Includes National Health Service Trusts.

Trade and the balance of payments

B46   The current account has deteriorated in recent years, mainly reflecting the increased deficit in trade in goods and services, which rose to £15.4 billion last year from a position of broad balance in 1997. This was compounded in 1999 by an estimated £7 billion fall in the surplus on investment income, exceptionally buoyed in 1998 by losses made by UK-based foreign-owned banks and oil companies in the wake of global financial turbulence. The current account deficit is now estimated at around £12 billion in 1999, as forecast in the Pre-Budget Report.

B47   A growing trade in goods deficit with non-EU countries has dominated performance since 1997, largely reflecting weak export growth. Excluding oil, growth in total goods export volumes fell to rates of under 3 per cent in both 1998 and 1999, driven first by sharp falls to non-EU countries as turbulence in Asia and other emerging markets reached its peak, and later compounded by weakening expansion in demand from EU countries. The deterioration partly reflected, though outpaced, the sharp slowdown in UK export markets growth from 10 per cent in 1997 to just 6 per cent last year. Thus UK exporters lost market share, particularly during the course of 1998 as the Asian currency devaluations and earlier appreciation of sterling against European currencies began to bite. Such losses have, however, been partly contained by reductions in export prices, which have fallen 12 per cent since 1996, and efforts to restore cost competitiveness. By late 1999, manufacturing productivity growth was up around $5^1/_2$ per cent on a year earlier with unit wage costs falling for the first time since 1994.

B48   The significant turnaround in UK export performance since last spring partly reflects a sharp upturn in UK export markets with growth in Europe and Asia surpassing expectations during the second half of 1999, bolstering a still remarkable expansion in US activity. These developments, together with continued falls in UK export prices, appear to have offset the effects of further sterling appreciation, particularly against the euro. Survey measures of export confidence and demand have risen further, though in the fourth quarter of 1999 export volumes eased from high levels. UK export markets are now expected to grow by $7^1/_2$ per cent in 2000 and $6^1/_2$ per cent in 2001, upward revisions of $^3/_4$ percentage points since the Pre-Budget Report forecast. Forecast growth in export volumes of goods and services has, however, been revised down to $5^1/_2$ to 6 per cent in 2000 reflecting sterling's recent strengthening. This still implies a sharp improvement on performance in 1998 and 1999, and growth in export volumes is expected to continue at the same rate in later years.

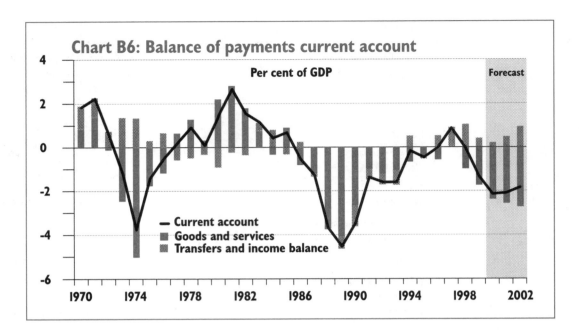

Chart B6: Balance of payments current account

Per cent of GDP

Forecast

— Current account
■ Goods and services
▨ Transfers and income balance

1970   1974   1978   1982   1986   1990   1994   1998   2002

B49   With import volumes boosted by falling prices and strong growth in domestic demand, net trade overall has continued to exert a significant drag on UK activity. Near-term strength in domestic spending will prolong this trend, though stronger export growth is expected to lower the negative contribution to growth from net trade to around 1 percentage point in 2000, unwinding further thereafter as import growth eases to trend rates. This implies some further widening in the trade in goods and services deficit, to around $2^1/_2$ per cent of GDP in 2000, which is $^3/_4$ percentage point more than forecast in November. The current account deficit is also forecast to be larger, stabilising at around $2^1/_4$ per cent of GDP in both 2000 and 2001 before starting to narrow.

Table B5: Trade in goods and services

	Percentage changes on previous year					£ billion
	Volumes		Prices[1]			Goods and services balance
	Exports	Imports	Exports	Imports	Terms of trade[2]	
1999	$2^1/_2$	$7^1/_4$	$-1^1/_4$	$-2^1/_2$	$1^1/_2$	$-15^1/_2$
Forecast						
2000	$5^1/_2$ to 6	$7^3/_4$ to $8^1/_4$	$^3/_4$	1	$-^1/_4$	$-22^1/_4$
2001	$5^1/_2$ to 6	$5^1/_2$ to 6	$2^1/_2$	$2^3/_4$	$-^1/_2$	$-25^1/_4$
2002	$5^1/_2$ to 6	$5^1/_2$ to 6	$3^1/_2$	$3^1/_2$	0	$-28^1/_4$

[1] *Average value indices.*
[2] *Ratio of export to import prices.*

B50   There are clear downside risks to the outlook. Despite improvements in Europe and elsewhere, global demand remains heavily reliant on the US economy which would falter if equity values fell sharply. Persistent strength in sterling might also lead to a sharper fall in UK exporters' market share and stronger import penetration. However, attempting to target both the inflation rate and exchange rate in the short term would lead back to the policies that caused economic instability in the past: maintaining low inflation and sound public finances is essential to secure a stable and competitive exchange rate in the medium term.

Table B6: Summary of economic prospects[1]

		Percentage changes on a year earlier unless otherwise stated			Average errors from past forecasts[3]	
			Forecast[2]			
	1999	2000	2001	2002	2000	2001
Output at constant market prices						
Gross domestic product (GDP)	2	2³/₄ to 3¹/₄	2¹/₄ to 2³/₄	2¹/₄ to 2³/₄	¹/₂	1
Manufacturing output	0	1³/₄ to 2¹/₄	1³/₄ to 2¹/₄	1³/₄ to 2¹/₄	³/₄	2¹/₂
Expenditure components of GDP at constant market prices[4]						
Domestic demand	3¹/₂	3³/₄ to 4	2¹/₂ to 3	2¹/₄ to 2³/₄	¹/₂	1¹/₄
Household consumption[5]	4	3¹/₂ to 3³/₄	2 to 2¹/₂	1³/₄ to 2¹/₄	³/₄	1¹/₄
General government consumption	3¹/₂	4	2³/₄	4¹/₄	1	1¹/₄
Fixed investment	5¹/₄	3¹/₄ to 3³/₄	3³/₄ to 4¹/₄	3³/₄ to 4¹/₄	1³/₄	2³/₄
Change in inventories[6]	−³/₄	¹/₄	0	−¹/₄ to 0	¹/₄	¹/₂
Export of goods and services	2¹/₂	5¹/₂ to 6	5¹/₂ to 6	5¹/₂ to 6	1³/₄	2¹/₂
Imports of goods and services	7¹/₄	7³/₄ to 8¹/₄	5¹/₂ to 6	5¹/₂ to 6	1³/₄	2³/₄
Balance of payments current account						
£ billion	−12¹/₄	−20¹/₂	−21	−19³/₄	7	9
per cent of GDP	−1¹/₂	−2¹/₄	−2¹/₄	−2	³/₄	1
Inflation						
RPIX (Q4)	2¹/₄	2¹/₄	2¹/₂	2¹/₂	³/₄	1
Producer output prices (Q4)[7]	1¹/₄	2	2	2¹/₄	1	1³/₄
GDP deflator at market prices (financial year)	2¹/₂	2¹/₄	2¹/₂	2¹/₂	³/₄	1
Money GDP at market prices (financial year)						
£ billion	901	946 to 951	990 to 1000	1037 to 1053	7	12
percentage change	5	5 to 5¹/₂	4³/₄ to 5¹/₄	4³/₄ to 5¹/₄	³/₄	1¹/₄

[1] The forecast is consistent with the national accounts and balance of payments statistics to the fourth quarter of 1999, released by the Office for National Statistics on 28 February 2000. See also footnote 1 on the first page of this chapter.

[2] The size of the growth ranges for GDP components may differ from those for total GDP growth because of rounding and the assumed invariance of the levels of public spending within the forecast ranges.

[3] Average absolute errors for current year and year-ahead projections made in spring forecasts over the past ten years. The average errors for the current account are calculated as a percent of GDP, with £ billion figures calculated by scaling the errors by forecast money GDP in 2000 and 2001.

[4] Further detail on the expenditure components of GDP is given in Table B7.

[5] Includes households and non-profit institutions serving households.

[6] Contribution to GDP growth, percentage points.

[7] Excluding excise duties.

Table B7: Gross domestic product and its components

	£ billion at 1995 prices, seasonally adjusted									
	Household consumption[1]	General government consumption	Fixed investment	Change in inventories	Domestic demand	Exports of goods and services	Total final expenditure	*Less* imports of goods and services	*Plus* statistical discrepancy[2]	GDP at market prices
1999	524.9	146.6	153.0	-1.7	823.1	248.2	1071.3	285.2	2.2	788.4
2000	542.7 to 544.8	152.5	158.1 to 158.7	0.2 to 0.8	853.5 to 856.9	262.2 to 263.2	1115.6 to 1120.1	307.3 to 308.5	2.4	810.8 to 814.0
2001	553.3 to 558.3	156.8	163.8 to 165.3	-0.1 to 1.3	873.8 to 881.6	276.3 to 278.8	1150.2 to 1160.4	324.0 to 326.9	2.4	828.5 to 835.9
2002	562.8 to 570.6	163.4	170.1 to 172.4	-1.7 to 0.5	894.5 to 906.8	291.8 to 295.8	1186.3 to 1202.6	342.2 to 346.9	2.4	846.4 to 858.1
1999 1st half	260.5	72.8	75.8	-1.0	408.2	120.4	528.6	138.8	1.0	390.8
2nd half	264.5	73.8	77.2	-0.7	414.9	127.8	542.8	146.4	1.2	397.5
2000 1st half	269.4 to 270.0	75.9	78.4 to 78.6	0.1 to 0.3	423.8 to 424.8	129.4 to 129.7	553.2 to 554.5	151.5 to 151.9	1.2	402.9 to 403.9
2nd half	273.3 to 274.8	76.6	79.6 to 80.1	0.1 to 0.6	429.7 to 432.1	132.8 to 133.5	562.4 to 565.5	155.8 to 156.7	1.2	407.8 to 410.1
2001 1st half	275.6 to 277.7	77.6	81.1 to 81.7	0.0 to 0.6	434.4 to 437.7	136.3 to 137.3	570.7 to 574.9	159.8 to 161.0	1.2	412.1 to 415.2
2nd half	277.7 to 280.5	79.2	82.7 to 83.6	-0.2 to 0.6	439.4 to 443.9	140.1 to 141.5	579.5 to 585.5	164.3 to 165.9	1.2	416.5 to 420.7
2002 1st half	280.0 to 283.5	81.2	84.3 to 85.3	-0.8 to 0.2	444.6 to 450.1	143.9 to 145.7	588.5 to 595.8	168.8 to 170.8	1.2	421.0 to 426.2
2nd half	282.8 to 287.1	82.2	85.8 to 87.1	–0·9 to 0·3	449.9 to 456.7	147·9 to 150.1	597.8 to 606.8	173.5 to 176.1	1.2	425.5 to 431.9
	Percentage changes on previous year[3,4]									
1999	4	3½	5¼	–¾	3½	2½	3¼	7¼	¼	2
2000	3½ to 3¾	4	3¼ to 3¾	¼	3¾ to 4	5½ to 6	4¼ to 4½	7¾ to 8¼	0	2¾ to 3¼
2001	2 to 2½	2¾	3¾ to 4¼	0	2½ to 3	5½ to 6	3 to 3½	5½ to 6	0	2¼ to 2¾
2002	1¾ to 2¼	4¼	3¾ to 4¼	–¼ to 0	2¼ to 2¾	5½ to 6	3¼ to 3¾	5½ to 6	0	2¼ to 2¾

[1] *Includes households and non-profit institutions serving households.*

[2] *Expenditure adjustment.*

[3] *For change in inventories and the statistical discrepancy, changes are expressed as a percent of GDP.*

[4] *The size of the growth ranges for GDP components may differ from those for total GDP growth because of rounding and the assumed invariance of the levels of public spending within the forecast ranges.*

THE WORLD ECONOMY

Overview

B51   The global recovery is gathering momentum with strengthening growth in the Eurozone, Asia surpassing expectations, and a hesitant recovery in Latin America. Continuing US strength has helped compensate for weakness in Japan, and fears of global recession have given way to concerns about inflationary pressures. Investor sentiment towards emerging markets has improved. Divergences in the pattern of global demand and associated exchange rate developments have led to substantial increases in external current account imbalances, particularly in the US.

Table B8: The world economy

| | Percentage changes on a year earlier | | | |
| | | Forecast | | |
	1999[1]	**2000**	**2001**	**2002**
Major 7 countries[2]				
Real GDP	$2^3/_4$	3	$2^1/_2$	$2^1/_2$
Consumer price inflation[3]	$1^3/_4$	2	$1^3/_4$	$1^3/_4$
World trade in goods	5	7	$6^1/_2$	$6^1/_4$
UK export markets[4]	6	$7^1/_2$	$6^1/_2$	6

[1] *Estimates, except consumer price inflation.*

[2] *G7: US, Japan, Germany, France, UK, Italy and Canada.*

[3] *Final quarter of each period. For UK, RPIX.*

[4] *Other countries' imports of manufactures weighted according to their importance in UK exports.*

G7 activity

B52   In 1999 the US expansion continued to show resilience, with a recent pick up in exports complementing robust consumer and investment spending. Strong productivity gains and moderate wage growth have so far ensured little upward pressure on unit labour costs. However, rapid domestic demand growth and higher oil prices have contributed to a widening current account deficit. Stock market valuations remain high by most traditional measures, increasing the risk of financial market instability if these imbalances were to unwind rapidly. The US economy is likely to slow this year and next, as monetary policy tightening takes effect and domestic demand growth moderates.

B53   The Eurozone recovery continues to strengthen, helped by low interest rates, the depreciation of the euro, and improved external demand. In Japan, the outlook remains uncertain, with limited evidence, as yet, of a sustained private sector recovery. Ongoing fiscal stimulus and higher exports, helped by the sharp recovery in Asia, should stabilise the Japanese economy this year.

B54   GDP growth in 2000 is expected to become more balanced among the three main industrial country blocks, as the European recovery takes hold, Japan's economy stabilises and the US begins to slow. G7 growth is projected to rise to 3 per cent in 2000, before falling back to $2^1/_2$ per cent in 2001.

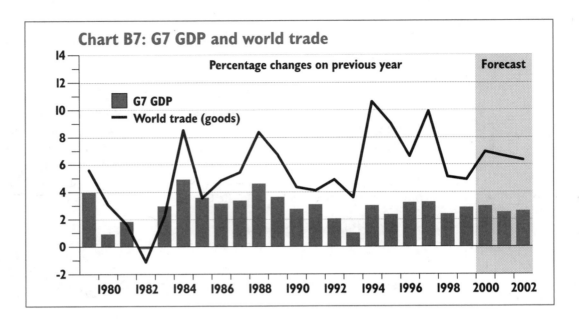

Chart B7: G7 GDP and world trade

G7 inflation

B55   Rising oil prices added to headline consumer price inflation in the major economies in 1999, and there was some upturn in the rate of growth of the prices of intermediate inputs. Nevertheless, core inflation – excluding energy and food prices – remained low. Stronger world growth and higher commodity prices are likely to continue to put pressure on G7 inflation in the short term. But considerable spare capacity in Japan and relatively subdued inflation in Europe should restrain the increase in international prices. Moreover, the overall impact of any given rise in commodity prices on the major industrialised economies has been lessened by the growing importance of services in total output and new energy-saving investments, which have helped to reduce the share of commodities in production and trade. G7 inflation is expected to rise in 2000 to an annual average of 2 per cent. Moderate increases in interest rates in the industrial countries are likely over the next 12 months, reflecting expected developments in activity and inflation.

Developing countries

B56   In developing countries, recoveries in Asian economies will progress and there are early signs of a turnaround in Latin America. The adjustment in some of the countries worst hit by the recent financial crisis, including Russia and Brazil, has been less severe than previously expected. Sharp increases in oil prices have clearly benefited the major oil-exporting developing countries.

B57   An improving external environment, rising commodity prices, ongoing adjustment and structural reform in emerging markets, and increasing confidence among both domestic and foreign investors, should help spur growth in developing countries this year. However, a sharp rise in world interest rates or a correction in global equity markets could trigger new financial disturbances which, together with necessary policy responses, would result in weaker shorter-term growth prospects.

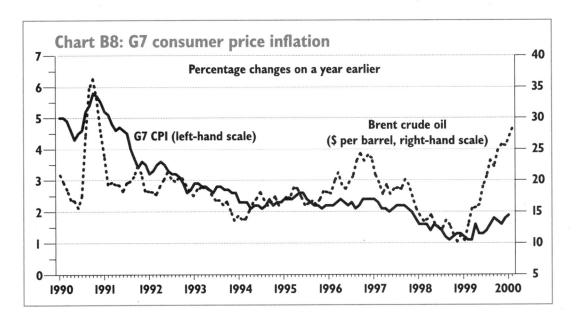

Chart B8: G7 consumer price inflation

World trade

B58 World trade grew by 5 per cent in 1999, driven by continued strength in US demand and the recovery in much of Asia. By contrast, trade in Europe remained sluggish. In 2000 world trade is expected to grow by 7 per cent, with the expansion in Asia and other emerging markets more than compensating for a modest slowing in US trade growth. World trade growth of 6^1/$_2$ per cent is forecast in 2001.

B59 UK export market growth slowed to 6 per cent in 1999, but still outstripped world trade growth due to the UK's relatively strong dependence on the US economy. Weaker imports in many of the UK's key export markets contributed to the slower growth. However, with improved prospects in Asia, Europe, Africa and the Middle East, UK export market growth is expected to increase to 7^1/$_2$ per cent this year, falling back to 6^1/$_2$ per cent in 2001 as the US economy slows.

C THE PUBLIC FINANCES

The latest projections of the public finances show that the underlying position remains sound. As a result of a continuing commitment to stability and prudence, the Government remains on track to meet its fiscal rules. This Budget locks in the fiscal tightening over the next two years, to a greater extent than projected in Budget 99, while releasing substantial new resources for the Government's priorities:

- the current budget surplus is estimated to be £17 billion (nearly 2 per cent of GDP) in 1999–2000. The surplus is projected to be around 1½ per cent of GDP over the two following years, and over ¾ per cent of GDP thereafter; and

- public sector net debt is projected to fall to 37.1 per cent of GDP by the end of financial year 1999–2000. It is projected to continue falling steadily as a percentage of GDP over the next three years, and to remain at about 32½ per cent of GDP after March 2003.

Cyclically-adjusted public sector net borrowing is estimated to be a repayment of 1.2 per cent of GDP in 1999-2000, and repayments of 0.5 and 0.3 per cent of GDP in the following two years. Modest deficits are projected from 2002-03, mostly reflecting the rapid growth of public investment.

INTRODUCTION

C1   Chapter 2 outlined the Government's fiscal framework, its fiscal rules, and how the latest projections of the public finances are consistent with meeting these rules. This chapter explains in more detail the Government's performance against the fiscal rules. It includes:

- five year ahead projections of the current budget surplus and public sector net debt, the key aggregates for assessing performance against the golden rule and the sustainable investment rule, respectively;

- projections of public sector net borrowing, the fiscal aggregate relevant to assessing the impact of fiscal policy on the economy;

- consistent projections of the cyclically-adjusted fiscal balances; and

- detailed analyses of the outlook for government receipts and expenditure.

MEETING THE FISCAL RULES

C2   The Government is on track to meet the fiscal rules throughout the next five years. Table C1 shows latest outturns for the key fiscal aggregates, together with estimates for the current year and projections up to 2004–05. Outturns and projections of other important measures of the public finances, including net borrowing and net worth, are also shown.

Table C1: Summary of public sector finances[1]

	Per cent of GDP						
	Outturn	Estimate	Projections				
	1998–99	1999–00	2000–01	2001–02	2002–03	2003–04	2004–05
Fairness and prudence							
Surplus on current budget	0.9	1.9	1.5	1.6	1.2	0.8	0.7
Cyclically-adjusted surplus on current budget	0.6	1.8	1.3	1.3	1.0	0.7	0.7
Average surplus since 1999–2000		1.9	1.7	1.7	1.5	1.4	1.3
Long-term sustainability							
Public sector net debt[2]	39.7	37.1	35.1	33.6	32.7	32.6	32.6
Net worth[2]	13.6	15.4	17.1	18.2	18.7	18.8	18.8
Primary balance	3.3	3.8	3.2	2.8	1.9	1.0	0.9
Economic impact							
Net investment	0.6	0.6	0.9	1.2	1.5	1.8	1.8
Public sector net borrowing (PSNB)	–0.3	–1.3	–0.7	–0.5	0.3	1.0	1.1
Cyclically-adjusted PSNB	–0.1	–1.2	–0.5	–0.3	0.5	1.1	1.1
Financing							
Central government net cash requirement[2]	–0.5	–0.6	–0.5	0.0	0.5	1.5	1.4
European commitments							
Maastricht deficit[3]	–0.6	–1.3	–0.6	–0.3	0.3	1.1	1.2
Maastricht debt ratio[4]	47.0	44.1	42.0	40.2	39.1	38.9	38.7
Memo: Output gap	0.2	0.1	0.4	0.3	0.2	0.1	0.0

[1] *Excluding windfall tax receipts and associated spending.*

[2] *Including windfall tax receipts and associated spending.*

[3] *General government net borrowing on an ESA95 basis. The Maastricht definition includes the windfall tax and associated spending.*

[4] *General government gross debt.*

C3   The current budget balance improved from a deficit of 3 per cent of GDP in 1996–97 to a surplus of nearly 1 per cent of GDP in 1998–99. The surplus is estimated to have risen to nearly 2 per cent of GDP in 1999–2000, despite the fact that non-oil GDP growth has been a little below its trend rate. Current budget surpluses of around 1¹/₂ per cent of GDP are projected over the next two years. Thereafter, surpluses are projected to fall gradually to around ³/₄ per cent of GDP by 2003–04. Consistent with the need to maintain a cautious approach, this profile shows that the Government is well on track to meet the golden rule over the projection period, with the average surplus on the current budget from 1999–2000 projected to be at least 1¹/₄ per cent of GDP throughout the next five years. The average current budget surplus over the period 1997–98 to 1999–2000, which early indications suggest may constitute a complete economic cycle, is estimated to have been ³/₄ per cent of GDP, indicating that the Government met the golden rule over this period.

C4   Net borrowing is equal to net investment minus the surplus on the current budget. Public sector net investment is projected to be a little over ¹/₂ per cent of GDP in 1999–2000, implying a repayment of net borrowing of 1¹/₄ per cent of GDP. The ratio of net investment to GDP is projected to more than double to 1³/₄ per cent by 2003–04. The rapid growth of net investment results in declining repayments of net borrowing over the next two years and, in conjunction with the effect of slower economic growth, and the Budget measures, modest deficits over the remainder of the period, consistent with meeting the sustainable investment rule.

C5   The primary balance is equal to net borrowing excluding net debt interest payments – thus abstracting from the implications of past fiscal deficits. If real interest rates exceed trend GDP growth, a primary surplus is required to stabilise the net debt ratio. The primary balance has swung from a deficit of $^1/_2$ per cent of GDP in 1996–97 to an estimated surplus of nearly 4 per cent of GDP in 1999–2000. It is projected to be in surplus by around 3 per cent of GDP during the next two years, and by 1-2 per cent of GDP thereafter.

C6   The central government net cash requirement was a repayment of $^1/_2$ per cent of GDP in 1998–99. Similar repayments are projected in 1999–2000 and the following year. From being in balance in 2001–02, the net cash requirement moves into deficit from 2002–03 onwards, mirroring the profile of public sector net borrowing. The approximate stock counterpart to the net cash requirement is public sector net debt. The projections of net cash repayments over the next two years implies a steady fall in the debt-GDP ratio, from 37.1 per cent in March 2000 to 32.7 per cent in March 2003. The debt-GDP ratio flattens out in 2003–04, as the public sector moves into deficit.

C7   The approximate stock counterpart to the current budget balance is public sector net worth. Current budget surpluses of about 1-2 per cent of GDP a year have begun to raise net worth. This follows a prolonged period in which the poor state of the public finances led to it falling below 15 per cent of GDP, from over 77 per cent of GDP in 1980–81. At present net worth is not used as a key indicator of the public finances, due mainly to the difficulties in measuring accurately many government assets and liabilities.

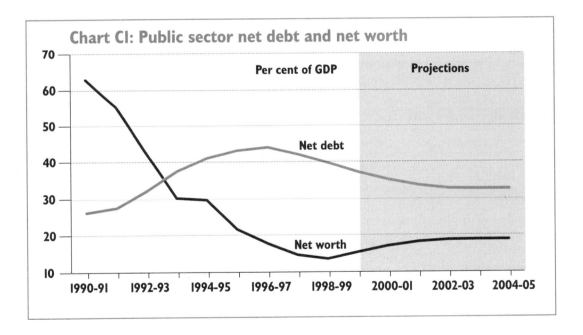

C8   Table C2 shows the updated estimates of the cyclically-adjusted current budget and net borrowing as a per cent of GDP, which allow underlying, or structural trends in the indicators to be seen more clearly, after the estimated effects of the economic cycle are removed.

Table C2: Fiscal balances[1]

	Outturns		Estimate	Projections				
	1997-98	1998-99	1999-00	2000-01	2001-02	2002-03	2003-04	2004-05
Budget balances								
Surplus on current budget	–0.7	0.9	1.9	1.5	1.6	1.2	0.8	0.7
Average surplus since 1999–2000			1.9	1.7	1.7	1.5	1.4	1.3
Net borrowing	1.2	–0.3	–1.3	–0.7	–0.5	0.3	1.0	1.1
Cyclically-adjusted budget balances								
Surplus on current budget	–0.6	0.6	1.8	1.3	1.3	1.0	0.7	0.7
Net borrowing	1.2	–0.1	–1.2	–0.5	–0.3	0.5	1.1	1.1
Memo: Output gap[2]	0.4	0.2	0.1	0.4	0.3	0.2	0.1	0.0

Per cent of GDP

[1] *Excluding windfall tax receipts and associated spending.*

[2] *Actual less trend output.*

C9   The cyclically-adjusted current balance has moved from a deficit of over 2 per cent of GDP in 1996–97 to a surplus of ¹/₂ per cent of GDP in 1998–99. It is estimated to have risen further in 1999–2000, to an estimated surplus of nearly 2 per cent of GDP. With the economy projected to be slightly above trend during most of the next five years, the cyclically-adjusted current budget surpluses are a little smaller than the unadjusted projections.

C10   There has been a corresponding improvement in cyclically-adjusted net borrowing, which is used to measure the fiscal stance. From a deficit of over 1 per cent of GDP in 1997–98, cyclically-adjusted net borrowing is estimated to be a repayment of 1¹/₄ per cent of GDP in 1999–2000. Repayments of around ¹/₂ per cent of GDP and ¹/₄ per cent of GDP, respectively, are projected in the following two years. Modest deficits are projected from 2002–03 onwards, as the share of net investment in GDP rises.

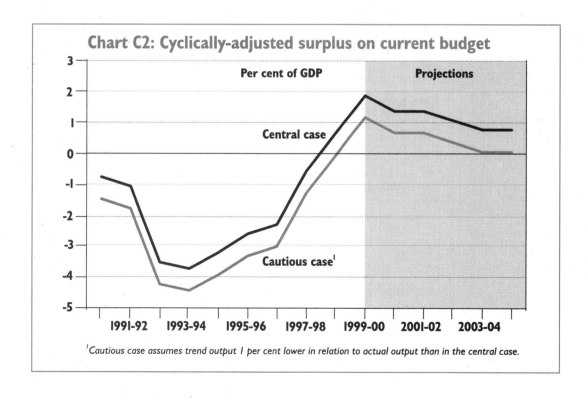

Chart C2: Cyclically-adjusted surplus on current budget

[1]*Cautious case assumes trend output 1 per cent lower in relation to actual output than in the central case.*

Forecast errors and risks

C11   The fiscal balances represent the difference between two large aggregates of spending and receipts, and forecasts of them are inevitably subject to wide margins of error. Over the past five years, the average absolute error (ie the average error irrespective of whether the errors have been positive or negative) for one-year ahead forecasts of net borrowing has been over 1 per cent of GDP, or plus or minus £9 billion at today's prices. The error tends to grow as the forecast horizon lengthens. (See Table B13 on page 122 of the November 1998 PBR.) Much of this error arises from errors in the forecasts of GDP.

C12   Short-term forecasts of the public finances are critically dependent on the path of the economy, as most tax revenues and some public expenditure (notably social security) vary directly with the economic cycle. If GDP growth were 1 per cent higher or lower than assumed over the coming year, net borrowing might be lower or higher by 0.4 per cent of GDP in the first year (equivalent to about £4 billion) and lower or higher by a further 0.3 per cent (£2 billion) in the second year.

C13   Errors in short-term growth forecasts may have only a temporary effect on the public finances. For a given path of trend output, higher or lower growth in the short-term will be followed by lower or higher growth later on, and the public finances may be little affected on average over the cycle. However, errors in estimating the cyclical position of the economy in relation to its trend – the output gap – will have a permanent effect on prospects.

C14   It is for this reason that projections in Chapter 2, and above, illustrate the effect of uncertainty over the cyclical position of the economy by showing a cautious case in which the output gap is 1 per cent higher than the central view.

C15   The fiscal projections are based on prudent and cautious assumptions (see paragraphs C16 to C19). Chart C2 above illustrates a still more cautious case, in which the level of trend output is assumed to be 1 per cent lower than in the central projection above. This scenario would imply that a greater proportion of the projected surplus on current budget was due to cyclical strength of the economy: a 1 per cent larger output gap reduces the structural surplus on current budget by about $^3/_4$ per cent of GDP a year. Even in this more cautious case, the cyclically-adjusted current budget is estimated to have been in balance in 1998–99, and is projected to remain comfortably in surplus or in balance over the forecast horizon.

ASSUMPTIONS

C16   The fiscal projections assume:

- the economy follows the path described in Chapter B. As always, and in the interests of caution, the fiscal projections are based on the lower end of the GDP growth ranges (which is based on a trend growth rate of $2^1/_4$ per cent a year);

- firm overall spending limits for the period of the 2000 Spending Review allowing:

    - current spending to increase by $2^1/_2$ per cent a year in real terms, in the three years to 2003–04, in line with the Government's neutral view of the economy's trend rate of growth; and

    - a more than doubling in net investment to 1.8 per cent of GDP by 2003–04. This makes a significant contribution to tackling the legacy of under-funding of Britain's public infrastructure while remaining consistent with the sustainable investment rule, with the debt to GDP ratio remaining well below 40 per cent in the medium term.

- there are no tax changes beyond those already announced in or before this Budget and the future indexation of rates and allowances.

Table C3: Economic assumptions for public finance projections

	Percentage changes on previous year						
	1998-99	1999-00	2000-01	2001-02	2002-03	2003-04	2004-05
Output (GDP)	$1^3/_4$	$2^1/_2$	$2^3/_4$	$2^1/_4$	$2^1/_4$	$2^1/_4$	$2^1/_4$
Prices							
RPIX	$2^3/_4$	$2^1/_4$	$2^1/_4$	$2^1/_2$	$2^1/_2$	$2^1/_2$	$2^1/_2$
GDP deflator	$3^1/_4$	$2^1/_2$	$2^1/_4$	$2^1/_2$	$2^1/_2$	$2^1/_2$	$2^1/_2$
RPI (September[1])	$3^1/_4$	$1^1/_4$	$3^1/_2$	$2^3/_4$	$2^1/_2$	$2^1/_4$	$2^1/_4$
Rossi[2] (September[1])	$2^1/_4$	$1^3/_4$	$1^1/_2$	2	$2^1/_4$	$2^1/_4$	2
Money GDP (£ billion)	857	901	946	990	1037	1086	1138

[1] Used for projecting social security expenditure over the following financial year.

[2] RPI excluding housing costs, used for uprating certain social security benefits.

C17 The key assumptions underlying the fiscal projections have been audited by the National Audit Office (NAO). The Chancellor of the Exchequer has asked the NAO to undertake a review of previously audited assumptions for the fiscal projections from this Budget onwards, on a three-year rolling basis. For this Budget the NAO was asked to review the assumptions on privatisation proceeds, trend GDP growth and interest rates and Spend to Save programmes which were last audited in July 1997. For the first three, the NAO concluded that the assumptions had "provided a reasonable basis for the elements of the fiscal projections to which they relate, and that they should continue to do so for future projections". However, as the Spend to Save programmes cover three years from 1997–98 to 1999-2000, the NAO concluded that they could not assess the reasonableness of the programmes until they had actual expenditure and revenue data for all three years. They will examine the outcome of the Spend to Save programme in their next report.

C18 The NAO was also asked to audit a new assumption for the Budget: that the additional revenue resulting from anti-tobacco smuggling measures announced in the Pre-Budget Report and the further measures the Government will be announcing on 22 March, should allow for the direct effect of these measures, including the deterrent effect of fiscal marks, but should exclude their indirect effects. The NAO concluded that the approach adopted is reasonably cautious.

C19 As a result of these reviews the key assumptions and conventions used for the Budget public finance projections are unchanged. In accordance with these assumptions and conventions, trend GDP growth is assumed to be $2^1/_4$ per cent a year. Details are given in Box C1.

Box C1: Key assumptions audited by the NAO

- **Privatisation proceeds**[1,6]
  Credit is taken only for proceeds from sales that have been announced.

- **Trend GDP growth**[1,6]
  2$\frac{1}{4}$ per cent a year.

- **UK claimant unemployment**[1,4]
  Constant at recent levels, 1.16 million.

- **Interest rates**[1,6]
  3 month market rates change in line with market expectations (as of March 14).

- **Equity prices**[2]
  FT-All share index rises from 3,126 in line with money GDP.

- **VAT**[2]
  Ratio of VAT to consumption falls by 0.05 percentage points a year.

- **GDP deflator and RPI**[2]
  Projections of price indices used to plan public expenditure are consistent with RPIX.

- **Composition of GDP**[3]
  Shares of labour income and profits in national income are broadly constant in the medium term.

- **Funding**[3]
  Funding assumptions used to project debt interest are consistent with the public finances forecast and with financing policy.

- **Oil prices**[5]
  $22.40 a barrel in 2000, the average of independent forecasts, and then constant in real terms.

- **Anti-tobacco smuggling measures**[6]
  Only direct effects, including deterrent effects of fiscal marks, are allowed for.

[1] See Audit of Assumptions for the July 1997 Budget Projections, 19 June 1997 (HC3693)
[2] Audit of Assumptions for the Pre-Budget Report, 25 November 1997 (HC361)
[3] Audit of Assumptions for the Budget, 19 March 1998 (HC616)
[4] Audit of the Unemployment Assumption for the March 1999 Budget Projections, 9 March 1999 (HC294)
[5] Audit of the Oil Price Assumption for the Pre-Budget Report November 1999 (HC873)
[6] Audit of Assumptions for the March 2000 Budget 21 March 2000 (HC348)

FISCAL AGGREGATES

C20   Tables C4 and C5 provide more detail on the projections of the current and capital budgets, in £ billion and as a per cent of GDP respectively. The tables show the current surplus and net borrowing, both including and excluding windfall tax receipts and associated spending. The latter gives a clearer picture of underlying trends. Latest estimates of associated spending are given in Table 4.1.

Table C4: Current and capital budgets

	£ billion						
	Outturn	Estimate			Projections		
	1998–99	1999–00	2000–01	2001–02	2002–03	2003–04	2004–05
Current budget							
Current receipts	335.9	356.2	376	395	412	428	448
Current expenditure	312.5	325.6	348	366	384	404	423
Depreciation	13.6	14.1	14	15	15	16	17
Surplus on current budget (including WTAS[1])	9.8	16.5	13	14	13	8	8
Surplus on current budget[2]	**7.5**	**17.1**	**14**	**16**	**13**	**8**	**8**
Capital budget							
Gross investment	22.8	24.1	26	30	35	39	41
less asset sales	−4.3	−4.5	−4	−4	−4	−4	−4
less depreciation	−13.6	−14.1	−14	−15	−15	−16	−17
Net investment	5.0	5.5	8	11	16	20	20
Net borrowing (including WTAS[1])	−4.9	−11.0	−5	−3	3	11	13
Net borrowing[2]	**−2.8**	**−11.9**	**−6**	**−5**	**3**	**11**	**13**
Public sector net debt – end year	348.6	342.6	340	340	347	363	379
Memos:							
General government net borrowing[3]							
ESA79	−7.3	−12.8	−9	−5	0	11	10
ESA95	−5.1	−11.4	−5	−3	3	12	13
General government gross debt[4]	403.2	396.8	397	398	406	422	440

[1] *Windfall tax receipts and associated spending.*

[2] *Excluding windfall tax receipts and associated spending.*

[3] *Maastricht measures of the government deficit and debt. From February 2000, the Maastricht measures moved from being reported under ESA79 to ESA95 accounting conventions.*

[4] *The stock of gross debt is not affected by the move to ESA95 accounting conventions.*

Table C5: Current and capital budgets

					Per cent of GDP		
	Outturn 1998–99	Estimate 1999–00	2000–01	2001–02	Projections 2002–03	2003–04	2004–05
Current budget							
Current receipts	39.2	39.6	39.7	39.9	39.8	39.4	39.3
Current expenditure	36.5	36.2	36.8	36.9	37.1	37.2	37.2
Depreciation	1.6	1.6	1.5	1.5	1.5	1.5	1.5
Surplus on current budget (including WTAS[1])	1.1	1.8	1.4	1.5	1.2	0.8	0.7
Surplus on current budget[2]	**0.9**	**1.9**	**1.5**	**1.6**	**1.2**	**0.8**	**0.7**
Capital budget							
Gross investment	2.7	2.7	2.8	3.0	3.4	3.6	3.6
less asset sales	–0.5	–0.5	–0.4	–0.4	–0.4	–0.3	–0.3
less depreciation	–1.6	–1.6	–1.5	–1.5	–1.5	–1.5	–1.5
Net investment	0.6	0.6	0.9	1.2	1.5	1.8	1.8
Net borrowing (including WTAS[1])	–0.6	–1.2	–0.5	–0.3	0.3	1.0	1.1
Net borrowing[2]	**–0.3**	**–1.3**	**–0.7**	**–0.5**	**0.3**	**1.0**	**1.1**
Public sector net debt – end year	**39.7**	**37.1**	**35.1**	**33.6**	**32.7**	**32.6**	**32.6**
Memos:							
General government net borrowing[3]							
ESA79	–0.9	–1.4	–0.9	–0.5	0.0	1.0	0.9
ESA95	–0.6	–1.3	–0.6	–0.3	0.3	1.1	1.2
General government gross debt[3, 4]							
ESA79	47.8	44.8	42.7	40.9	39.8	39.5	39.3
ESA95	47.0	44.1	42.0	40.2	39.1	38.9	38.7

[1] Windfall tax receipts and associated spending.

[2] Excluding windfall tax receipts and associated spending.

[3] Maastricht measures of the government deficit and debt. From February 2000, the Maastricht measures moved from being reported under ESA79 to ESA95 accounting conventions.

[4] The move to ESA95 accounting conventions does not affect the stock of gross debt, but it does increase money GDP by about £8 billion in 1998–99.

C21   The current budget surplus in 1999–2000 is estimated to be over £17 billion. Net investment is estimated to be £5½ billion, giving a repayment of net borrowing of nearly £12 billion.

C22   The current budget surplus is projected to fall slightly in 2000–01, to £14 billion, reflecting the relatively strong growth of current expenditure. Together with the planned rapid increase in net investment, this reduces the repayment of net borrowing to £6 billion in 2000–01.

C23   The current budget surplus is projected to rise to £16 billion in 2001–02, but to decline slightly thereafter, to about £8 billion from 2003–04 onwards. The profile of a modest decline in the current budget surplus from 2001–02 reflects the planned real increase in current expenditure of 2½ per cent a year, together with receipts projections that are based on a cautious projection of real GDP growth of 2¼ per cent a year. Together with a rising ratio of net investment to GDP, this results in a projection of net borrowing rising to 1 per cent of GDP in 2003-04, well within the limit on public sector net borrowing set by the sustainable investment rule.

C24   The profile of significant repayments of net borrowing up to 2001–02 results in a declining net debt-GDP ratio. Public sector net debt falls from 37.1 per cent of GDP in March 2000, to 32.7 per cent of GDP in March 2003. The debt-GDP ratio stabilises at around this level in the remainder of the projection period.

C25   The Maastricht Treaty and stability and growth pact provide reference values for general government net borrowing (3 per cent of GDP) and general government gross debt (60 per cent of GDP). Table C5 shows the Maastricht measures of the deficit and debt used in the Excessive Deficits Procedure of the Maastricht Treaty, as a per cent of GDP. From February 2000, the Maastricht measures moved from being reported under ESA79 to ESA95 accounting conventions, and are thus now fully consistent with the UK national accounts, which moved to being on an ESA95 basis in September 1998. Table C5 shows the Maastricht measures under both the ESA79 and ESA95 accounting conventions. The reference levels of 3 per cent of GDP for the deficit and 60 per cent of GDP for debt are achieved comfortably throughout the projection period, on either definition.

C26   Table C6 shows the latest projections of the main fiscal aggregates, and projections made in the November 1999 Pre-Budget Report (PBR) and March 1999 Budget. The table shows that the projected current budget surplus and repayment of net borrowing in 1999–2000 increased by £7^1/$_2$ billion and £6^1/$_2$ billion respectively between Budget 99 and the PBR last November. Much of this improvement reflected a stronger than expected economy: whereas the projected current budget surplus increased from 0.3 per cent of GDP at Budget time to 1.1 per cent of GDP in the PBR, the cyclically-adjusted projections showed an improvement of just 0.3 per cent of GDP between the Budget and the PBR. The public finances have improved further since November. Latest estimates of the current budget surplus and the repayment of net borrowing are at least £7^1/$_2$ billion higher than in the PBR. But, unlike the improvement between Budget 99 and PBR99, much of this seems to reflect structural factors. The cyclically-adjusted current budget surplus has risen by 0.9 per cent of GDP since the PBR, slightly more than the rise in the unadjusted surplus.

C27   The increase in the current budget in 1999–2000 since the projection last March is largely carried forward over the next two years. This reflects both an upward revision to economic prospects over the next two years since last March, together with an underlying, structural improvement in the public finances: the cyclically-adjusted current budget surplus is about ^{1}/$_4$ per cent of GDP higher over the next two years than projected a year ago. A similar improvement is projected for cyclically-adjusted net borrowing over the next two years.

Table C6: Fiscal balances comparison with PBR 99 and Budget 99[1]

	Outturn[2]	Estimate[3]	Projections				
	1998–99	1999–00	2000–01	2001–02	2002–03	2003–04	2004–05
Fiscal balances (£ billion)							
Surplus on current budget – Budget 99	4.1	2	4	8	9	11	
Surplus on current budget – PBR 99	7.2	9.5	11	13	13	12	11
Surplus on current budget – Budget 2000	**7.5**	**17.1**	**14**	**16**	**13**	**8**	**8**
Net borrowing – Budget 99	–1.0	3	3	1	3	4	
Net borrowing – PBR 99	–2.5	–3.5	–3	–3	1	4	6
Net borrowing – Budget 2000	**–2.8**	**–11.9**	**–6**	**–5**	**3**	**11**	**13**
Cyclically-adjusted budget balances (per cent of GDP)							
Surplus on current budget – Budget 99	0.2	0.6	1.0	1.1	0.9	1.0	
Surplus on current budget – PBR 99	0.6	0.9	1.0	1.2	1.2	1.1	1.0
Surplus on current budget - Budget 2000	**0.6**	**1.8**	**1.3**	**1.3**	**1.0**	**0.7**	**0.7**
Net borrowing – Budget 99	0.1	0.0	–0.2	–0.1	0.3	0.4	
Net borrowing – PBR 99	0.0	–0.2	–0.2	–0.2	0.1	0.4	0.5
Net borrowing – Budget 2000	**–0.1**	**–1.2**	**–0.5**	**–0.3**	**0.5**	**1.1**	**1.1**

[1] *Excluding windfall tax receipts and associated spending.*
[2] *The 1998–99 figures were estimates in Budget 99.*
[3] *The 1999–2000 figures were projections in Budget 99.*

RECEIPTS

C28   Table C7 gives projections of receipts as a percentage of GDP. Changes in the receipts projections since the November PBR and March Budget are shown in Table C8. A more detailed breakdown of receipts, in £ billion, for 1999–2000 and 2000–01 is given in Table C9. Table C10 sets out the projections of the tax-GDP ratio.

Table C7: Current receipts

	Outturn	Estimate		Projections			
	1998–99	1999–00	2000–01	2001–02	2002–03	2003–04	2004–05
				Per cent of GDP			
Income tax (gross of tax credits)	10.3	10.6	10.7	10.8	10.9	11.0	11.2
Income tax credits[1]	–0.2	–0.3	–0.5	–0.8	–0.8	–0.8	–0.8
of which:							
Working Families' Tax Credit		–0.1	–0.5	–0.5	–0.5	–0.5	–0.5
Corporation tax	3.5	3.8	3.6	3.9	3.8	3.6	3.5
Windfall tax	0.3						
Value added tax	6.1	6.3	6.3	6.3	6.2	6.2	6.1
Excise duties[2]	4.2	3.8	3.9	3.9	3.9	3.8	3.7
Social security contributions	6.4	6.3	6.2	6.2	6.1	6.1	6.1
Other taxes and royalties[3]	6.5	6.6	6.8	6.9	6.9	6.8	6.8
Net taxes and social security contributions[4]	37.1	37.0	36.9	37.3	37.1	36.7	36.6
Accrual adjustments on taxes	0.1	0.4	0.3	0.1	0.1	0.1	0.1
less own resources contribution to EU budget	–0.7	–0.6	–0.6	–0.5	–0.4	–0.4	–0.3
Income tax credits[5]	0.2	0.3	0.5	0.6	0.6	0.6	0.6
Other receipts	2.5	2.4	2.5	2.4	2.4	2.4	2.3
Current receipts (including windfall tax)[6]	39.2	39.6	39.7	39.9	39.8	39.4	39.3
Current receipts (excluding windfall tax)[6]	38.9	39.6	39.7	39.9	39.8	39.4	39.3
Memo:							
Current receipts (£bn)	335.9	356.2	376	395	412	428	448

[1] Mainly MIRAS and tax reliefs under the Working Families' Tax Credit and Children's Tax Credit schemes.

[2] Fuel, alcohol and tobacco duties.

[3] Includes Council Tax and money paid into the National Lottery Distribution Fund, as well as other central government taxes.

[4] Includes VAT and 'own resources' contributions to EU budget. Net of income tax credits. Cash basis.

[5] Excludes Children's Tax Credit, which scores as a tax repayment in the national accounts.

[6] Accruals basis.

C29   Excluding the windfall tax, total receipts are estimated to rise by nearly 7 per cent in 1999–2000, and by 5¹/₂ per cent in 2000–01. This compares with projected money GDP growth of just over 5 per cent in both years. The relative buoyancy of receipts in 1999–2000 was highlighted in the PBR last November (see paragraph B23 on page 148 of the 1999 PBR). At that time, it appeared that the composition of GDP had been more favourable than expected for tax revenues. Recent developments have reinforced that analysis. While money GDP growth this year may be a little over ¹/₂ per cent higher than expected in November, income tax and VAT receipts have both been higher than expected by around 1³/₄ per cent.

Table C8: Changes in current receipts since Budget 99 and PBR 99

| | £ billion | | | |
| | 1999-00 | | 2000-01 | |
	Budget 99	PBR99	Budget 99	PBR 99
Income tax (gross of tax credits)	4.4	1.2	5.1	1.0
Income tax credits	–0.1	0.4	–0.1	–0.1
Non-North Sea corporation tax	3.8	0.5	0.1	0.9
North Sea revenues	1.4	0.1	3.0	0.9
Capital taxes[1]	–0.8	–0.1	–0.2	0.4
Stamp duty	0.9	0.5	1.1	1.1
Value added tax	2.7	1.0	2.8	1.6
Excise duties[2]	–1.9	0.0	–2.9	0.2
Social security contributions	0.6	0.2	1.3	–0.1
Other taxes and royalties[3]	0.8	0.6	–0.4	–0.5
Net taxes and social security contributions	11.8	4.3	9.8	5.4
Other receipts and accounting adjustments	–0.4	–0.1	1.7	0.2
Current receipts	**11.4**	**4.2**	**11.5**	**5.6**

[1] *Capital gains tax and inheritance tax.*
[2] *Fuel, alcohol and tobacco duties.*
[3] *Includes Council Tax and money paid into the National Lottery Distribution Fund, as well as other central government taxes.*

Income tax   C30   Income tax receipts (net of tax credits) are expected to be about £92$\frac{1}{4}$ billion in 1999–2000, about £4$\frac{1}{4}$ billion higher than in the Budget 99 forecast. Most of the increase stems from higher PAYE (Pay as you Earn) which in turn reflects higher than expected growth in wages and salaries. Receipts are also higher than in the PBR, by about £1$\frac{1}{2}$ billion. This is again mainly due to higher PAYE and especially to tax on the high bonus payments of recent months. Income tax receipts in 2000–01 increase to £96 billion but fall slightly as a share of GDP. This is mainly a result of measures announced in this Budget and earlier. These measures lead to a further fall in the share of GDP in 2001–02, but there are small increases in subsequent years as a result of real fiscal drag.

Corporation tax   C31   Receipts of corporation tax in 1999–2000 are expected to be just over £34 billion, about £0.6 billion higher than forecast in the PBR. Receipts in January 2000 of mainstream tax on profits in 1998 of industrial and commercial companies were higher than expected and repayments of surplus advance corporation tax (ACT) paid with foreign income dividends have been lower than forecast.

C32   Corporation tax receipts in 1999–2000 exceeded the Budget 99 forecast for several reasons:

- profits of companies in both the financial and the industrial and commercial sectors in 1998 were higher than forecast leading to higher tax payments by about £1.7 billion in 1999–2000;

- similarly profits in 1999 have been above forecast leading to the first year's instalment payments by large companies exceeding expectations by £1.4 billion, including £0.3 billion higher payments by oil extraction companies which are attributed to the rise in the oil price; and

- the yield of ACT was £1.1 billion higher than forecast because many companies with foreign parents paid dividends before the date of abolition, in order to benefit from tax credits which were reduced from the same date. On the other hand, the number of companies delaying dividends to avoid ACT was less than forecast. Also, repayments of ACT on foreign income dividends have been lower than expected.

C33   Corporation tax receipts in 2000–01 are expected to be slightly lower than in 1999–2000. The yield from Budget 98 tax changes (the transition to instalments and the rate cuts) is expected to be less than in 1999–2000. The yield will also depend on how close instalments paid by large companies are to the 18 per cent set for the second year of transition. Receipts are forecast to grow rapidly in 2001–02 as a result of substantial profit growth and the yield from the third year of transition to instalments. Receipts may decline slightly in 2003–04 as the transition to instalments finishes.

North Sea   **C34**   Receipts from companies engaged in North Sea oil and gas extraction are estimated to
revenues   be £2.5 billion in 1999–2000, slightly up on the PBR estimate. Receipts in 2000–01 are projected to rise to £4.3 billion, nearly £1 billion higher than the PBR forecast. This reflects both higher oil prices (the audited assumption is for oil prices of $22.40 a barrel in 2000, compared with the PBR assumption of $18.70) and higher production levels. Receipts are projected to rise to over £5 billion in the following two years, but to decline a little thereafter, as North Sea production levels begin to fall.

Capital taxes   **C35**   Current year receipts for capital gains and inheritance tax are much as expected in the PBR. However, receipts in 2000–01 and subsequent years are higher than in the PBR mainly because of higher assumptions for equity and house prices and transaction volumes.

Stamp duty   **C36**   Stamp duty receipts in 1999–2000 are about £½ billion higher than expected in the PBR and £1 billion higher than in the Budget 99 forecast. This reflects the buoyancy of the equity and housing markets. Stamp duty receipts are expected to rise further in 2000–01 reflecting both the continuing strength of the equity and housing markets and the effects of Budget measures; the forecast level is some £1 billion above that in the PBR.

VAT receipts   **C37**   VAT receipts in 1999–2000 are expected to be £1 billion higher than in the PBR and £2³/₄ billion higher than in the Budget 99 forecasts. Some of the increase is due to higher consumer spending, but VAT receipts are estimated to grow by 8½ per cent this year, compared with growth in nominal consumer spending of around 6¼ per cent. This implies a significant increase in the VAT effective tax rate in 1999–2000, the causes of which are not yet clear. While the composition of consumer spending may have increased the tax base, it seems unlikely that this could account fully for the current strength of VAT receipts. The forecast continues to assume a steady fall in the effective tax rate of 0.5 per cent a year, in line with the National Audit Office audited assumption. Compared with a flat VAT ratio, this cautious assumption reduces receipts by about £1½ billion by 2004–05.

Excise duties   **C38**   Cash receipts from fuel, tobacco and alcohol duties are estimated to be about £34.4 billion in 1999–2000, little changed since the PBR. Cash receipts are projected to grow strongly (up 8½ per cent to £37.4 billion) in 2000–01. This reflects additional tobacco duty receipts, which have been depressed temporarily in 1999–2000 by changes to the timing of forestalling activity by cigarette manufacturers after the Budget 99 measures. (Accruals of tobacco duty have not been affected by these timing effects. These developments were explained in more detail in paragraph B27 on page 156 of the 1999 FSBR.) Thereafter, excise duties fall slightly as a proportion of GDP largely reflecting the relatively slow growth in the demand for excise goods. The tobacco forecast takes into account the impact on revenues of the direct effects of additional anti-smuggling measures, including the deterrent effects of fiscal marks (as reviewed by the NAO), to be announced on 22 March 2000.

Social security **C39** Social security (national insurance) contributions are estimated to be nearly £56$\frac{1}{2}$
contributions billion in 1999–2000, little changed from the PBR estimate. Receipts are projected to grow
relatively strongly in 2000–01, in part reflecting the effects of real fiscal drag. Thereafter, the
ratio of social security contributions to GDP is projected to fall, in part reflecting assumed
higher rates of contracting out of the state pension scheme, as individuals increasingly make
use of stakeholder pensions.

Table C9: Public sector current receipts

	£ billion		
	Outturn 1998–99	Estimate 1999–00	Projection 2000–01
Inland Revenue			
Income tax (gross of tax credits)	88.4	95.2	101.0
Income tax credits	–2.0	–2.9	–5.1
Corporation tax[1]	30.0	34.1	33.8
Windfall tax	2.6		
Petroleum revenue tax	0.5	0.9	1.2
Capital gains tax	1.8	2.4	3.4
Inheritance tax	1.8	2.0	2.3
Stamp duties	4.6	6.6	7.2
Total Inland Revenue (net of tax credits)	**127.7**	**138.2**	**143.8**
Customs and Excise			
Value added tax	52.3	56.7	59.6
Fuel duties	21.6	22.3	23.3
Tobacco duties	8.2	5.7	7.4
Spirits duties	1.6	1.8	1.8
Wine duties	1.5	1.6	1.7
Beer and cider duties	2.8	2.9	3.1
Betting and gaming duties	1.5	1.5	1.4
Air passenger duty	0.8	0.9	1.0
Insurance premium tax	1.2	1.4	1.6
Landfill tax	0.3	0.4	0.4
Customs duties and levies	2.1	2.0	2.0
Total Customs and Excise	**94.0**	**97.4**	**103.3**
Vehicle excise duties	4.7	4.9	4.9
Oil royalties	0.3	0.4	0.5
Business rates[2]	15.3	15.5	16.2
Social security contributions	55.1	56.4	58.8
Council Tax	12.1	12.8	13.6
Other taxes and royalties[3]	8.3	8.0	8.2
Net taxes and social security contributions[4]	**317.7**	**333.6**	**349.4**
Accrual adjustments on taxes	1.2	3.8	3.0
less own resources contribution to EU budget	–6.2	–5.5	–5.4
less PC corporation tax payments	–0.4	–0.4	–0.4
Income tax credits[5]	2.0	2.9	5.1
Interest and dividends	4.3	3.2	4.4
Other receipts[6]	17.3	18.7	19.6
Current receipts	**335.9**	**356.2**	**375.6**
Memo:			
North Sea revenues[7]	2.5	2.5	4.3

[1] *Includes advance corporation tax (net of repayments):* — 11.0 — 1.8 — –0.2
Also includes North Sea corporation tax after ACT set off, and corporation tax on gains.
[2] *Includes district council rates in Northern Ireland.*
[3] *Includes money paid into the National Lottery Distribution Fund.*
[4] *Includes VAT and 'traditional own resources' contributions to EU budget. Net of income tax credits. Cash basis.*
[5] *Excludes Children's Tax Credit, which scores as a tax repayment in the national accounts.*
[6] *Mainly gross operating surpluses and rent.*
[7] *North Sea corporation tax (before ACT set-off), petroleum revenue tax and royalties.*

Total taxes   **C40**   Chart C3 and Table C10 show the tax-GDP ratio, measured as net taxes and social security contributions, as a percentage of GDP. The tax ratio is estimated to fall both in 1999-2000 and the following year. The increase in the tax ratio projected for 2001–02 largely reflects the timing effects on receipts of the new corporation tax system. The tax ratio is projected to fall in each year after 2001–02, and is lower on average over the next five years than the estimate for the current year. By April 2001, when personal tax and benefit measures from this and previous Budgets have come into effect, the tax burden on a typical family with two children will fall to its lowest level since 1972.

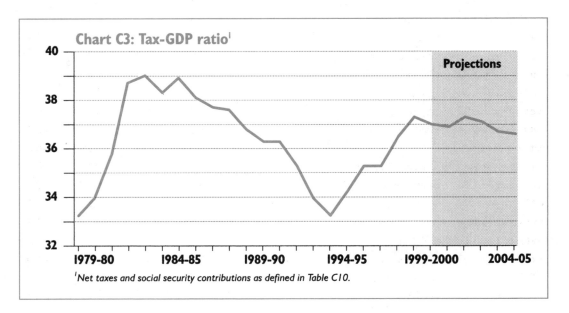

Chart C3: Tax-GDP ratio[1]

[1] Net taxes and social security contributions as defined in Table C10.

Table C10: Net taxes and social security contributions[1]

	Outturn 1998–99	Estimate 1999–00	Projections 2000–01	2001–02	2002–03	2003–04	2004–05
Budget 99	37.2	36.6	36.7	37.0	37.0	37.1	
PBR 99	37.4	37.0	36.8	37.2	37.2	37.0	36.8
Budget 2000	**37.1**	**37.0**	**36.9**	**37.3**	**37.1**	**36.7**	**36.6**

[1] Net of income tax credits; cash basis.

PUBLIC EXPENDITURE

C41   Table C11 shows the projections for public expenditure for the three years covered by the Comprehensive Spending Review (CSR). These projections cover the whole public sector, using the aggregate Total Managed Expenditure (TME). TME is split into Departmental Expenditure Limits (DEL) and Annually Managed Expenditure (AME). In 2001–02 TME is derived by assuming 2.5 per cent real growth in current expenditure and net investment at 1.2 per cent of GDP, forming the envelope for the first year of the Spending Review. The additional spending this implies, over and above the existing DEL plans and AME projections, is shown separately in the table.

Table C11: Total Managed Expenditure 1998–99 to 2001–02

	£ billion						
	Outturn 1998–99	Estimated Outturn 1999–00	2000–01	Projections 2001–02	Changes since Budget 99 1999–00	2000–01	2001–02
Departmental Expenditure Limits	167.2	178.9	193.7	202.6	–0.3	4.0	3.1
Annually Managed Expenditure							
Social Security Benefits	93.3	97.1	99.6	104.5	–2.1	–2.0	–1.9
Housing Revenue Account subsidies	3.5	3.4	3.3	3.3	–0.1	–0.1	–0.2
Common Agricultural Policy	2.7	2.6	2.5	2.6	0.1	–0.2	–0.3
Export Credits Guarantee Department	–0.2	0.9	0.3	0.4	0.4	–0.5	–0.5
Net Payment to EC Institutions[1]	3.6	2.6	2.7	2.5	–0.1	0.1	–0.4
Self-financing Public Corporations	–0.2	0.2	0.2	–0.1	0.4	0.4	0.3
Locally Financed Expenditure	16.1	17.2	18.1	19.1	0.2	–0.2	–0.7
Net Public Service Pensions	4.7	5.6	5.7	5.6	–0.5	–0.3	–0.5
National Lottery	1.6	2.0	2.3	2.0	–0.6	–0.4	–0.8
Central government gross debt interest	29.5	25.5	27.8	27.1	–0.5	0.1	0.0
Accounting and other adjustments	9.1	9.3	13.7	14.5	0.1	2.0	1.7
AME Margin	0.0	0.0	1.0	2.0	–1.0	–1.0	–1.0
Annually Managed Expenditure	163.8	166.3	177.2	183.6	–3.7	–1.9	–4.2
Budget 2000 addition				5.9			5.9
Total Managed Expenditure	331.0	345.2	370.9	392.1	–4.0	2.1	4.8
of which:							
Public sector current expenditure	312.5	325.6	348.2	365.8	–3.3	2.1	3.8
Public sector net investment	5.0	5.5	8.2	11.4	0.0	0.7	1.8
Public sector depreciation	13.6	14.1	14.5	15.0	–0.7	–0.7	–0.7

[1] Net payments to EC institutions exclude the UK's contribution to the cost of EC aid to non-Member States (which is attributed to the aid programme). Net payments therefore differ from the UK's net contribution to the EC Budget, latest estimates for which are (in £ billion).

	1998–99	1999–00	2000–01	2001–02
Figures from 2000–01 are trend estimates.	4.1	3.0	3.3	3.4

C42   There have been a number of changes to DEL since Budget 99. The underspend in 1998–99 on DEL items of £0.7 billion was carried forward into 1999–2000 under the End Year Flexibility arrangements. It is now estimated that the revised DEL total for 1999–2000 will be underspent by £1.0 billion. The tables assume that this underspend is carried forward into the 2000–01 DEL, together with additional allocations of £3.0 billion. These additional allocations are described in Chapter 5. The 2001–02 DEL has increased with new allocations to health expenditure of £3.1 billion. Plans for 2001–02 for other departments will be reviewed in the Spending Review.

C43   The components of AME were reviewed at the time of the PBR and have been reviewed again for this Budget. Table C11 shows the detailed changes since Budget 99 for the current year and the next two years. The AME margin has been set to zero in 1999–2000, to £1 billion in 2000–01 and to £2 billion in 2001–02.

C44   Total AME for the years 1999–2000 to 2001–02 is now nearly £10 billion lower than in Budget 99. The biggest reductions have been on social security. This is forecast to be lower by around £2 billion in each year. This is due primarily to lower unemployment in 1999–2000 than assumed at Budget 99 and a lower unemployment assumption for the next two years. The lower assumption reflects lower recent levels of unemployment (see Box C1).

C45   Chart C4 shows the ratio of TME to GDP. The ratio rises over the next two years, to just under 40 per cent.

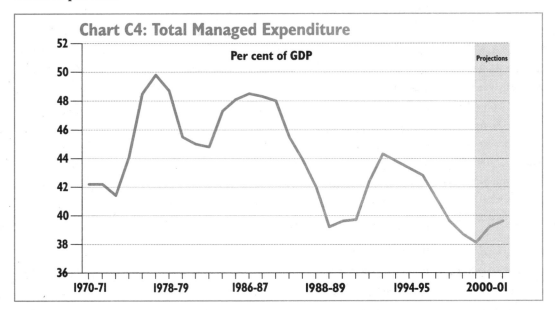

Chart C4: Total Managed Expenditure

Per cent of GDP

Projections

C46   Central government gross debt interest is estimated at £25.5 billion, or 2.8 per cent of GDP, for 1999–00. It is expected to rise next year reflecting projections of higher short-term interest rates and RPI inflation increasing from its unusually low level in 1999–2000. The estimate for 1999–2000 is lower than was forecast at Budget 99 due to improvements in government borrowing. Forecasts of debt interest for the next two years remain broadly unchanged as predicted lower borrowing is offset by the effects of higher interest rate and RPI projections.

C47   Other significant changes to the AME projections since the PBR include lower projections for Export Credit Guarantee Department and National Lottery expenditure. The former is due to a revised profile of lending by ECGD over future years. The latter reflects new information on planned expenditure by the Lottery Distribution Bodies.

C48   The main accounting adjustments, those items within TME but outside DEL and AME main programmes, are shown in Table C12. There have been small increases across a number of adjustments since Budget 99. The adjustments increase over the next two years mainly because of the introduction of the Working Families' Tax Credit.

Table C12: Accounting and other adjustments

	£ billion			
	1998–99	1999–00	2000–01	2001–02
1 Non-trading capital consumption	7.0	7.1	7.3	7.6
2 VAT refunded on general government expenditure	5.3	5.4	5.7	6.0
3 EC contributions	–6.0	–5.5	–5.4	–5.1
4 Income tax credits	2.0	2.9	5.3	5.8
of which Working Families' Tax Credit and Disabled Persons' Tax Credit:	*0.0*	*0.9*	*4.9*	*5.4*
5 Other programme spending in AME	0.2	0.6	0.4	0.5
6 Adjustments for public corporations	3.1	3.4	4.0	3.9
7 Intra-public sector debt interest	–2.3	–2.1	–1.6	–2.1
8 Financial transactions in DEL and AME	0.0	–2.4	–2.2	–2.2
9 Other accounting adjustments	–0.3	–0.1	0.3	0.2
Total	**9.1**	**9.3**	**13.7**	**14.5**

C49   Table C13 gives a breakdown of public sector net investment. Compared to Budget 99, reductions in expected capital expenditure by Lottery distribution bodies have been more than offset by additional allocations elsewhere.

Table C13: Public sector capital expenditure

	£ billion			
	1998–99	**1999–00**	**2000–01**	**2001–02**
CG spending and LA support in DEL	10.7	12.0	15.1	16.6
Locally financed spending	0.8	0.8	0.7	0.7
National Lottery	1.4	1.5	1.4	1.2
Public corporations[1]	4.4	4.7	4.7	5.2
Other capital spending in AME	1.2	0.5	0.5	0.5
Reserve allocation and Budget 2000 addition	0.0	0.0	0.2	2.1
Public sector gross investment[2]	**18.5**	**19.6**	**22.7**	**26.4**
Less depreciation	−13.6	−14.1	−14.5	−15.0
Public sector net investment[2]	**5.0**	**5.5**	**8.2**	**11.4**
Proceeds from the sale of fixed assets[3]	4.3	4.5	3.8	3.8

[1] *Public corporations' capital expenditure is partly within DEL and partly within AME.*

[2] *This and previous lines are all net of sales of fixed assets.*

[3] *Projections of total receipts from the sale of fixed assets by public sector. These receipts are taken into account in arriving at public sector gross and net investment, which are net of sales of fixed assets.*

PRIVATE FINANCE INITIATIVE

C50   Table C15 shows a forecast of the estimated payments for services flowing from new private investment over the next twenty five years. Actual expenditure will depend on the details of the payment mechanism for each contract. Payments may be lower than estimated due to deductions from the service payments caused by either the supplier's failure to make the service available or a failure to meet the required performance standards. In addition variances may occur due to changes in the service requirements agreed during the course of the contacts. Payments may also vary as a result of the early termination of a contract triggering contractual arrangements for compensation on termination.

Table C14: Private Finance Initiative: estimated capital spending by the private sector-signed deals

	£ million			
	1999-00	2000-01	2001-02	2002-03
Defence	319	177	0	0
FCO and International Development	0	33	4	7
Agriculture[1]	0	0	0	0
Trade and Industry	0	54	34	33
Environment, Transport and Regions[2,3]	0	793	636	706
Education and Employment[4]	0	28	32	9
Home Office	73	90	35	4
Legal Departments	8	13	32	26
Culture, Media and Sport	0	0	13	1
Health	177	320	468	336
Social Security	0	69	26	39
Scotland	51	69	205	293
Wales	0	89	50	19
Northern Ireland	12	36	74	52
Chancellor's Departments	0	125	20	21
Local authorities[5,6]	800	1200	1200	1200
Total	**1432**	**2971**	**2829**	**2746**

[1] Includes Forestry Commission

[2] Includes the private sector capital investment in Channel-Tunnel Rail Link.

[3] In addition, substantial private investment is levered in through housing, urban regeneration and other programmes.

[4] Excludes PPP/PFI activity in the further and higher education (FHE) sectors, which are classified to the private sector. For FHE, the total estimated capital value of major PPP/ PFI projects which have signed or expected to sign is £65 million for 1999-2000 and £165 million for 2000-2001. Includes projects in VA schools only: schools projects funded through Revenue Support Grant are included in the Local Authority figures.

[5] Figures represent spending on projects signed, and expected to be signed, up to the end of 1998-99 only.

[6] PFI activity in local authority schools is included in the local authorities line.

Table C15: Estimated payments under PFI contracts- March 2000

	£ million		£ million
1998–99	1030	2012–13	2568
1999–00	1650	2013–14	2451
2000–01	2060	2014–15	2362
2001–02	2054	2015–16	2234
2002–03	2478	2016–17	2227
2003–04	2922	2017–18	2216
2004–05	3152	2018–19	2185
2005–06	3254	2019–20	1786
2006–07	3183	2020–21	1754
2007–08	3139	2021–22	1758
2008–09	3145	2022–23	1696
2009–10	2986	2023–24	1704
2010–11	2935	2024–25	1588
2011–12	2671	2025–26	1583

Table C16: Private Finance Initiative: estimated capital spending by the private sector-preferred bidder

	£ million			
	1998-99	**1999-00**	**2000-01**	**2001-02**
Defence	0	374	415	273
FCO and International Development	0	20	30	0
Agriculture[1]	0	3	18	0
Trade and Industry[6]	0	0	0	0
Environment, Transport and Regions[2,3]	0	63	65	50
Education and Employment[4]	0	330	0	0
Home Office	146	161	50	0
Legal Departments	0	11	26	38
Culture, Media and Sport	0	2	10	0
Health[6]	0	0	0	0
Social Security	0	0	0	7
Scotland	70	360	540	300
Wales	0	0	0	0
Northern Ireland	1	48	62	21
Chancellor's Departments[6]	0	0	0	0
Local authorities[5,6,7]	0	0	0	0
Total	**217**	**1372**	**1216**	**689**

[1] Includes Forestry Commission

[2] Includes the private sector capital investment in Channel Tunnel Rail Link

[3] In addition, substantial private investment is levered in through housing, urban regeneration and other programmes.

[4] Excludes PPP/PFI activity in the further and higher education (FHE) sectors, which are classified to the private sector. For FHE, the total estimated capital value of major PPP/ PFI projects which have signed or expected to sign is £65 million for 1999–2000 and £165 million for 2000–2001. Includes projects in VA schools only: schools projects funded through Revenue Support Grant are included in the Local Authority figures.

[5] Figures represent spending on projects signed and expected to be signed, up to the end of 1998–99 only.

[6] Preferred bidder information cannot be disaggregated from the information in the signed-deals tables as it refers solely to RSG payments.

[7] PFI activity in local authority schools is included in the local authorities line.

C51   Table C17 shows receipts from asset and loan sales from 1998–99 to 2001–02. Planned sales of fixed assets by central government remain on course to reach £1 billion in each of the three years to 2001–02.

Table C17: Loans and sales of assets

	£ billion			
	Outturn	Estimate	Projections	
	1998–99	**1999–00**	**2000–01**	**2001–02**
Sales of fixed assets				
Central Government	1.5	1.1	1.0	1.0
Local Authorities	2.8	3.4	2.8	2.8
Total sales of fixed assets	**4.3**	**4.5**	**3.8**	**3.8**
Loans and sales of financial assets				
Sale of student loans portfolio	1.0			
Other loans and sales of financial assets	–2.0	–2.5	–2.3	–2.7
Total loans and sales of financial assets	**–1.0**	**–2.5**	**–2.3**	**–2.7**
Total loans and sales of assets	**3.3**	**1.9**	**1.4**	**1.0**

C52   The figures for sales of financial assets include proceeds from the sale of British Energy debt and from the Public Private Partnerships for National Air Traffic services, the Defence Evaluation and Research Agency and Belfast Port.

C53 Table C18 shows a full analysis of public sector recipts and expenditure by economic category, with a breakdown between central government, local authorities and public corporations.

Table C18: Public sector transactions by sub-sector and economic category

		£ billion				
		1999-00				
		General government				
	Line	Central government	Local authorities	Total	Public corporations	Public sector
Current receipts						
Taxes on income and wealth	1	133.4	0.0	133.4	–0.4	133.0
Taxes on production and imports	2	126.3	0.1	126.4	0.0	126.4
Other current taxes	3	3.4	12.8	16.2	0.0	16.2
Taxes on capital	4	2.0	0.0	2.0	0.0	2.0
Social contributions	5	56.4	0.0	56.4	0.0	56.4
Gross operating surplus	6	4.4	8.7	13.0	4.6	17.6
Rent and other current transfers	7	0.8	0.0	0.8	0.6	1.4
Interest and dividends from private sector and abroad	8	2.3	0.6	2.9	0.2	3.2
Interest and dividends from public sector	9	6.2	–3.9	2.3	–2.3	0.0
Total current receipts	10	**335.1**	**18.3**	**353.4**	**2.8**	**356.2**
Current expenditure						
Current expenditure on goods and services	11	100.9	63.6	164.5	0.0	164.5
Subsidies	12	4.4	0.8	5.2	0.0	5.2
Net social benefits	13	98.6	13.8	112.3	0.0	112.3
Net current grants abroad	14	–0.9	0.0	–0.9	0.0	–0.9
Current grants (net) within public sector	15	63.7	–63.7	0.0	0.0	0.0
Other current grants	16	18.9	0.0	18.9	0.0	18.9
Interest and dividends paid	17	25.5	0.4	25.9	–0.3	25.6
Apportionment of DEL reserve and AME margin	18	0.0	0.0	0.0	0.0	0.0
Total current expenditure	19	**311.0**	**14.8**	**325.9**	**–0.3**	**325.6**
Depreciation	20	3.9	6.2	10.0	4.0	14.1
Surplus on current budget	21	**20.2**	**–2.7**	**17.5**	**–1.0**	**16.5**
Capital expenditure						
Gross domestic fixed capital formation	22	4.5	5.8	10.4	4.7	15.1
Less depreciation	23	–3.9	–6.2	–10.0	–4.0	–14.1
Increase in inventories	24	–0.2	0.0	–0.2	0.0	–0.1
Capital grants (net) within public sector	25	4.6	–3.3	1.3	–1.3	0.0
Capital grants to private sector	26	3.9	1.2	5.1	0.0	5.1
Capital grants from private sector	27	0.0	–0.4	–0.4	0.0	–0.4
Apportionment of DEL reserve	28	0.0	0.0	0.0	0.0	0.0
Net capital expenditure	29	**9.0**	**–2.9**	**6.1**	**–0.6**	**5.5**
Net borrowing	30	**–11.2**	**–0.2**	**–11.4**	**0.4**	**–11.0**

Table C18: Public sector transactions by sub-sector and economic category

	£ billion					
	2000-01					
	General government					
Line	Central government	Local authorities	Total	Public corporations	Public sector	
						Current receipts
1	140.5	0.0	140.5	−0.4	140.1	Taxes on income and wealth
2	131.8	0.1	131.9	0.0	131.9	Taxes on production and imports
3	3.4	13.6	17.0	0.0	17.0	Other current taxes
4	2.2	0.0	2.2	0.0	2.2	Taxes on capital
5	60.1	0.0	60.1	0.0	60.1	Social contributions
6	4.6	8.9	13.5	4.8	18.3	Gross operating surplus
7	1.0	0.0	1.0	0.6	1.6	Rent and other current transfers
8	3.6	0.6	4.2	0.2	4.4	Interest and dividends from private sector and abroad
9	5.6	−3.4	2.2	−2.2	0.0	Interest and dividends from public sector
10	**352.8**	**19.8**	**372.6**	**3.0**	**375.6**	**Total current receipts**
						Current expenditure
11	107.7	67.0	174.8	0.0	174.8	Current expenditure on goods and services
12	3.9	0.8	4.7	0.0	4.7	Subsidies
13	103.2	14.6	117.7	0.0	117.7	Net social benefits
14	−1.3	0.0	−1.3	0.0	−1.3	Net current grants abroad
15	66.6	−66.6	0.0	0.0	0.0	Current grants (net) within public sector
16	21.4	0.0	21.4	0.0	21.4	Other current grants
17	27.8	0.4	28.1	−0.2	27.9	Interest and dividends paid
18	3.0	0.0	3.0	0.0	3.0	Apportionment of DEL reserve and AME margin
19	**332.3**	**16.2**	**348.5**	**−0.2**	**348.2**	**Total current expenditure**
20	4.0	6.3	10.3	4.2	14.5	Depreciation
21	**16.5**	**−2.6**	**13.8**	**−0.9**	**12.9**	**Surplus on current budget**
						Capital expenditure
22	6.3	6.7	13.1	4.7	17.7	Gross domestic fixed capital formation
23	−4.0	−6.3	−10.3	−4.2	−14.5	*Less* depreciation
24	0.1	0.0	0.1	0.0	0.1	Increase in inventories
25	4.0	−3.3	0.6	−0.6	0.0	Capital grants (net) within public sector
26	3.9	1.3	5.2	0.0	5.2	Capital grants to private sector
27	0.0	−0.5	−0.5	0.0	−0.5	Capital grants from private sector
28	0.2	0.0	0.2	0.0	0.2	Apportionment of DEL reserve
29	**10.5**	**−2.1**	**8.3**	**−0.1**	**8.2**	**Net capital expenditure**
30	**−6.0**	**0.5**	**−5.5**	**0.8**	**−4.7**	**Net borrowing**

Table C19: Departmental Expenditure Limits – Current and Capital Budgets

		£ billion			
			Estimated		
	Outturns		Outturn	Plans	
	1997–98	1998–99	1999–00	2000–01	2001–02
Current Budget					
Education and Employment	14.0	13.6	14.8	16.6	17.1
Health	35.1	37.5	40.5	44.2	47.4
of which: NHS	34.5	36.8	39.9	43.5	46.6
DETR – Main programmes	4.1	4.0	4.6	4.7	4.9
DETR – Local Government and Regional Policy	31.1	32.4	33.9	35.3	36.6
Home Office	6.2	6.5	7.3	7.6	7.7
Legal Departments[1]	2.6	2.6	2.7	2.8	2.7
Defence	20.1	20.8	21.6	21.3	21.4
Foreign and Commonwealth Office	1.0	1.0	1.1	1.0	1.0
International Development	1.8	2.1	2.2	2.5	2.7
Trade and Industry[2]	2.7	2.6	3.0	3.2	3.2
Agriculture, Fisheries and Food[3]	1.4	1.2	1.2	1.1	1.0
Culture, Media and Sport	0.8	0.8	0.9	0.9	1.0
Social Security (administration)	3.2	3.3	3.3	3.2	3.2
Scotland [1,4]	11.5	11.6	12.3	13.0	13.4
Wales[4]	5.6	5.9	6.4	6.9	7.2
Northern Ireland[4]	4.9	5.1	5.5	5.5	5.6
Chancellor's Departments	2.6	3.1	3.5	3.6	3.5
Cabinet Office	1.0	1.0	1.1	1.1	1.1
Welfare to Work[5]	0.0	0.3	0.5	0.8	1.0
Invest to Save Budget				0.0	0.0
Capital Modernisation Fund					
Reserve[6]				2.0	2.1
Allowance for Shortfall			–1.4		
Total Current Budget	**149.7**	**155.3**	**165.1**	**177.3**	**184.1**
Capital Budget					
Education and Employment	0.7	0.8	1.1	1.7	2.1
Health	0.2	–0.1	0.2	0.8	1.4
of which: NHS[7]	0.1	–0.2	0.2	0.7	1.3
DETR – Main programmes	5.5	5.0	5.7	6.2	6.9
DETR – Local Government and Regional Policy	0.3	0.4	0.3	0.0	0.0
Home Office	0.5	0.4	0.4	0.5	0.5
Legal Departments[1]	0.1	0.1	0.0	0.1	0.1
Defence	0.9	1.6	1.2	1.5	1.5
Foreign and Commonwealth Office	0.1	0.1	0.1	0.1	0.1
International Development	0.2	0.2	0.3	0.3	0.4
Trade and Industry[2]	0.4	0.3	0.4	0.5	0.5
Agriculture, Fisheries and Food[3]	0.3	0.1	0.2	0.2	0.2
Culture, Media and Sport	0.1	0.1	0.1	0.1	0.1
Social Security (administration)	0.0	–0.3	0.0	0.0	0.0
Scotland [1,4]	1.4	1.4	1.7	1.9	2.1
Wales[4]	0.9	0.8	0.8	0.8	0.8
Northern Ireland[4]	0.5	0.5	0.5	0.7	0.7
Chancellor's Departments	0.1	0.1	0.1	–0.1	0.1
Cabinet Office	0.2	0.2	0.3	0.2	0.2
Welfare to Work[5]	0.1	0.3	0.3	0.6	0.3
Invest to Save Budget				0.0	0.0
Capital Modernisation Fund			0.0	0.2	0.3
Reserve[6]				0.2	0.2
Total Capital Budget	**12.6**	**12.0**	**13.8**	**16.5**	**18.5**
Departmental Expenditure Limits	**162.3**	**167.2**	**178.9**	**193.7**	**202.6**
Total education spending	37.2	38.4	41.1	45.8	48.0

[1] The Crown Office is included in the Lord Chancellor's Department figures up to 1998–99, and in the Scotland figures from 1999–2000, reflecting a machinery of government change. See Chapter 22 of the CSR White Paper for further details.

[2] Includes the capital expenditure of the Export Credits Guarantee Department.

[3] Includes spending on BSE related programmes.

[4] For Scotland and Wales, the split between current and capital budgets is decided by the respective Executives. For Northern Ireland, during any period when the Assembly ceases to operate, this is a matter for the Secretary of State.

[5] Expenditure financed by the Windfall Tax.

[6] Reserve has been arbitrarily apportioned between current and capital, with 10% allocated to capital.

[7] Excludes the element of NHS trust capital expenditure which is funded through charges to health purchasers. Plans for total net capital spending on health are £1.5 billion in 1999–2000, £2.0 billion in 2000–01 and £2.9 billion in 2001–02.

FINANCING REQUIREMENT

C54   Table C20 presents projections of the net cash requirement by sector, giving details of the various financial transactions that do not affect net borrowing (the change in the sector's net financial indebtedness) but do affect its financing requirement.

Table C20: Public sector net cash requirement[1]

	£ billion							
	1999–2000				**2000–01**			
	General government				General government			
	Central government	Local authorities	Public corporations	Public sector	Central government	Local authorities	Public corporations	Public sector
Net borrowing	**–11.2**	**–0.2**	**0.4**	**–11.0**	**–6.0**	**0.5**	**0.8**	**–4.7**
Financial transactions								
Net lending to private sector and abroad	2.7	–0.1	0.0	2.7	2.4	–0.1	0.0	2.3
Cash expenditure on company securities (including privatisation proceeds)	–0.1	0.0	0.0	–0.1	0.0	0.0	0.0	0.0
Accruals adjustments on receipts	3.8	0.0	0.0	3.8	0.1	0.0	0.0	0.1
Other accruals adjustments	–1.3	0.0	0.0	–1.3	–2.8	0.0	0.0	–2.8
Miscellaneous financial transactions	–1.4	0.6	0.3	–0.5	0.0	0.0	0.0	0.0
Own account net cash requirement	–7.5	0.3	0.6	–6.5	–6.3	0.4	0.8	–5.1
Net lending within the public sector	1.6	–1.4	–0.2	0.0	1.4	–1.0	–0.4	0.0
Net cash requirement[2]	–5.8	–1.1	0.5	–6.5	–4.9	–0.6	0.4	–5.1

[1] The figures in this table include the windfall tax and associated spending. Excluding windfall tax receipts and associated spending, the public sector net cash requirement is projected to be £-7.4 billion (-0.8 per cent of GDP) for 1999–2000. It is projected at £–6.9 billion (–0.7 per cent of GDP) for 2000–01 and £–2 billion (–0.2 per cent of GDP) for 2001–02.

[2] Market and overseas borrowing for Local Government and Public corporation sectors.

C55   Table C21 updates the financing arithmetic for 1999–2000 to allow for the latest forecast of the central government net cash requirement, and sets out the arithmetic for 2000–01.

Table C21: Financing requirement forecast

	1999–2000				2000–01
	March 1999	Revised remit	November 1999	March 2000	March 2000
£ billion	Original remit	April 1999[1]	Pre-Budget Report	Budget	Budget
Central government net cash requirement	**6.2**	**6.2**	**1.1**	**–5.8**	**–4.9**
Expected net financing of official reserves[2]	2.4	2.3	2.3	2.2	3.5
Expected gilt redemptions	14.8	14.9	14.9	14.9	18.6
Debt buy-backs					3.5
Gilt sales residual	–2.3	–4.1	–4.1	–4.1	–9.5
Financing Requirement	**21.0**	**19.3**	**14.2**	**7.2**	**11.2**
Less assumed net National Savings contribution	0.1	0.1	–0.9	–1.0	–0.8
Less increase in T-bills and other short term debt[3]	3.6	1.9	0.8	–5.7	–0.2
Gross gilt sales requirement	**17.3**	**17.3**	**14.2**	**13.8**	**12.2**
Change in short-term debt from orginal remit (residual)				**–9.5**[4]	

Note: Figures may not sum due to rounding.

[1] Remit revised following outturn of the 1998–99 central government net cash requirement.

[2] The Reserves require financing in 1999–2000 to replace Euro 3.5billion of Euro Treasury bills. In 2000–01 the Euro 2 billion Euronote, the Euro 2.5 billion Eurobond and expiring forward contracts will be replaced. Future refinancing estimated at current exchange rate.

[3] This increase less the 1998–99 overfinancing shows the increase in the stock of T-bills and other short-term debt during 1999–2000 in advance of the DMO taking over responsibility for cash management.

[4] Adjusted for financing of the cash deposit at the Bank of England.

C56   The gilts issuance programme for 1999–2000 was revised following the Pre-Budget Report in November 1999. At that time the Government had announced that it would hold an auction of long conventional gilts, and needed a further auction of index-linked gilts if it was to meet its commitment to issue a minimum of £2.5 billion to support the move to index-linked auctions. Keeping to these plans implied gilt sales of around £14$^{1}/_{4}$ billion. This requirement was met by a reduction in the expected stock of Treasury bills at 31 March 2000, reflecting the later transfer of cash management from the Bank of England to the Debt Management Office. The Budget forecast shows a further improvement in the public finances and a consequent further reduction in the level of short term debt. The residual adjustment to rebuild the stock of short term debt reduces the requirement for gilt sales in 2000–01.

C57   The central government net cash requirement in 2000–01 is again forecast to be in surplus. This and the planned increase in the stock of short term debt reduces gilt sales to below the level required to refinance gilts redeemed during the year. As in 1999–2000, financing of the foreign currency reserves through sterling and foreign currency swaps to replace maturing foreign currency debt should represent better value for money. This and some restructuring of sterling debt through buy-backs adds to the financing requirement. Together these measures provide additional sales to help address current illiquidity in the gilts market. Details of the debt management plans for 2000–01, including the remits to the Debt Management Office and National Savings, are published today in the 2000–01 Debt Management Report.

HISTORICAL TABLES

C58   Table C22 and C23 set out historical data for the main fiscal aggregates.

Table C22: Historical series of public sector balances, receipts and debt

	Per cent of GDP								
	Public sector current budget[1]	Public sector net borrowing[1]	Public sector net cash requirement[1]	General government net borrowing[2]	Net taxes and social security contributions	Public sector current receipts	Public sector net debt[3]	General government gross debt[4]	Public sector net worth[5]
1970–71	7.0	–0.5	1.3	–2.0		42.7	69.6	77.7	41.7
1971–72	4.5	1.1	1.5	–0.7		41.1	65.2	74.8	48.1
1972–73	2.1	2.9	3.8	2.3		38.5	58.5	67.6	60.0
1973–74	1.0	4.5	5.9	4.1		39.7	58.4	65.9	76.8
1974–75	–0.6	6.3	9.1	4.0		42.2	52.4	60.5	78.0
1975–76	–1.4	7.1	9.4	4.8		42.7	54.2	59.5	66.5
1976–77	–1.0	5.7	6.5	4.3		43.0	52.6	58.9	63.9
1977–78	–1.1	4.3	3.7	3.5		41.3	49.2	57.5	58.6
1978–79	–2.2	4.8	5.2	4.0	33.3	40.1	47.3	56.1	64.9
1979–80	–1.5	3.9	4.8	2.8	34.0	40.8	44.1	52.0	71.8
1980–81	–2.7	4.6	5.3	3.7	35.8	42.6	46.2	53.6	77.1
1981–82	–1.1	2.2	3.5	3.2	38.7	45.9	46.4	51.8	74.7
1982–83	–1.4	3.0	3.2	3.2	39.0	45.4	44.9	50.5	67.1
1983–84	–1.9	3.8	3.2	3.8	38.3	44.5	45.2	50.6	65.5
1984–85	–2.5	4.2	3.2	3.8	38.9	43.8	45.4	50.5	61.4
1985–86	–1.0	2.4	1.6	2.6	38.1	43.2	43.6	49.6	61.0
1986–87	–1.4	2.1	1.0	2.4	37.7	41.8	41.2	48.8	66.6
1987–88	–0.3	1.0	–0.7	1.3	37.6	41.0	36.9	46.6	69.1
1988–89	1.8	–1.4	–3.0	–1.0	36.8	40.6	30.7	40.6	82.4
1989–90	1.6	–0.3	–1.3	0.2	36.3	39.9	27.9	35.6	74.5
1990–91	0.8	0.7	–0.1	1.3	36.3	39.0	26.3	33.3	62.8
1991–92	–1.7	3.6	2.4	3.5	35.3	38.8	27.6	34.6	55.3
1992–93	–5.7	7.8	5.9	7.6	34.0	36.5	32.2	40.5	42.4
1993–94	–6.2	7.8	7.2	7.8	33.3	35.9	37.5	46.1	30.2
1994–95	–4.8	6.3	5.3	6.6	34.4	36.9	41.1	49.5	29.7
1995–96	–3.5	4.9	4.4	5.1	35.3	37.9	43.2	52.2	21.6
1996–97	–2.9	3.6	3.0	3.8	35.3	37.6	44.1	52.2	17.8
1997–98	–0.7	1.2	0.4	0.9	36.5	38.7	42.1	49.6	14.7
1998–99	0.9	–0.3	–0.6	–0.6	37.1	39.2	39.7	47.0	13.6
1999–00	1.9	–1.3	–0.8	–1.3	37.0	39.6	37.1	44.1	15.4

[1] Excluding windfall tax receipts and associated spending.

[2] UK national accounts definition (ESA95).

[3] At end-March, GDP centred on end-March.

[4] Expressed as a ratio to money GDP (ESA95).

[5] At end-December; GDP centred on end-December.

Table C23: Historical series of government expenditure

	£ billion (1998–99 prices)				Per cent of GDP			
	Public sector current exoenditure	Public sector net capital expenditure	General government expenditure	Total Managed Expenditure	Public sector current expenditure	Public sector net capital expenditure	General government expenditure	Total Managed Expenditure
1970–71	148.8	30.1	190.1	195.5	32.1	6.4	41.0	42.2
1971–72	155.7	26.2	195.6	199.3	32.9	5.5	41.3	42.2
1972–73	163.5	25.4	204.0	207.2	32.7	5.0	40.8	41.4
1973–74	180.0	28.5	219.7	229.1	34.7	5.5	42.3	44.1
1974–75	199.1	29.9	246.8	251.1	38.4	5.8	47.6	48.5
1975–76	203.6	29.5	246.9	255.4	39.7	5.7	48.1	49.8
1976–77	209.5	24.3	240.7	256.9	39.7	4.6	45.6	48.7
1977–78	206.1	17.0	229.4	246.2	38.1	3.1	42.4	45.5
1978–79	212.3	14.9	240.2	250.8	38.0	2.7	43.0	45.0
1979–80	218.7	14.1	246.7	256.6	38.1	2.4	43.0	44.8
1980–81	225.7	11.0	254.5	261.5	40.8	2.0	46.0	47.3
1981–82	235.3	6.1	258.0	265.9	42.6	1.1	46.7	48.1
1982–83	241.4	9.5	264.1	274.6	42.6	1.6	46.6	48.5
1983–84	248.3	11.3	267.2	283.4	42.3	1.9	45.5	48.3
1984–85	255.0	10.0	272.6	287.7	42.5	1.6	45.5	48.0
1985–86	255.7	8.3	271.5	284.5	41.0	1.3	43.5	45.5
1986–87	259.8	5.2	271.0	285.8	40.0	0.8	41.6	43.9
1987–88	263.2	5.2	272.2	287.3	38.5	0.7	39.8	42.0
1988–89	256.9	3.0	265.3	279.7	36.0	0.4	37.2	39.2
1989–90	258.1	9.5	277.9	287.3	35.6	1.3	38.3	39.6
1990–91	259.5	10.8	278.8	287.7	35.8	1.5	38.5	39.7
1991–92	275.1	13.8	291.9	303.5	38.4	1.9	40.8	42.4
1992–93	289.6	15.1	308.3	318.4	40.3	2.1	42.8	44.3
1993–94	298.5	12.5	317.8	324.3	40.3	1.7	42.9	43.8
1994–95	309.1	11.7	326.4	334.6	40.0	1.5	42.2	43.3
1995–96	313.7	10.6	333.6	338.8	39.6	1.3	42.1	42.8
1996–97	315.9	5.5	328.1	335.5	38.8	0.7	40.3	41.2
1997–98	315.0	4.7	329.2	333.5	37.4	0.6	39.1	39.6
1998–99	312.5	5.0	328.4	331.3	36.5	0.6	38.3	38.7
1999–00	317.7	5.4	334.0	335.1	36.2	0.6	38.0	38.1

CONVENTIONS USED IN PRESENTING THE PUBLIC FINANCES

FORMAT FOR THE PUBLIC FINANCES

The June 1998 Economic and Fiscal Strategy Report (EFSR), set out a new format for presenting the public finances that corresponded more closely to the two fiscal rules. The three principal measures are:

- the surplus on *current budget* (relevant to the golden rule);

- public sector *net borrowing,* and

- the public sector *net debt ratio* (relevant to the sustainable investment rule).

These measures are based on the national accounts and are consistent with the new European System of Accounts 1995 (ESA95). Estimates and forecasts of the public sector *net cash requirement* (formerly called the public sector borrowing requirement) are still shown in the FSBR, but they are given less prominence.

The fiscal rules are similar to the criteria for deficits and debt laid down in the Maastricht treaty but there are important definitional differences:

- UK fiscal rules cover the whole public sector, whereas Maastricht only includes general (ie: central and local) government;

- the fiscal rules apply over the whole economic cycle, not year-to-year;

- the current budget excludes capital spending, which is included in the Maastricht deficit measure; and

- the UK debt measure is net of liquid assets, whereas Maastricht uses gross debt.

From February 2000 the Maastricht deficit moved to being reported on an ESA95 basis.

NATIONAL ACCOUNTS

The national accounts record most transactions, including most taxes (although not corporation tax), on an accruals basis, and impute the value of some transactions where no money changes hands (for example, non-trading capital consumption). The principal measures drawn from the national accounts are described below.

The current budget (formerly known as the current balance) measures the balance of current account revenue over current expenditure. The definition of the current balance presented in this chapter is very similar to the national accounts concept of net saving. It differs only in that it includes taxes on capital (mainly death duties) in current rather than capital receipts.

Public sector net borrowing (formerly known as the financial deficit in the UK national accounts) is the balance between expenditure and income in the consolidated current and capital accounts. It differs from the public sector net cash requirement because it is measured on an accruals basis and because certain financial transactions (notably net lending and privatisation proceeds, which affect the level of borrowing but not the public sector's net financial indebtedness) are excluded from public sector net borrowing but included in the public sector net cash requirement.

General government net borrowing, which excludes net borrowing of public corporations, is the most internationally comparable measure of the budget deficit. It is reported to the European Commission under the Maastricht Treaty.

CASH BASIS

The cash approach measures the actual cash transactions between the public sector and the rest of the economy. It is the starting point for monthly estimates of net borrowing. Table C20 shows the financial transactions that are deducted to reach net borrowing.

MONTHLY DATA

In July 1998 the joint Treasury/ONS monthly First Release on the public finances was expanded to include monthly estimates of *net borrowing* (previously the release showed only the public sector *net cash requirement*). In January 1999 it was expanded further to include monthly estimates of *net public sector debt*. The release still shows the cash measures, which remain of interest for measuring financing requirements for the purpose of debt management.

In February 1999, ONS began publication of a new quarterly First Release *Provisional Public Sector Accounts*. This gives quarterly information on the public sector in national accounts, such as the surplus on current budget, some three or four weeks before the publication of the main quarterly national accounts.

In November 1999, the ONS produced the first monthly estimates of the current budget surplus. This meant that for the first time, all the key measures needed to assess progress against the Government's fiscal framework were published together on a monthly and timely basis.

Monthly Statistics on Public Sector Finances – A methodological guide was published in January 1999 as No. 12 in the GSS Methodology Series. This describes in detail the derivation of the monthly estimates of net borrowing, net debt and net cash requirement that now appear in the ONS's monthly *Public sector finances* First Release.

PUBLIC SECTOR CURRENT RECEIPTS

Net taxes and social security contributions in Table C10 are measured on a cash basis, rather than a national accounts (accruals) basis, and, as far as possible, relate to actual cash flows. Income tax credits are netted off. VAT is net of refunds to the public sector. Social security contributions are scored gross of amounts netted off by employers as reimbursement in respect of statutory sick pay and statutory maternity pay. (These payments count as expenditure rather than negative receipts.). "Good causes" receipts from the National Lottery are included.

The accounting adjustments put these cash figures on to a national accounts (accruals) basis. Tax credits which score as expenditure in the national accounts are added back. VAT refunded within the public sector is added back. Those elements of the UK contribution to the EC budget which relate to the UK tax base are deducted as, under ESA95, they are treated for national accounts as taxes imposed directly by the EU.

Certain income tax reliefs are payable regardless of an individual's liability to income tax; thus some payments are made to non-taxpayers. Examples are mortgage interest relief paid under the MIRAS (mortgage interest relief at source) scheme, life assurance premium relief on pre-1984 policies and private medical insurance premium relief for over-60s. The working families tax credit also falls into this category. Total tax relief paid under these schemes is shown as income tax credits in Tables C7 and C9. Income tax receipts in these tables are shown gross of these tax credits. All such tax credits are shown in the national accounts as expenditure. From 2001–02, income tax credits (Table C9) include the new Children's Tax Credit.

TOTAL MANAGED EXPENDITURE (TME)

Public expenditure control regime

The Economic and Fiscal Strategy Report (EFSR) in June 1998 also reformed the planning and control regime for public spending.

- Overall plans are based on sound economic principles, with a new distinction between current and capital spending;

- Firm 3-year plans (Departmental Expenditure Limits – DEL) will provide certainty and flexibility for long-term planning and management;

- Spending outside DEL, which cannot reasonably be subject to firm multi-year limits commitments, will be reviewed annually as part of the Budget process. This Annual Managed Expenditure (AME) is also subject to constraints;

- Large public corporations, not dependent on government grants, will have more flexibility.

Detailed plans under this regime were given in the Comprehensive Spending Review in July 1998 for the years 1999–2000 to 2001/02.

Public sector capital expenditure is shown in Table C13. It includes:

(i)   gross domestic fixed capital formation (ie expenditure on fixed assets – schools, hospitals, roads, computers, plant and machinery, intangible assets etc) net of receipts from sales of fixed assets (eg council houses and surplus land);

(ii)   grants in support of capital spending by the private sector; and

(iii)   the value of the physical increase in stocks (for central government, primarily agricultural commodity stocks).

Net investment in Table C1 nets off depreciation of the public sector's stock of fixed assets.

Departmental Expenditure Limits (DEL) have distinct current and capital budgets, shown in Table C19. The departmental groupings used in this table are defined at the end of the Annex.

Annually Managed Expenditure (AME) components are shown in Table C11. These include all of social security spending, housing revenue account subsidies, the Common agricultural policy, export credits, net payments to EC institutions, spending by self financing public corporations, public service pensions net of contributions, spending financed by the national lottery and central government gross debt interest.

Total Managed Expenditure (TME), the sum of DEL and AME, is shown in Table C11.

Export Credits Guarantee Department programme includes a classification change since the CSR. The activities of the Guaranteed Export Finance Corporation (GEFCO), whose sole business is to refinance export loans guaranteed by ECGD, thus reducing the cost to Government, have been reclassified to central government and are now included. GEFCO's past activities are now regarded as agency transactions undertaken for the government, as is the funding raised by GEFCO. Its future activities will be funded through ECGD. However, the refinancing activities are financial transactions affecting only the net cash requirement and so are netted out in the accounting adjustments.

Locally financed expenditure comprises local authority self-financed expenditure (LASFE) and Scottish spending financed by local taxation (non-domestic rates and, if and when levied, the Scottish variable rate of income tax). LASFE is the difference between total local authority expenditure, including most gross debt interest but net of capital receipts, and central government support to local authorities (ie Aggregate External Finance (AEF), specific grants and credit approvals).

Central government debt interest is shown gross. Only interest paid within central government is netted off; all other receipts of interest and dividends are included in current receipts. The capital uplift on index-linked gilts is scored as interest at the time it accrues, whereas the cash tables record the actual payments of capital uplift on index-linked gilts, and includes the amortisation of discounts on gilts at issue. Following the GEFCO reclassification, interest is included on the net funds raised by that body (£118 million in 1998/99).

The accounting adjustments include various items within TME but outside DEL which are not shown separately in table C11. These details are shown in table C12. The definition of each line is as follows:

- *Line one* adds the value of general government non-trading capital consumption.

- *Line two* adds back VAT refunded to central government departments and local government. Departmental Expenditure Limits and Annually Managed Expenditure programme expenditure are measured net of these refunds, while Total Managed Expenditure is recorded including the VAT paid. Adds VAT refunded to NHS trusts, BBC and ITN in respect of contracted out services for non-business purposes, and adds VAT refunds to DIY house-builders.

- *Line three* deducts traditional own resources (ie payments of Customs duties and agricultural and sugar levies) and VAT contributions to the European Community, which are included in the net payments to EC institutions line in AME, but excluded from TME.

- *Line four* adds income tax credits which score as public expenditure under national accounting conventions. Includes Mortgage Interest Relief, Life Assurance Premium Relief, and (from 1999–00) Working Families' Tax Credit and Disabled Persons' Tax Credit.

- *Line five* includes the Valuation Office, Financial Services Authority and Redundancy Payments Scheme.

- *Line six* shows accounting adjustments to move to a national accounts basis for scoring public corporations' current and capital spending; adds capital expenditure and debt interest payments outside the public sector and removes capital grants from general government.

- *Line seven* removes intra-public sector debt interest and dividend payments and receipts which are included elsewhere in Departmental Expenditure Limits and Annually Managed Expenditure.

- *Line eight* deducts thos financial transactions which are scored in Departmental Expenditure Limits and Annually Managed Expenditure.

- *Line nine* shows other adjustments and include, amongst others, the deduction of grants paid to local authorities by non-departmental public bodies classified to the central government sector and the inclusion of utilities levies netted off in Departmental Expenditure Limits.

DEBT AND WEALTH

Public sector net debt is approximately the stock analogue of the public sector net cash requirement. It measures the public sector's financial liabilities to the private sector and abroad, net of short-term financial assets such as bank deposits and foreign exchange reserves.

General government gross debt is the measure of debt used in the European Union's excessive deficits procedure. As a general government measure, it excludes the debt of public corporations. It measures general government's total financial liabilities before netting off short- term financial assets.

Public sector net worth represents the public sector's overall net balance sheet position. It is equal to the sum of the public sector's financial and non-financial assets less. The estimates of tangible assets are subject to wide margins of error, because they depend on broad assumptions, for example about asset lives, which may not be appropriate in all cases. The introduction of resource accounting for central government departments will lead in time to an improvement in data quality, as audited information compiled from detailed asset registers becomes available.

LIST OF ABBREVIATIONS

AEI	Average Earnings Index
AME	Annually Managed Expenditure
APPs	Appropriate personal pensions
BAA	British Agrochemicals Association
BCC	British Chamber of Commerce
BCS	British Crime Survey
CAT	Charges Access Terms
CBI	Confederation of British Industry
CCL	Climate change levy
CED	Consumers' expenditure deflator
CFCs	Controlled Foreign Companies
CGT	Capital Gains Tax
CHP	Combined Heat and Power
CMF	Capital Modernisation Fund
COMPS	Contracted-out money purchase schemes
COSRS	Contracted-out salary related schemes
CSR	Comprehensive Spending Review
DEL	Departmental Expenditure Limits
DETR	Department of the Environment, Transport and the Regions
DfEE	Department for Education and Employment
DIS	Departmental Investment Strategy
DLA	Disability Living Allowance
DPTC	Disabled Person's Tax Credit
DTI	Department of Trade and Industry
DVLA	Driver and Vehicle Licensing Agency
DWA	Disability Working Allowance
EAC	Environmental Audit Committee
EA(PC)	Cabinet Committee on Productivity and Competitiveness
EC	European Commission
EEA	European Economic Area
EFSR	Economic and Fiscal Strategy Report
EIS	Enterprise Investment Scheme
EMA	Education Maintenance Allowance
EMIs	Enterprise Management Incentives
EMU	Economic and Monetary Union
ES	Employment Service
ESA79	European Systems of Accounts 1979
ESA95	European Systems of Accounts 1995
ETG	Emissions Trading Group
ETC	Employment Tax Credit
EU	European Union
FE	Further education
FEFC	Further Education Funding Council
FRES	Federation of Recruitment and Employment Services
FSA	Financial Services Authority
FSMB	Financial Services and Markets Bill
FSBR	Financial Statement and Budget Report

G5	Group of Five. A group of five major industrial nations (comprising: France, Germany, Japan, UK and US).
G7	Group of Seven. A group of seven major industrial nations (comprising: Canada, France, Germany, Italy, Japan, UK and US).
GDP	Gross Domestic Product
HEES	Home Energy Efficiency Scheme
HICP	Harmonised Index of Consumer Prices
HIPC	Heavily Indebted Poor Countries
HRA	Human Rights Act
ICC	Integrated Child Credit
ICT	Information and Communications Technology
ICTA	Income and Corporation Tax Act
IFS	Institute for Fiscal Studies
IIP	Investors in People
ILO	International Labour Organisation
IMF	International Monetary Fund
IPPC	Integrated Pollution and Prevention Control
IPRs	Intellectual Property Rights
IRB	Income Related Benefits
IRU	Indefeasible Right of Use
ISMI	Income Support for Mortgage Interest
ISA	Individual Savings Account
IT	Information Technology
ITCE	Information Technology and Communication Engineers
JSA	Jobseekers' Allowance
LEL	Lower earnings limit
LFS	Labour Force Survey
LPG	Liquefied Petroleum Gas
MA	Maternity Allowance
MCA	Married Couple's Allowance
MCT	Mainstream corporation tax
MDR	Marginal Deduction Rate
MIT	Massachusetts Institute of Technology
MIRAS	Mortgage Interest Relief at Source
MPC	Monetary Policy Committee
MtC	Million tonnes of carbon
NAIRU	Non-accelerating inflation rate of unemployment
NAO	National Audit Office
NAR	National Asset Register
NDLP	New Deal for Lone Parents
NESI	New Enterprise Support Initiative
NFC	Non-financial company
NHS	National Health Service
NICs	National Insurance Contributions
NOx	Nitrogen Oxides
OECD	Organisation for Economic Cooperation and Development
OFT	Office of Fair Trading
OFTEL	Office of Telecommunications
OGC	Office of Government Commerce

OLS	Overseas Labour Service
ONS	Office for National Statistics
PAT	Policy Action Team
PAYE	Pay As You Earn
PBR	Pre-Budget Report
PEP	Personal Equity Plan
PFI	Private Finance Initiative
PPC	Pollution Prevention and Control
PPI	Pooled Pension Investment
PPPs	Public Private Partnerships
PRT	Petroleum Revenue Tax
PSA	Public Service Agreement
PSNB	Public sector net borrowing
PT	Primary threshold
PUK	Partnerships UK
RAB	Resource Accounting and Budgeting
R&D	Research and Development
RDAs	Regional Development Agencies
RPI	Retail Prices Index
RPIX	Retail Prices Index excluding mortgage interest payments
RSLs	Registered Social Landlords
SBIT	Small Business Investment Task-force
SBS	Small Business Service
SEE	Small Earnings Exception
SERPS	State Earnings Related Pensions Scheme
SEU	Social Exclusion Unit
SME	Small and medium-sized enterprise
SMP	Statutory Maternity Pay
SRA	Strategic Rail Authority
TESSA	Tax Exempt Special Savings Account
TME	Total Managed Expenditure
TTWA	Travel To Work Area
UEL	Upper earnings limit
UfI	University for Industry
UK	United Kingdom
ULSD	Ultra Low Sulphur Diesel
ULSP	Ultra Low Sulphur Petrol
US	United States of America
VAT	Value Added Tax
VCTs	Venture Capital Trusts
VED	Vehicle Excise Duty
VOCs	Volatile Organic Compounds
WFTC	Working Families' Tax Credit
WTAS	Windfall Tax and Associated Spending

LIST OF TABLES

Economic and Fiscal Strategy Report

Financial Statement and Budget Report

LIST OF CHARTS

Economic and Fiscal Strategy Report

Financial Statement and Budget Report

Printed in the UK by the Stationery Office Limited
on behalf of the Controller of Her Majesty's Stationery Office
Dd 144792   19585   461591